SOURCES O[illegible]ERING

SOURCES OF SUFFERING
Fear, Greed, Guilt, Deception, Betrayal, and Revenge

Salman Akhtar

KARNAC

Chapter One has previously appeared in S. Akhtar (Ed.), *Fear: A Dark Shadow Across The Life Span* (pp. 3–34). London: Karnac, 2014.

Portions of Chapter Three are taken from Salman Akhtar's paper, "Guilt: an introductory overview", which appeared in S. Akhtar (Ed.), *Guilt: Origins, Manifestations, and Management* (pp. 1–13). Lanham, MD: Jason Aronson, 2013.

Portions of Chapter Four are taken from Salman Akhtar's paper, "Lies, liars, and lying: an introductory overview", which appeared in S. Akhtar and H. Parens (Eds.), *Lying, Cheating, and Carrying On: Developmental, Clinical, and Sociocultural Aspects of Dishonesty and Deceit* (pp. 1–15). Lanham, MD: Jason Aronson, 2009.

Chapter Five has previously appeared in S. Akhtar (Ed.), *Betrayal: Developmental, Literary, and Clinical Realms* (pp. 117–134). London: Karnac, 2013.

All this material is reprinted here with the author's and the corresponding publishers' explicit permission.

First published in 2014 by
Karnac Books Ltd
118 Finchley Road
London NW3 5HT

British Library Cataloguing in Publication Data

A C.I.P. for this book is available from the British Library

ISBN-13: 978-1-78220-069-7

Typeset by V Publishing Solutions Pvt Ltd., Chennai, India

www.karnacbooks.com

To
RAMA RAO GOGINENI & APRIL FALLON
in friendship

CONTENTS

PART II: SUFFERING INFLICTED

ACKNOWLEDGEMENTS

Writing a book only appears to be a solo endeavour. Behind the scenes, the writer always has heroes, peers, and critics accompanying him in this journey. I too have been fortunate to have had the helpful input of many psychoanalytic colleagues, especially Drs Jennifer Bonovitz, Ira Brenner, Ralph and Lana Fishkin, Rao Gogineni, Axel Hoffer, Henri Parens, and Vamik Volkan. Drs Rajnish Mago and Stephen Schwartz were helpful in subtle and, occasionally, not-so-subtle ways in reading and reviewing some of the material contained in this book. My assistant, Jan Wright, prepared the manuscript of this book with diligence and good humour. My personal friends, especially Drs April Fallon, Naresh Julka, Saida Koita, Harish Malhotra, Tahir Maqsood, Roomana Sheikh, and J. Anderson Thomson kept me in good humour during easy and difficult times. To all these individuals, my sincere thanks, indeed.

Salman Akhtar
Philadelphia, PA

ABOUT THE AUTHOR

Salman Akhtar, MD, is professor of psychiatry at Jefferson Medical College and a training and supervising analyst at the Psychoanalytic Center of Philadelphia. He has served on the editorial boards of the *International Journal of Psychoanalysis* and the *Journal of the American Psychoanalytic Association*. His more than 300 publications include fifteen books—*Broken Structures* (1992), *Quest for Answers* (1995), *Inner Torment* (1999), *Immigration and Identity* (1999), *New Clinical Realms* (2003), *Objects of Our Desire* (2005), *Regarding Others* (2007), *Turning Points in Dynamic Psychotherapy* (2009), *The Damaged Core* (2009), *Comprehensive Dictionary of Psychoanalysis* (2009), *Immigration and Acculturation* (2011), *Matters of Life and Death* (2011), *The Book of Emotions* (2012), *Psychoanalytic Listening* (2013), and *Good Stuff* (2013)—as well as forty-two edited or co-edited volumes in psychiatry and psychoanalysis. Dr Akhtar has delivered many prestigious addresses and lectures including, most recently, the inaugural address at the first IPA-Asia Congress in Beijing, China (2010). Dr Akhtar is the recipient of the *Journal of the American Psychoanalytic Association*'s Best Paper of the Year Award (1995), the Margaret Mahler Literature Prize (1996), the American Society of Psychoanalytic Physicians' Sigmund Freud Award (2000), the American Psychoanalytic Association's Edith Sabshin Award (2000), the American College of Psychoanalysts' Laughlin Award (2003), Columbia University's Robert Liebert Award for Distinguished Contributions to Applied Psychoanalysis (2004), the American Psychiatric Association's Kun Po Soo Award (2004), the Irma Bland Award for being the Outstanding Teacher of Psychiatric Residents in the country (2005), and the Nancy Roeske Award (2012). Most recently, he received the Sigourney Award (2013), which is the most prestigious honour in the field of psychoanalysis. Dr Akhtar is an internationally sought speaker and teacher, and his books have been translated in many languages, including German, Turkish, and Romanian. His interests are wide and he has served as the film review editor for the *International Journal of Psychoanalysis*, and is currently serving as the book review editor for the *International Journal of Applied Psychoanalytic Studies*. He has published seven collections of poetry and serves as a scholar-in-residence at the InterAct Theatre Company in Philadelphia.

INTRODUCTION

Suffering is integral to life. Alongside joy and excitement, it permeates our existence as we pass from infancy through adulthood to old age. It accompanies us at each developmental epoch and at every maturational milestone. It is even there after a successful psychoanalytic treatment. Indeed, Freud admitted that all psychoanalysis can do is to "transform hysterical misery into common unhappiness" (1950a, p. 305). And, he was not alone in coming to the conclusion that a certain amount of emotional pain is inevitable in the course of life. Buddha's first Noble Truth, Ghalib's equation of *qaid-e-hayat* (prison of existence) with *bund-e-ghum* (bondage to pain), and David Thoreau's declaration that all men live a life of "quiet desperation"—all speak to this very point. This is ordinary suffering: irreducible and inherent in life. Elsewhere, I have delineated its components under the rubric of "burdens of sanity" (Akhtar, 2009, p. 42).

However, such suffering is not the topic of my book, which deals with suffering that is unfortunate, unnecessary, excessive, pathological, and is remediable. To be sure, the book is not exhaustive; the fact that it does not address the distress emanating from envy, shame, regret, hate, and boredom attests to its modest scope. Within that limited reach, however, it seeks to underscore the multifaceted ways in which we encounter suffering in clinical and social settings. The book identifies six such "sources of suffering". The first three, namely, fear, greed, and guilt, cause an individual to suffer privately, though not entirely without interpersonal consequences. The second three, namely, deception, betrayal, and revenge, lead others to suffer, though not entirely without subjective distress on the part of the individual himself.

In elucidating the intricacies of these six sources of suffering I have attempted to deal with each emotion's phenomenological, developmental, and sociocultural aspects. Wherever possible, I have included pertinent information from the related fields of anthropology, sociology, ethology, and evolutionary sciences. I have included literary references as well as clinical vignettes to highlight the nuances of fear, greed, guilt, deception, betrayal, and revenge. My aim is to help the clinicians empathise with these complex human experiences, recognise their emergence within the transference-countertransference axis, and facilitate ego dominance and mastery on the part of their patients. Though not a guidebook or a therapeutic manual, my book is unabashedly pragmatic. Its purpose is to help psychoanalysts and psychotherapists become more skilful in helping their patients renounce, reduce, or reframe their suffering. The novice in our field is my main audience but if those who are more experienced find something of benefit in my scribblings, I will be delighted.

PART I

SUFFERING TOLERATED

CHAPTER ONE

Fear

Fear is ubiquitous. All of us experience it at one time or another. The sound of footsteps approaching us from behind in a dark alley, an unexpected visit to the city morgue, eye contact with a large alligator in the zoo, and a precipitous "fall" of a rollercoaster can all give us goose bumps of terror. We shriek, scream, or simply become paralysed with fear. We readily recognise its dark arrival in the pit of our stomachs and feel its movement in our blood.

But do we understand the actual nature of fear? Do we know the purpose it serves? Do we agree upon the circumstances under which it is "normal" to be afraid? And, when does fear become abnormal or morbid? Is fear to be avoided at all costs or can this bitter gourd of emotion be transformed into a sweet mango of cultural delight? Questions like these suggest that fear is simple and self-evident only on the surface. Examined carefully, it turns out to be a complex and nuanced phenomenon.

Fear

Webster's dictionary defines fear as "an unpleasant, often strong emotion caused by anticipation or awareness of danger" (Mish, 1998,

p. 425). While the source of the threat is not identified, the tone makes it clear that the danger referred to resides in external reality. Fear, in other words, is a dysphoric reaction to an actual object (e.g., a wild animal, a knife-wielding drunkard), event (e.g., an earthquake, a stampede), or situation (e.g., watching a horror movie, losing control of a car on an icy road) that is felt to be threatening. The extent of dysphoria in the face of approaching danger varies and four levels of fear's severity are identified in the English language: (a) *apprehension*, which refers to a mild anticipation of a bad occurrence; (b) *dread*, which blends the conviction that one is facing danger with a powerful reluctance to encounter the scary object or situation; (c) *panic*, which denotes an overwhelming sense of being scared, coupled with alarmed hyperactivity (e.g., pacing, running away) and physiological arousal (e.g., increased heartbeat, laboured breathing); and (d) *terror*, which signifies an extreme degree of consternation, a feeling of doom, "catastrophic aloneness" (Grand, 2002), and psychomotor paralysis.

The fact that fear is ubiquitous in the animal kingdom suggests that it is a "needed emotion", that is, one that is important for the organism's survival and functioning. For all living beings, including humans, the emotion of fear serves as a protective device; it warns them that some danger is approaching and they had better undertake measures to avoid it. This could be in the form of actively combating the "enemy" or rapidly escaping from it, meaning the well-known "fight-or-flight" response to threats.

Some fears are widespread over the animal kingdom and seem "hard-wired". Others are the result of developmentally unfolding, epigenetic sequence of fantasies that are specific to human beings. Among the former are fear of loud noises, sudden and jerky movements, looking down from heights, and animals that have fangs, claws, sharp teeth, and can jump or move at great speed (Abraham, 1913a; Akhtar & Brown, 2005). Present from birth onwards and persistent throughout life (even if in attenuated forms and at a preconscious level), these fears give testimony to man's essential kinship with animals since their function is self-protective and oriented towards survival. Among the latter are the developmentally derived fears of loss of love objects, loss of love, and castration (Freud, 1926d); fear of death joins this list somewhat later during the course of psychic development. These "hard-wired" and developmentally derived fears exist in both sexes though there is some evidence (Horner, 1968; Miller, 1994; Symonds, 1985) that, owing to socialisation patterns and internalised cultural biases, fear of becoming alone and fear of success are somewhat more prevalent among women.

Another point needs mention here. The experience of fear is mediated through two different routes: a shorter, rapid, and subcortical route which goes directly through the amygdala and a longer, slower, and more complex route that includes hippocampal and cortical participation (Damasio, 1999; Emanuel, 2004; Pally, 2000). Each route has an identical output: a fear response. However, the shorter route lacks the benefit of contextual information that the longer route provides. As a result, the shorter route produces a direct and simple fear response which can be tempered or even entirely inhibited by the longer route. The profound implications of this for psychic development and for therapeutic intervention are nowhere better illustrated than in the "visual cliff" experiment devised by Gibson and Walk (1960).

This experiment consists of having the glass floor of a room papered, from below, with a chequerboard design up to its midpoint. As a result, the first half of the floor does not appear any different from ordinary floors but, as the paper affixed from below runs out, the floor suddenly appears threatening due to the depth perception through the transparent glass. The point at which the transparent glass begins is the "visual cliff". Now, a toddler is placed on the papered end of the floor and his or her mother is asked to watch him from across the room. The toddler begins to make his way towards her but abruptly stops at encountering the "visual cliff". If the mother remains impassive, the child does not move forward. However, if the mother smiles, spreads her arms, and vocally encourages the child to come to her, the child crawls or walks over the transparent glass. Mother's loving support activates the hippocampal-cortical system that dampens the fear aroused by the amygdala-sponsored pathway mentioned above.

While this is a salutary consequence of environmental modulation of "hard-wired" childhood fears, adverse and even sinister interplays of childhood vulnerability and caregiver input also exist. Children (more so than adults) need company and

> ... their needs for attachment experiences and even moments of intimacy will lead them to shadow, seek out, and submissively engage the parents who, for the most part, cause them pain and disappointment. Their avidity for exploration and assertion will

> lead them to follow a ball out into a dangerous street, climb up an unstable support, or put fingers in electric plugs. Their love of sensual enjoyment from fondling, kissing, and rocking will result in their participating in sexually over-exciting play or overt seductions by older children and adults. The pleasure of social contact will expose older children to the smiling-faced inducements of a kidnapper, and the same desire coupled with greed leaves adults exposed to psychopathic salesmen and con men. Thus, parents must inculcate a sense of danger as an active educative effort. (Lichtenberg, 1991, pp. 396–397)

Such nuanced interplay of "nature versus nurture" variables in the genesis and modulation of fear undergirds the epigenetic unfolding of phase-specific fears throughout childhood development. "Natural" fears of starvation and physical injury are given specific "human" colouring via the potential danger of anaclitic betrayal and loss during infancy, castration and genital mutilation during early childhood, and moral anxiety (the internalised consequence of the preceding fear) during later childhood and adolescence (Freud, 1926d). Still later, in the course of adult life, fear of death appears on the psychic horizon; multiply determined and culturally variable, this fear combines fears of physical infirmity, separation from love objects, and loss of self (Akhtar, 2010; Chadwick, 1929; Freud, 1923b; Hoffman, Johnson, Foster & Wright, 2010; Natterson & Knudson, 1965; Zilboorg, 1943).

Anxiety

Fear and anxiety share some characteristics. Both evoke a sense that something bad is about to happen. Both are unpleasant and undesirable experiences. Both can serve as alarms and thus protect us from danger. However, in other ways, the two experiences are different. Fear is a response to external danger; anxiety to dangers emanating from the internal world. As early as 1895, Freud noted the relationship between "unpleasure" (not yet delineated as anxiety) to earlier painful experiences. He wrote:

> If the memory image of the hostile object is in any manner freshly cathected (e.g., by fresh perceptions), a condition arises which is not pain but has a similarity to pain. It includes unpleasure and the

> inclination to discharge corresponding to the experience of pain. Unpleasure is released from the interior of the body—is freshly provoked—by the cathexis of memories. (1950a, p. 381)

Thirty years later, Freud (1926d) published his major work on the problem of anxiety and restated this thesis. However, this time, he linked the cathexis of previous traumata and their memories to the specific affect of anxiety. He stated:

> Anxiety is not newly created in repression; it is reproduced as an affective state, in accordance with an already existing mnemic image. If we go further and enquire into the origin of that anxiety—and of affects in general—we shall be leaving the realm of pure psychology and entering the borderland of physiology. Affective states have become incorporated in the mind as precipitates of primeval traumatic experiences and when a similar situation occurs, they are revived like mnemic symbols. (p. 93)

In the same contribution, Freud also delineated the seminal "danger situations" causing anxiety. These included threats of (a) loss of a love object, (b) loss of the love object's love, (c) castration, and (d) moral condemnation from within oneself. "Each situation or danger corresponds to a particular period of life or a particular developmental phase of the mental apparatus and appears to be justifiable to it" (p. 146). Some "danger situations" lose their evocative power as the individual matures while others survive by acquiring more up-to-date forms. Still others (e.g., superego's attack) accompany people throughout their lives. "Danger situations" mobilise anxiety and set ego defences in motion. This is "signal anxiety". It contrasts with "automatic anxiety" that results from the ego being overwhelmed by threats from within. The feeling in anxiety that something bad is about to happen is due to the ego's sense that one might give in to id impulses that would lead to physical harm, others' disapproval, or rebuke from one's own conscience. However, since the impulse in question is almost always repressed, the nature of danger felt remains vague. This explanatory model, however, applies only to what is generally called "neurotic anxiety". It does not address anxiety that presumably arises from the infantile era where a coherent ego and hence a wishful intentionality is not yet in place. In such anxiety, the dread is not of an instinctual breakthrough but that of psychic "breakdown" (Winnicott, 1974). Variously termed "psychotic anxiety" (Klein, 1932), "unthinkable anxiety" (Winnicott, 1962), and "annihilation anxiety" (Hurvich, 2003), such dysphoria threatens to disorganise mental functioning altogether. Elsewhere, I have noted the main characteristics of this anxiety.

> ... (i) it originates in early infancy; (ii) it can, however, be reactivated by later phase-specific anxieties; (iii) a combination of excessive constitutional aggression and severe traumatic experiences leads to ego weakness which, in turn, increases the vulnerability to such anxiety; (iv) it might exist in pre-verbal forms or might acquire retrospective fantasy content from later developmental phases; (v) it is generally associated with propensity towards psychosis but might also underlie non-psychotic conditions especially those of addictive, psychosomatic, and perverse varieties; and, (vi) it mobilizes defenses that are particularly recalcitrant. (Akhtar, 2009, p. 22)

Regardless of whether it is "neurotic" or "psychotic" in nature, the intrapsychic origin of anxiety also precludes its control by physical flight; one can run away from fear, not from anxiety. Fear and anxiety are thus both similar and dissimilar. The phenomenological terrain is further muddled by the fact that the two often coexist. External threats are played up by internal vulnerabilities and intrapsychic threats can readily be externalised. Some admixtures of fear and anxiety are commonplace, others curious.

Phobia

By itself, fear is a rational response and therefore poses few problems. When it gets fuelled by anxiety in a regressive blurring of external and internal realities, difficulties of clinical proportions begin to arise. The most well known among these conditions is phobia. A term derived the Greek word *phobos* (meaning flight, dread, and panic), phobia stands for "marked and persistent fear that is excessive or unreasonable, cued by the presence or anticipation of a specific object or situation" (*DSM-IV-TR*, 2000, p. 449). In effect, both anxiety (internal danger) and fear (external danger) coexist within phobia, although in their pure forms, anxiety and fear are quite different (see Table 1). Phobia is distinct from

Table 1. Fear, anxiety, and phobia.

Variables	*Fear*	*Anxiety*	*Phobia*
Source	External	Internal	Externalised
Risk	Actual	Unknown	Imagined
Threat	Clear	Vague	Clear
Danger	Plausible	Implausible	Exaggerated
Avoidance	Helpful	Futile	Helpful
Prevalence	Universal	Limited	Limited

fear because it is out of proportion with the situation in reality. Indeed, a fear must meet the following criteria in order to qualify as a phobia: (i) it should not be age-specific, (ii) it should not be widely accepted as normal within a culture or subculture, (iii) it should be noticeably out of proportion with the plausible danger from the object or the situation, (iv) it should result in impairment of psychosocial functioning, (v) it should be associated with active avoidance of the dreaded stimulus, and (vi) such avoidance should provide symptomatic relief.

Phobia also needs to be distinguished from the paranoid fear insofar as there is no motive assigned in phobia to the frightening object; the statement "I am afraid of pigeons" represents phobia and the statement "Pigeons are out to get me" represents paranoia. The former is the result of displacement, the latter that of projection.

Phobias can be of many types, as is attested by the profusion of specific phobias with Greek prefixes,[1] and many classifications exist. While a bit older, the classification by the British psychiatrist, Marks (1970), seems not only to be valid today but perhaps most sensible. According to him, phobias can be grouped into the following categories:

- *Agoraphobic syndrome*: is the commonest variety, constituting about sixty per cent of all phobias. The agoraphobic patients have fears not only of open spaces but also of shopping, crowds, travelling, and even of closed spaces. Other neurotic symptoms including panic attacks, dizziness, compulsive rituals, and feelings of depersonalisation are also often present. Most agoraphobics are women and the majority develop their symptoms after puberty.
- *Animal phobia*: constitutes the most clear-cut variety of phobia but, in its pure form, is infrequently encountered in clinical practice. The

symptom usually develops at the onset of latency, that is, around six to eight years of age. There is little tendency for its "generalisation" and there is little tension in the absence of the phobic object.

- *Social phobia*: involves fear of public speaking, blushing, shaking, writing, eating, drinking, vomiting, or becoming incontinent in public. It occurs with equal frequency among men and women and usually starts after puberty, with a peak of incidence in the late teens.
- *Miscellaneous specific phobias*: start any time in life and persist fairly consistently. The phobic situations vary from one case to another but remain fairly specific for a given individual. The dreaded situations include travel, heights, wind, thunderstorms, darkness, bridges, and large bodies of water.

Of these four types, animal phobias and miscellaneous specific phobias have received the most attention from psychoanalysis. Beginning with Freud's (1909b) widely known study of Little Hans, to numerous subsequent contributions (e.g., Campbell & Pile, 2011; Kulish, 1996; Lewin, 1952; Rangell, 1952; Sandler, 1989; Tyson, 1978; Wangh, 1959), psychoanalysts have sought to discern what underlies such focal reigns of terror upon the ego. Freud traced Little Hans's fear of being bitten by a horse to his dread of castration by his father; this, in turn, was the talion punishment for the boy's incestuous longings for his mother. Freud's early followers (Abraham, 1913a; Deutsch, 1933; Fenichel, 1945) fervently subscribed to this explanation and began to view all phobias as derived from castration anxiety. However, as psychoanalytic theory advanced and attention shifted towards the vicissitudes of pre-Oedipal development, the "danger situation" (Freud, 1926d) of loss of love gained explanatory ascendance.[2] The centrality of castration anxiety came under question and anxiety over good internal objects getting drowned by the aggression within (in a newer rendition of the "loss of love" hypothesis) became an equally, if not more, important motivating force for symptom formation.

Regardless of their source, till such anxieties remained repressed, one simply failed to see, hear, or otherwise attend to threatening internal (wishes, impulses) or external (triggers, temptations) stimuli. Nonetheless, the repressed material continued to seek expression. In Freud's (1915e) words, "The repressed exercises a continuous pressure in the direction of consciousness" (p. 51). This tendency becomes stronger in the face of a reactive increase in the intensity of drives. Many "simple phobias" (Fenichel, 1945) can thus be explained.

> In certain cases there is not much displacement; anxiety is simply felt in situations where an uninhibited person would experience either sexual excitement or rage ... For such cases, a formula is valid which would be an oversimplification in more complicated cases: what a person fears, he unconsciously wishes for ... In other and still simple phobias, the feared situation does not represent a feared temptation; rather, it is the threat that causes the temptation to be feared: castration or loss of love. There are knife and scissor phobias, the implication of which is that the touch or even the sight of these instruments awakens the feared thought of a possible castration (and, it is true, in most cases, also an unconscious temptation for a repressed hostility). Certain persons are afraid of seeing cripples or of witnessing accidents, which means: "I do not want to be reminded of what might happen to me" (and again, the fear may also arise from such sights being a temptation for unconscious hostile wishes). (pp. 195–196)

The psychodynamics of most phobias is, however, far more complicated. But before going into these details, it should be noted that many non-analytic aetiological models of phobia also exist. Modelling, vicarious learning, and observational conditioning are alternative pathways by which animals acquire their phobic potential (Cook & Mineka, 1987; Emde, 1984; Eysenck, 1965, 1976; Marks, 1987; Mineka, Davidson, Cook & Keir, 1984; Solyom, Beck, Solyom & Hugel, 1974; Wolpe & Rachman, 1960). This perspective reports cases of phobias arising after a child observes a parent responding fearfully to an animal (Solyom, Beck, Solyom & Hugel, 1974), or, as in Mineka, Davidson, Cook, and Keir's (1984) experiments, after laboratory-reared rhesus monkeys view wild-caught monkeys reacting fearfully to snakes. More recently, learning theory has been challenged and broadened by biological research in animal phobias (Bennett-Levy & Marteau, 1984; Davey, 1992; Davey, Forster, & Mayhew, 1993; McNally & Steketee, 1985; Mineka, Davidson, Cook & Keir, 1984). This view suggests that learning is "biologically prepared" in that there are anatomic portions of the brain preprogrammed to perceive specific, fear-evoking animal movements much like the nondominant parietal lobe perceives faces. Sudden movement and speed are "chosen" as fearful. Some of these authors have pointed to the fact that most animal phobias involve harmless (spider, cockroach, maggot, snake, and rat) rather than predatory animals (lions, tigers, sharks); they postulate that animal phobias correlate more with contamination and disgust rather than with fear. Together, these three aetiological perspectives, namely modelling, vicarious learning, and observational conditioning, along with consideration of potential hereditary determinants of fear and phobias (Delprato, 1980), might explain why specific animals have remained both "chosen" phobia objects and symbols in mythology in almost every culture.

Returning to the psychoanalytic perspective on phobias, one notes that the complexity of their dynamics is due to the fact that repression alone becomes incapable of keeping the threat sufficiently removed from awareness. As a result, displacement, symbolism, and regression come into play. Displacement, the process by which an affect or attitude is unconsciously transferred from one object to a more acceptable substitute, is then added to repression. Now, it is not the *sexual* situations but the *sexualised* situations that are feared. The diffuse anxiety becomes bound to a specific object/situation. This makes life easier, since the specificity of the fear now makes matters manageable through the active process of avoidance. The advantage offered by displacement is that the original offensive idea/affect does not become conscious. Also, by binding the hostile vector of ambivalence towards one's father, for instance, into a fear of horses, the displacement tends to resolve conflicts of ambivalence. Also, as Freud (1909b) pointed out, displacement by itself renders avoidance easier.

The feared object/situation often represents an exquisitely unique and symbolic crystallisation of all the important determinants of the phobia, including the predominant impulse of threat against which the phobia is a defence. Jones (1948) emphasised the role of symbolism in phobia, noting that there is a certain affinity between the individual and the icons he chooses to express his instrapsychic concerns. Lewin (1952) likened the process determining the specific phobia to the dream work, sharing the same overdetermination and other parallel phenomena, including traces of early experiences. Although universally symbolic meanings for various phobias may be suggested, these are not invariably valid. It is therefore better not to approach the patient's phobia with preconceived ideas about its meaning. The true meaning of any symbol to an individual patient can be determined only by listening to his/her associations.

A certain amount of regression is also central to all phobias. The phobic's cognition, in the restricted area of his neurotic symptom, is strikingly similar to the child's animistic perception of the world as threatening and overwhelming. Regression also is evident insofar as

> ... all phobics behave like children, whose anxieties are soothed if the mother sits by the bedside and holds their hand. Such a demand for reassuring measures on the part of parent substitutes is especially evident in those agoraphobics who feel protected in the presence of a companion ... in phobias in which the companion is essential, the relationship to this companion is of basic importance. The companion not only represents the protecting parent but also the unconsciously-hated parent; his presence serves the purpose of diverting the patient's mind from unconscious fantasies to reality, that is, of reassuring him that he has not killed this person who is walking safely at his side. In such cases, the fear that something may happen to the patient is often preceded by a fear for the safety of the same person who, later on in the agoraphobia, is used as a companion. (Fenichel, 1945, pp. 206–207)

Agoraphobia, the roots of which were traced to a repressed prostitution fantasy by Freud (1897, cited in Masson, 1985, p. 253), is actually more often the result of conflicts pertaining to "optimal distance" (Akhtar, 1992b; Escoll, 1992; Mahler, Pine & Bergman, 1975). In an early paper on "locomotor anxiety", Abraham (1913b) noted that neurotic inhibitions of motility emanate not only from defences against constitutionally strong pleasure in movement and unconscious sexual concerns but also from difficulty in separating from love objects. They fear going out but also are unhappy at being left alone indoors. Speaking of such "'topophobia", Abraham said that in patients with this malady:

> ... anxiety prevents them from becoming free from themselves and from the objects upon which their love was fixed in childhood, and from finding the way to objects belonging to the external world. Every path which leads them away from the charmed circle of those people upon whom they are fixated, is closed to them. (p. 241)

Some years later, Deutsch (1929) declared the involvement of a partner to be the crucial determinant of the agoraphobic's malady. However, she felt that hostile and controlling fantasies were frequently hidden underneath the consciously experienced need for libidinal attachment. Following this, Mittleman (1957) observed the confinement of the agoraphobic to a "limited circumference" (p. 289) and Weiss (1964) noted that such patients grow more anxious the farther they go from their home. This led him to define agoraphobia as an anxiety reaction to abandoning a fixed point of support. More recently, Kohut (1980) concluded that the agoraphobic's consciously felt need for a reassuring companion is the key to what lies in a psychic depth, namely, the continued search for a maternal self object.

Clearly, all these authors regard agoraphobia as a malady of distance. My own elucidation of the ubiquitous, though unconscious, fantasy of a "psychic tether" (Akhtar, 1992b) lends support to such formulation. How far can one go away from one's objects without endangering the cohesion of one's self, seems to be the question.[3] The opposite question, how close can one get to another person without risking one's autonomy, applies to claustrophobia. And, just like in agoraphobia, in claustrophobia, too, anxieties regarding optimal distance (from love objects) are intermingled with psychosexual anxieties and other dreads pertaining to Oedipal conflicts. Lewin's (1935) declaration that there is a close connection between claustrophobia and being inside the mother and the fear of being buried alive is a transformed wish to return to the womb, can be interpreted in both Oedipal and pre-Oedipal ways. The fact is that almost all psychopathology comes from both sources. It is rarely an "either-or" matter. A phobic symptom is derived from diverse sources and contains tributaries from multiple phases of development. This statement applies to monosymptomatic phobia as well as to the diffuse agoraphobic syndrome. It is even more true when phobic concerns pervade the entire character.

Phobic character

Introduced by Fenichel (1945), the designation "phobic character" is reserved for individuals "whose reactive behavior limits itself to the avoidance of situations originally wished-for" (p. 527). Those with severe inhibitions of sexuality and aggressiveness also display a similar picture of generalised apprehension and social withdrawal. Elaborating on Fenichel's proposal, Mackinnon and Michels (1971) emphasised that more common than ego-dystonic, monosymptomatic phobia is the use of fearful avoidance as a character defence, adding that such an individual is "constantly imaging himself in situations of danger while pursuing the course of greatest safety" (p. 49). More recently, Stone (1980) recognised a "phobic-anxious" personality type that displays extremes of "fearfulness and avoidance of the most harmless objects and situations" (p. 332). While resembling schizoid individuals in their restricted life style, phobic characters are different in significant ways. They are not "shy" and idiosyncratic like schizoid people. They avoid situations (and physical objects), not people. Their avoidance of certain situations (e.g., visiting an amusement park, watching a pornographic movie, going to a new restaurant), can lead to the false appearance of discomfort with people in general. The fact is that outside the dreaded situations, they can have empathic and meaningful affective interchanges with others. Phobic characters are not associated with "identity diffusion" (Akhtar, 1984; Kernberg, 1975) and extensive reliance upon splitting mechanisms. They do not therefore represent a borderline personality organisation (Kernberg, 1967); they are organised at a higher level with fears emanating from the externalisation and symbolic reification of their internal conflicts. Their fears are imaginary. Cowardice, in contrast, involves a recoil from plausible, if not actual, threats. Symbolism lies at the heart of phobic character and anxiety about object loss forms the bedrock of cowardice.

Cowardice

A habitual reaction to threat and danger, cowardice—at least on the surface—is a response to fear of actual harm. It involves a "crippling of the will" (Menaker, 1979, p. 93); one succumbs to fear and withdraws from the "combat".[4] Cowardice can be evident in physical, intellectual, and moral realms. Physical cowardice involves an inordinate fear of injury and the resulting restriction of exploratory and playful motor activity; one avoids athletics, amusement park rides, and any possibility of physical altercation. Intellectual cowardice results in inhibition of mental activity; one cannot think "outside the box" and gets scared if new insights do pop up in the mind. Moral cowardice manifests as the inability to uphold ethical standards and speak the truth under difficult circumstances; one lies, suddenly seems to lack words, and adopts the "silence of the complicit" (Akhtar, 2013a).

The coward reacts to confrontation with distress. In part, this is due to "automatic anxiety" (Freud, 1926d), the spontaneous reaction of helpless dread in the face of a massively traumatic situation. And, in part, this is due to projection of the coward's own anger. Unable to express his resentment directly, the coward attributes vicious intent to his opponent and gets terrified. Consequently, he postpones the "debate", falsely concurs with his adversary, or, worse, flees the situation in reality. Recognition of his timidity fills him with shame and self-disgust; these are often drowned in drink or covered over by the narcissistic fantasy of having deliberately engineered his defeat. The spineless combatant of yesterday thus transforms himself into the lofty bestower of victory to others.

But there is more to cowardice than its narcissistic dynamic. The base of cowardice is formed by a "thin-skinned" (Rosenfeld, 1971) psyche which is the consequence of weak maternal containment of early infantile anxieties (Bick, 1968). The cowardly individual tends to become affectively overwhelmed while facing a narcissistic threat; withdrawal from a full encounter with it follows. Deficient identification with the same-sex parent also contributes to such psychic vulnerability. The most important aetiological factor in cowardice, however, is a condensation of body mutilation anxieties (including, of course, castration anxiety) and a dread of separation and aloneness. An "ocnophile" (Balint, 1968) par excellence, the coward clings to his objects and is willing to sacrifice dignity at the altar of relatedness. All cowardice, when it comes down to it, is the fear of being disliked and being alone. Meltzer (1973) notes:

> Where dependence on good internal objects is rendered infeasible by damaging masturbatory attacks and where dependence on a good external object is unavailable or not acknowledged, an addictive relationship to a bad part of the self—the submission to tyranny takes place. An illusion of safety is promulgated by the omniscience of the destructive part ... Where a dread of loss of an addictive relation to a tyrant is found in psychic structure, the problem of terror will be found at its core, as the force behind the dread and the submission. (p. 78)

Meltzer's proposal has implications for the technical handling of individuals trapped in relationships with narcissistic-sadistic partners. However, before discussing them, it is pertinent to take a few steps back and consider the myriad ways in which fear is exploited, used, marketed, and enjoyed by societal institutions created by man.

A cultural digression

Although fear is ubiquitous in human existence, it does have a deep and complex relationship with culture. Their relationship is often dialectical in nature. Fear can disturb a culture's slumber and mobilise adaptive and maladaptive responses. Cultural narratives can embellish existing fears, create new ones, and offer rich iconography for both. All this becomes evident in the realms of regional concerns, prejudice, politics, literature, and even entertainment. The following passages address these matters in brief.

Some fears (e.g., looking down from a great height, fast-moving animals) seem so widely spread across the globe as to appear independent of cultural influences. Like "universal dreams" (Freud, 1900a),[5] such "universal fears" combine phylogenetic predisposition, evolutionary advantages, and precipitates of early childhood experiences. Other fears are idiosyncratic, limited to some people, and, at times, restricted to regions and eras. Fear of ghosts and evil spirits, for instance, has largely gone from modernised societies while persisting in less educated, less industrialised, rural and sub-rural communities of the world. Fears of earthquakes, floods, and tornadoes are generally restricted to areas with vulnerability to such disasters. Similarly, animal phobias are regionally anchored; it is hardly conceivable for one living in Saudi Arabia to be afraid of polar bears.

The phenomenology of "culture-bound psychiatric syndromes" (Guarnaccia & Rogler, 1999; Meth, 1974; Yap, 1969) is replete with observations that support this line of thought. Not only animals that populate a specific region are chosen as phobic objects by people living there, they can also become the suitable containers of projections of the attributes of bravery and cowardice. In colloquial English, for instance, a coward is referred to as "chicken-hearted" or merely a "chicken" and in Spanish, as *gallina* (hen). In Arabic, a brave man is called an *assag* (lion) while in Urdu, such a person is called *sher-dil* (one with a lion's heart); in contrast, a coward is called *buz-dil* (one with a goat's heart). What all this demonstrates is that not only are the objects of fear but even the metaphors of bravery and cowardice often regionally determined.

Fear plays in important role in prejudice as well. The "unmentalized xenophobia" (Akhtar, 2007c) that results in bland indifference towards and avoidance of those different from oneself is merely the tip of the proverbial iceberg here. The relentless need to externalise aggression and the deployment of paranoia as a "psychic vitamin for threatened identity and a powerful anodyne against the pain that results from genuine self-reflection" (ibid., p. 17) results in the creation of frightening outside figures. Since minorities are often "suitable reservoirs for projection" (Volkan, 1988), all sorts of dread and danger are seen as emanating from them. Blacks, homosexuals, and Muslims are frequent targets of hostile projection and therefore objects of fear; this, in turn, is utilised as a rationalisation for discrimination and prejudice. Mesmerising oratory of hatred by charismatic though paranoid leaders fuels the imaginary dangers posed by the other and sanctions acts of cruelty and violence. No wonder fear and politics are often intertwined with each other.

Monarchies and totalitarian regimes are customarily prone to create a "culture of fear" for their citizens. The term "terrorism" —used these days mostly to designate the political violence of small groups—actually originated in the context of state-sponsored intimidation. First used in 1795, "terrorism" denoted the French Revolutionary statesman Maximilien de Robespierre's Reign of Terror (1785–1794). Robespierre defended his fear-mongering, iron-fisted control, and terrorising of the masses by claiming that the Revolution enacted the despotism of liberty against tyranny. He was, however, not an exception. More recent times have witnessed Adolf Hitler's Holocaust, Joseph Stalin's gulags and purges, and Pol Pot's killing fields. Government, turned mercenary, can be a source of great fear, indeed.

Unfortunately, even democratic nations can regress and make people tremble while expressing their opinions or, worse, become altogether mute. The so-called "emergency rule" enforced by India's prime minister, Indira Gandhi (1917–1984), before she was assassinated, and the unauthorised wire-tapping and "extraordinary renditions" by the CIA during the post-9/11 era of George W. Bush's presidency were no less terrorising to the people of their respective nations.[6] Within psychoanalysis itself, there have been prominent individuals and organisations that have inculcated a "culture of fear". This ranges from Freud's authoritarian suppression of dissent (Rudnytsky, 2012) to the pervasive sense in the field that openly expressing a pro-Palestinian stance is risky if not tantamount to professional suicide. Needless to add that when such dread pervades the tissue of an organisation, its advance is seriously compromised.

Evoking and fuelling large group fears is a favourite strategy of political leaders with narcissistic and paranoid tendencies (Volkan, 1997). Hitler's pronouncement that Jews were a threat to the European economy, Slobodan Milosevic's poisonous reminder to the Serbs that some of their fellow citizens were actually Turks, and the constant evocation of mortal danger from Arabs by Israelis and vice versa, are some prominent illustrations of fearmongering as a tactic for strengthening one's political hand. Fear then becomes a ploy for oppression, disenfranchisement, and even genocide of hated others.

A dramatically different interaction between fear and culture occurs when judiciously titrated and aesthetically cleansed fear forms the basis of literature. The oral tradition of telling scary tales dates back to antiquity and the written genre of fear-laced fiction has seen steady output over centuries. Essentially such sagas belong to two categories, namely those of supernatural horror (e.g., ghost stories, tales from beyond the grave, satanic machinations, attacks by aliens and zombies), and of evil lying within the human heart itself (e.g., murder stories, sadomasochistic cliffhangers). Reading such novels and short stories stirs up psychic terror; this is often accompanied by a sense of helplessness (a result of identification with the victimised protagonist). There is also a feeling of being immersed in the goings-on and yet experiencing a bit of uncanniness. Freud's (1919h) discussion of *unheimlich* or the uncanny clearly stated that it derives its terror not from something externally alien or unknown but—on the contrary—from something strangely familiar which defeats our effort to separate ourselves from it. There is a quality of something "fateful and inescapable" (p. 237) being forced upon one. Freud goes on to state that:

> An uncanny effect is often easily produced when the distinction between imagination and reality is effaced, as when something that we have hitherto regarded as imaginary appears before us in reality, or when a symbol takes over the full functions of the thing it symbolizes, and so on. It is this factor which contributes not a little to the uncanny effect attaching to magical practices. (p. 244)

Writers of terrifying fiction, ranging from Clara Reeves (1729–1807) and Ann Radcliffe (1764–1823) through Edgar Allan Poe (1809–1849) and Bram Stoker (1847–1912) to Ann Rice (b. 1941) and Stephen King (b. 1947) are deft in evoking an uncanny response by straddling the line between reality and unreality within the plot and the details of its characters. They succeed in collapsing the boundary between mind and matter, mundane and strange, and natural and diabolical.

However, for some individuals menace in print is not sufficient. They require visual images and sound effects to experience fear. Enter horror movies. A genre which emerged at almost the inception of commercial cinema (circa 1910), horror movies exploit many ubiquitous human tendencies, even if these are ordinarily banished from conscious awareness. Among these are the need for excitement, novelty-seeking, the pleasure of an adrenaline rush, counterphobic pressure to master fear, and the vicarious gratification of repressed perverse fantasies and impulses to defy social norms (Goldstein, 1998).[7] Especially appealing to young men, such movies become an engrossing topic of conversation and a glue for peer bonding. It must, however, be added that horror movies are not uniform and many sub-genres exist. These include themes pertaining to:

- Demon-child, e.g., *The Exorcist* (1973), and *The Omen* (1976).
- Alien invasion, e.g., *War of the Worlds* (1953), and *Puppet Masters* (1994).
- Dangerous animals, e.g., *The Birds* (1963), and *Jaws* (1975).
- Gory violence, e.g., *Texas Chainsaw Massacre* (1974), and *A Clockwork Orange* (1971).
- Perverse and psychotic ruthlessness, e.g., *Psycho* (1960), and *The Shining* (1980).

The common element in all such movies is the evocation of fear, often to an unsettling and near-traumatic extent.[8] They provide an encounter with the "uncanny" (Freud, 1919h) by disrupting routine and by transforming the all-too-familiar into the bizarre and unpredictable. While gratuitous throat-slitting violence can elicit tormented joy from filmgoers, it is the helpless anticipation that truly terrifies them. The great maestro of fear, Alfred Hitchcock (1899–1980), recognised this and declared: "There is no excitement in the bang, only in the anticipation of it." Hitchcock knew that while fear is unpleasant, playing with fear, if done artistically, can yield pleasure.

Back to the clinical realm

Having discussed the differential diagnoses in the realm of fear (i.e., fear, anxiety, phobia, cowardice), I wish now to comment upon the management of fear and fear-related phenomena in the clinical situation.[9] That such work involves a great deal of countertransference vigilance and can be taxing for the analyst's ego goes without saying. Indeed, all interventions in such work require patience, tact, and forbearance from the analyst (besides, of course, his or her interpretive skill) and the categorisation of such interventions here is largely for didactic ease. That being said, three main tasks in working with those afflicted with fear and those capable of inducing fear in the analyst are (i) sensing fear, assessing dangerousness, and setting limits, (ii) bearing and containing the patient's fear, and (iii) managing one's own fear and learning from it. My selecting these three areas to focus upon is by no means dismissive of the customary interpretive and reconstructive work that forms the basic material of all psychoanalyses. Defence and resistance analysis, confrontation with the repudiated preconscious material, linking-up of derivatives, and helping decipher what underlies the symbolic and displaced forms of fear constitute the bread and butter of psychoanalytic work. Such work is needed regardless of whether the patient's fears are neurotic, paranoid, or self-annihilatory. The three areas chosen to be addressed are additional and not alternative to the customary work of psychoanalysis.

Sensing fear, addressing dangerousness, and setting limits

Since most analysts and psychoanalytically oriented therapists screen their patients for possessing "a fairly reliable character" (Freud, 1905a, p. 263) and only take into treatment those individuals who are not sociopathic and are not suicidal or homicidal, assessment of the patient's dangerousness does not figure in their usual repertoire of concerns. Nonetheless, situations can—and do—evolve where the analyst has to decide whether it is safe to continue working in the customary manner. The following declaration by Hoffer (1985) is pertinent in this context.

> The analyst's neutrality with respect to conflict may be suspended in situations the analyst feels are (a) emergencies for the patient—e.g. suicidality, psychosis, toxic state, etc.; (b) emergencies for someone potentially vulnerable to the patient's destructiveness—e.g. the analysand's children; and, (c) emergencies for the analyst—physical or psychological threats. (p. 786)

Under such circumstances, the analyst might feel afraid and rationally worry about the safety of himself, others, or the patient. This might happen in the course of an ongoing treatment or, at times, in the very first encounter between the patient and the analyst.[10]

Clinical vignette: 1

> Sarah Green, a forty-five-year-old librarian made an appointment to see me upon her sister's insistence. She appeared overwhelmed with pain at the break-up of a romantic relationship. Having lived alone most of her life, she found this belated attachment profoundly significant. The man she was involved with was married. He abruptly left her saying that he could no longer continue cheating on his wife. She was destroyed. Heartbroken, she came to see me.
>
> We began the first hour of consultation in a customary history-taking way. However, within twenty minutes of the session, she announced that she had decided to blow her head off with a gun which she had bought earlier that day. Alarmed by the earnestness of her tone, I suggested that we take immediate steps to get the gun removed from her apartment, obtain some collateral information regarding the extent of her depression, and consider beginning our work on an inpatient basis. The patient reacted sharply to my suggestion and, refusing to let me contact her sister who could remove the gun, got up to leave the office. At this point, I said to her, "Look, everybody gets about ten candles' worth of life and inside you eight have already gone off. The wind is blowing hard and to protect the remaining two candles, you came here and put them in my heart. Now, since you have enlisted me for this purpose, it is my duty to keep these two candles protected from the wind. When the storm settles, I will return them to you so that you can light the other eight candles back with their help." The patient broke down in tears and after some thinking gave me the permission to contact her sister who subsequently removed the gun from the patient's apartment and encouraged the patient to stay at her house for the next few days.

Such admixture of limit-setting, supportive measures, environmental interventions, and interpretive approach might tilt in favour of one or the other component given the seriousness and/or urgency of threatened violence (towards self or others). Generally speaking, in psychoanalytic practices, supportive and interpretive measures carry the day while in psychiatric clinics (especially in the Casualty Department settings), limit-setting, hospitalisation, and medications might become necessary to manage the patient's aggression and the fear induced into others by such aggression.[11] Kernberg's (1984) guidelines for the management of hatred in severely borderline patients allow for assuring safely by strict limit-setting. Frightening outbursts of rage in such patients have to be met not only by holding and containment but also by explicitly informing the patient of what he or she can and cannot do within the clinical setting.

Clinical vignette: 2

> Bob Dolinski, a borderline young man in twice weekly psychotherapy, exploded with rage when I refused to comply with his demand for painkillers. In a menacing tone, he threatened to take my eyeballs out and crush them under his feet. Alarmed by his emotional flooding and rapidly disintegrating reality-testing, I firmly told him to stay put in his chair. I added that if he as much as laid a finger on me I would terminate the treatment and never see him again. I told him that he needed someone who could listen to him peacefully, not someone who was afraid of him and that I would be afraid of him if he acted even once on his impulse to hurt me. Noticing that he was settling down, I added that the idea that he could take my eyeballs out was both unrealistic and intriguing. He could not do it; I would not let him. And, why did he think of eyeballs in the first place? Could it have something to do with the memory of his mother looking contemptuously at him? Interventions along these lines calmed him down and soon the session was progressing in a more mutually related manner.

Similar to the technical interventions in the preceding vignette, my stance during this frightening episode, with imminent risk of physical violence, included firm limit-setting coupled with comments to improve reality-testing. In addition, I also made an attempt to link the content of his threat with certain memories he had reported during an earlier phase of our work. While such active efforts were needed here, in cases where the threat is subtle and slow, one can maintain relative neutrality and, just by bearing the fear induced by the patient, prepare the ground for customary interpretive work.

Bearing and containing the patient's fear

Prominent among the analyst's tasks is to hold and contain the fears that the patient can feel and verbalise as well as those fears that remain unspeakable for the patient. Discerning such "beta elements" (Bion, 1967a) through his reverie, his resonance with the patient's projective identification, and his empathy-driven "trial identifications" (Fliess, 1942) with the patient, the analyst senses the patient's fears but does not hurriedly unmask them. Instead, he allows himself to be the depository of such affects, waiting for the process of defence analysis and for the patient's resulting ego-growth to permit the verbalisation of hitherto repudiated anxieties. Stated in the language of contemporary relational psychoanalysis, fear is an intersubjective response which, like any other countertransference reaction, helps the analyst understand himself, his patient, and the nature of their interaction. Moreover, since the patient and the analyst need to feel safe, a modicum of mutual regulation is important for the dyad in "setting and re-calibrating the danger-safety balance in their analytic work" (Kafka, 1998, p. 102).

Such is the process in most ongoing analyses. However, there are occasions when the dreaded fragments of the patient's psyche burst through the rational mind of the ego and result in a state of "emotional flooding" (Volkan, 1976). Under such circumstances, the analyst's containing capacity acquires a greater importance; this capacity then prepares the ground for an interpretive deconstruction of what just took place.

Clinical vignette: 3

> Rebecca Cohen, twenty-six-year-old daughter of a Holocaust survivor father, was in analysis with me. The course of early treatment was filled with anxiety-laden fantasies about her father's experience in the Nazi concentration camp. Dreaded scenarios of ethnic hatred and violence preoccupied Rebecca and this readily spread to the transference. She feared and hated me, regarded me as a Jew-hating Muslim or Arab, and suspected that I supported anti-Israeli violence by Palestinians. Projections of her own transgenerationally given post-traumatic Jew-Nazi split of the self were constantly active in her relatedness with me. One day, I was hated and viciously attacked. Next day, I was deeply feared.

> During one session while talking of the Holocaust, she suddenly jumped up from the couch and ran to the corner of the office that was farthest from me, trembling and obviously shaken by something she had just experienced internally. Rebecca stood there crying. I remained silent. Then she found a box of tissues on the desk nearby, cleaned her face, and began to look a bit composed. I did not say anything and waited patiently for things to unfold. Rebecca jumped up, sat on my desk, and asked me if I knew what had happened. I shook my head, telling her that I did not. She then revealed that she had felt that I was going to take out a knife and stab her while she was on the couch and that's why she had to get away from me. As she was narrating this, I noted that she had become much calmer. I remained quiet. Rebecca went on to say, "You know, I have never seen your office from this end. It looks so strange … You know, what it looks like … It looks so still. Everything is unmoved, quiet. It is like a dust cover jacket of a bestseller murder mystery. And you know what, sometimes when you read the whole book, you find out that all the clues were already shown in the photograph on the cover of the book. Yes, your office, from this side, looks like a photograph of just that sort, with all the clues intact." Now I spoke. I said, "And, I guess I would be the corpse in this murder scene." Rebecca smiled, stretched her arms, and aiming her clasped hands at me, made a noise indicating that she was shooting me with a gun. I responded by saying, "You know what, a little while ago you thought that I was going to kill you and now that you have taken some distance from that position, you find yourself killing me. Look, this murder and murderer are both parts of your own self and, for the work we have mutually undertaken, it is my hope that we hold on to both these views and see how they are related to each other, where they came from, and what purposes do they serve." Rebecca got off the desk, walked back to the couch, and lay down. The session continued in the "usual" way.

This clinical exchange illustrates a number of interventions, including the interpretation of splitting and projective identification. However, what I wish to emphasise here is how my unperturbed and non-intrusive stance facilitated the unfolding of the clinical material. My verbal interventions were important but these were possible only because of the material that became available due to my containing her terror by an unshaken and quiet stance.

Managing one's own fear and learning from it

During the course of his clinical work, the psychoanalyst experiences a vast array of emotions and fear figures prominently in that list. Poland (cited in Mathias, 2008) has described four different ways in which fear arises within the analyst: (i) elicited by the patient, (ii) originating within the analyst himself, (iii) pertaining to the analytic process, and (iv) from the realities of the human condition. Finding these categories to be overlapping, I classify the analyst's fear into (i) his fear of the patient, (ii) his fear of acting out and making mistakes, (iii) his fear that the analysis will fail, and (iv) his fear of making unusual interventions. Acknowledging that such things cannot be neatly catalogued and one classification might clarify some things and muddle some others, in the following passages, I will follow my scheme.

First is the analyst's fear of the patient. This is most marked when he is working with paranoid or borderline individuals, especially if they are given to outbursts of rage (see clinical vignette 2). Those who are chronically at the verge of committing suicide can also induce fear in the analyst. Fears of being sued and of damage to one's professional reputation can become quite powerful under such circumstances. These concerns might constitute rational responses to the patient's self-destructiveness and be accentuated by the projection of the analyst's own unconscious hatred of the patient (Maltsberger & Buie, 1974). At times the analyst is successful in bearing such fears for long periods of time and continuing to work with the patient in a holding-interpretive mode. His decision to not set limits but allow the process to unfold is based upon a sense that the patient needs him to tolerate being afraid and that this transference demand is going to become amenable to interpretive resolution. Then something happens and the whole edifice falls apart.

Clinical vignette: 4

As the treatment proceeded, Sarah Green (the patient mentioned in clinical vignette 1) recounted details of her long-term suicidal wishes and her constant sense, while growing up, that her mother hated her and wanted her dead. She also talked about the harsh criticism her mother directed at her; she repeatedly called Sarah a "monster" and an "evil one". Not surprisingly, Sarah was terrified of her mother and made few demands on her time and attention.

As these details unfolded, Sarah stole a revolver from her sister's house and started sleeping with it—fully loaded—in her hand. I was terrified and yet felt prompted to stay away, this time, from insisting that she get rid of the gun immediately. I had a vague sense that the fear I was experiencing was the consequence of projective identification with her frightened child-self, as well as a direct result of her revenge-seeking fantasies. In other words, due to the effect of her projection, I had become "scared little Sarah" while she had adopted the role of her terrifying mother. And, at the same time, she had transformed herself from poor little Sarah to intimidating Sarah and I, as the mother, had to be tormented for what I had done to her as a child.

The very fact that I could conceptualise the enactment and put what was, most likely, going on into mental words, told me that there was something containable and, ultimately, interpretable here. The risk (for her) was high and the fear (in me) palpable but session after session, we talked about the potential underlying what was taking place—feelings, somewhere deep in our hearts, that we did not need to rupture the enactment by behavioural limit-setting, that she needed me to bear the anxiety. We felt that all that was happening was in the "pretend mode" (Fonagy & Target, 1997).

Then one afternoon, Sarah called me, saying that she was feeling truly suicidal again. I had another patient in the waiting room and asked her if she could assure me that she would not do anything impulsive and self-destructive for the next hour. She promised and we agreed that I would call her as soon as the patient I was about to see left. However, when I called, the phone kept ringing and ringing and Sarah did not pick it up. I was horrified, and thought that she had killed herself. Trembling with fear and cursing myself for being unduly heroic and adventuresome in my clinical work, I called her sister, who immediately departed for Sarah's apartment. The next thirty minutes were the longest thirty minutes I have ever lived. Then, I got a call from her sister that she had found Sarah fast asleep and that everything was fine and under control. Sarah came on the phone and profusely apologised for what had happened. I accepted

> her apology but, feeling that a certain line had been crossed (and, that from a containing mother, I was becoming an ignoring and destructive mother), I insisted that the sister not only take the gun away but immediately dispose of it in a manner that Sarah would never be able to get her hands on it again. This intervention and its subsequent discussion in the clinical setting paved the way for the deepening of our therapeutic work.

Second is the fear of the analyst's own impulses to act out. If the analyst is under great personal stress (e.g., bereavement, divorce, serious illness), his fear of acting out with his patients, using his patients to diminish his loneliness, and venting sexual or aggressive effects (even if in a mild and aim-inhibited manner) is plausible and worthy of attention; consultation with a trusted colleague or return to some treatment must be considered under such circumstances. However, there are other times when the analyst is functioning optimally and yet develops a fear of doing something odd or strange with his patient. This is the stuff of countertransference and restraint coupled with self-reflection often reveals the nature of transference that is putting such pressure on the analyst. Here is a clinical example of such an occurrence.

Clinical vignette: 5

> Melanie Wright, a boyish young woman had sought treatment owing to feelings of anxiety and some marital tension. She had panicked when her husband was laid off from his job and, even though he was able to find gainful employment soon afterwards, remained anxious; in fact, she feared that they would become destitute. She and her husband frequently argued over this fear of hers and the friction between them was growing.
>
> What struck me most when I first met her, however, was not this undue anxiety but the fact that she—a young woman in her mid-twenties—looked like a teenage boy. Making a mental note of it, I proceeded with gathering some background history. It turned out that her parents were divorced when she was six years old and that she had been raised by a loving but industrious and busy professional mother. Two other important facts were that the divorce had been precipitated by her father's announcement that he was gay and that young Melanie had to grow up with a very difficult

> older brother who constantly, and, at times, physically hurt—her. All sorts of factors, it seemed, worked in unison and led to the compromise of her femininity. The fact that she had been married for three years and seemed to love her husband appeared a little out of place.
>
> As we began an analysis, I found myself experiencing something I had never felt during a clinical hour before. With Melanie talking—sometimes haltingly and at other times freely—about this or that issue, I experienced a peculiar discomfort in my rib cage and upper abdominal area. It is as if someone was tickling me very hard (my mind went to some childhood memories that involved my older brother). I repeatedly wanted to change my position in the chair, as if to evade this tickling. Alongside such physical unease, I also felt impulses to interrupt her by saying something absurd and totally unrelated to what Melanie was talking about. If, for instance, she was talking about her parents' divorce, I felt like asking her if she knew the capital of Iowa and if she ruminated on her financial future, or I had the urge to tell her about the intricacies of Urdu poetry.
>
> While I kept such impulses in check, the experience was nonetheless unnerving. I kept wondering what it was about. What would be the impact upon her were I to utter my passing thoughts? To be sure, she would be shocked. She might experience me as bizarre, if not outright mad.
>
> A few weeks of sitting upon such impulses, waiting, allowing the material to evolve further, and conducting piecemeal defence analysis, led to her revealing that her father had not only become gay but quite "crazy": he had painted the living and dining room ceilings purple, had started inviting his gay lovers to their home and would have sex in front of Melanie and her brother (when the mother was out working). Once or twice, he invited the children to join him and his lover in the bed while they were making love. As this material emerged—amid much distress and crying—I found a sudden reduction in my impulses to "act crazy"!

With the countertransference tension more in control, I became better able to think about what had transpired between the patient and myself. My "conjecture" (C. Brenner, 1976) was that the patient had been shocked by her father's perverse behaviour and had internalied this traumatic object relations scenario. It remained "unmetabolised", however, and needed to be deposited into me, like Bion's (1962) beta elements, for my containing and processing. She could retrieve it only after her capacity to bear the trauma and to "mentalise" (Fonagy & Target, 1997) grew. Meanwhile, I had to bear the noxious experience alternately as the victim (e.g., my feeling mercilessly tickled) and the perpetrator (e.g., my wishing to shock her by uttering absurdities) of the psychic violence.

A *third* fear experienced by the analyst is that of analytic failure. While exceptions exist, generally this fear reflects that the patient was not really suitable for analysis (e.g., too concrete, too paranoid, too lonely), and was taken into treatment by misjudgment or for the wrong reasons (e.g., analyst's need for money, patient's seductiveness). Generally this becomes evident via the concreteness of thought, the unrelenting inability or refusal to free associate, and/or the poverty of affective life displayed by the patient. A different sort of scenario unfolds with patients who flood their clinical situation with their "militant hopelessness" (Poland, cited in Jordan, 2002, p. 989). Session after session they complain about how futile their lives are, how the analyst is not helping them, and how they are certain that the analysis will fail. They might pay lip service to recognising that the analyst is devoted and doing his best but their way of relating remains dismissive of all his interventions. Possessed by a sort of "daemonic force" which Freud (1920g, p. 35) talked about in his elucidation of the death instinct, such patients suffer greatly while making the analyst suffer as well. Anticipating their suicide (which seems imminent each day), the analyst feels a bone-chilling fear at the destruction of his professional reputation and his personal well-being. Chused also mentions the fear generated by feeling utterly helpless as an analyst and acknowledges being haunted by memories of failed analyses which "make [her] afraid not of these patients but of the limited value of what we do" (cited in Jordan, 2002, p. 992). Yet another situation where the fear of failed analysis appears is when the patient carries a tenacious "someday …" fantasy (Akhtar, 1996). The patient keeps hoping, reflecting a state of pathological optimism, that his or her longed-for wish (e.g., a deceased parent to come back alive, for the analyst to marry the patient) will "someday" come true. And, having worked interpretively for a very long time, the analyst begins to feel the terror that this hope will not be renounced by the patient and the analysis will either go on forever or be abruptly ended; in either case, it will be a failure. Under such circumstances, consultation with a colleague or supervisor is indicated. And, it might become necessary to convert psychoanalysis to psychotherapy (see Akhtar, 2009, pp. 57–58).

Finally, the analyst (especially the novice analyst) fears making what for the lack of a better term might be designated as "unusual interventions" (Akhtar, 2012). Here, the fear is one of attitude from supervisors, mentors, and analytic heroes internalised into the analyst's superego, rather than his "working self" (Bolognini, 2011). "What will they say?" becomes the driving injunction rather than what the truth of a particular clinical moment demands. Clearly, this is a murky area and the inexperienced analyst is safe in erring on the side of caution but the fear of acting in an "unusual" manner has to be put aside sooner or later if the analyst has to work with a "free-floating responsiveness" (Sandler & Sandler, 1998) and authenticity of participation. In an edited volume (Akhtar, 2011b), I have collated nine so-called unusual interventions, including (i) making extraordinary monetary arrangements, (ii) conducting treatment outside the office, (iii) changing the frequency, length, and timing of sessions, (iv) refusing to listen to certain kinds of material, (v) giving advice, (vi) interpreting in the form of action, (vii) talking about oneself, (viii) touching the patient, and (ix) giving mementos and gifts to the patient. The volume also elucidates the pros and cons of their deployment and the reader might benefit by looking up that material.

Concluding remarks

In this chapter, I have described fear, categorised its intensities, and traced its developmental origins. I have delineated the similarities and differences between fear and anxiety while showing how the two coexist in the state of phobia. Following this, I have made a brief foray into the cultural realm and attempted to demonstrate how the unpleasant emotion of fear can be turned into the excitement of horror movies, gothic literature, and thrill-seeking games, while, on the negative side of things, forming a part of ethno-racial prejudice and political oppression. Returning to the clinical realm, I have discussed the presence of fear in the transference-countertransference matrix and outlined the strategies to deal with the resulting problems.

Before concluding, however, it seems only fair to make some comments about psychic states that seem to be the opposite of fear. There are three such conditions: (i) fearlessness, (ii) counterphobia, and

(iii) courage. Fearlessness is of two varieties. Primary fearlessness exists in infants and young children who are not aware of the dangers that surround them; they can put potentially poisonous items in their mouths and insert fingers in electric sockets. Being hurt a few times and being repeatedly instructed by parents gradually curtails such "un-fear". Secondary fearlessness is seen among low-level operatives in a criminal ring; they carry out nefarious and risky acts under the protection of a powerful boss and feel that nothing can and will happen to them.

The state of counterphobia refers to that unconscious attitude of the ego which propels the individual to undertake, and even enjoy, the very activities that arouse fear and anxiety in him. However, there is a rigid and exaggerated quality to such behaviour. According to Fenichel (1945),

> The obsessive manner of the search for the once-feared situations shows that the anxiety has not been completely overcome. The patients continuously try to repeat the way in which in childhood other anxieties gradually had been mastered by active repetitions of exciting situations. The counterphobic pleasure is a repetition of the child's "functional" pleasure of "I do not need to be afraid anymore" (Silberer, 1909). And, as in the child, the type of pleasure achieved proves that the person is by no means really convinced of his mastery, and that before engaging in any such activity, he passes through an anxious tension of expectation, the overcoming of which is enjoyed. (p. 480)

A common example of counterphobic attitude is the social and motoric daredevilry of adolescents (e.g., driving at high speeds, experimenting with drugs, defying social etiquette, confronting the high school principal). Another illustration is the strikingly rapid assimilation into the host culture on the part of some immigrants (Akhtar, 1999b). They adopt the new local customs in a magical way in order to deflect the social anxiety of being "different". More examples can be given. An individual who accepts the recommendation of a major surgical operation in the blink of an eye is most likely showing a counterphobic attitude. The grotesque youthfulness of some aging narcissists (Kernberg, 1980) and the "gallows humour" of some terminally ill individuals also belies a defensive avoidance of approaching threats. In all these situations, there is a suspicious absence of expectable fear. The fact is that fear exists but is kept in abeyance by forceful self-assurances to the contrary.

Finally, there is courage. Hardly synonymous with fearlessness, courage implies that the person knows that his stance (physical, intellectual, or moral) and his actions can have adverse consequences: financial loss, social isolation, personal ridicule, physical punishment, and so on. And yet, he braces himself to encounter their impending onslaught. Only then can he face destruction and death and not betray the meaningful core of his existence. John Wayne, the movie actor who personified boldness in his roles, quipped that "[C]ourage is being scared to death and saddling up anyway" (downloaded from *www.Thinkexist.com*). General William T. Sherman (after whom the Sherman tank is named) declared courage to be "a perfect sensibility of the measure of danger and a mental willingness to endure it" (cited in Kidder, 2006, p. 9).

The courageous man accords great weight to his own thoughts and perceptions. He needs no consensus and does not depend upon others' approval. He can stand on his own even when others do not agree with him or oppose him. Courage becomes for him "an exceptional state of mind allowing and producing an extraordinary form of behavior" (Coles, 1965, p. 85).

In essence, courage is a particular variety of response to fear, as are counterphobia and cowardice. And, the fact is that we—all of us—are capable of reacting to fear in all three ways. Which one predominates, when, and with what consequences ultimately gives shape to our adaptation to inner and outer reality, our overall character, and the direction our life takes.

Notes

1. An admittedly incomplete list includes *ablutophobia* (fear of washing), *acrophobia* (fear of heights), *agoraphobia* (fear of open spaces), *arachnophobia* (fear of spiders), *batrachophobia* (fear of frogs), *claustrophobia* (fear of enclosed spaces), *homophobia* (fear of homosexuals), *Islamophobia* (fear of Muslims), *photophobia* (fear of lights), and so on. The list, frankly, can be endless; one internet site contains 530 entries!
2. This affected the later reconstructions of Little Hans's childhood as well (Joseph, 1990; Silverman, 1980), which gave more attention to his pre-Oedipal development.

3. The childhood disorder commonly known as "school phobia" has little to do with school per se; the anxiety aroused by separating from parents (usually, the mother) and from the familiar environment of home mostly contributes to such fear.
4. A curious overlap seems to exist between cowardice and procrastination. Biswas-Diener (2012) observes that not finishing a task that one undertook is associated with a kind of "minor cowardice" (p. 7) in many people's minds.
5. According to Freud (1900), the following dreams were so widely prevalent as to be considered 'universal': the dreams of (i) flying, (ii) falling, (iii) being chased, (iv) being inoptimally dressed or naked in public, (v) the death of a loved one, (vi) having difficulty performing in an examination or test and, (vii) teeth falling out.
6. The colour-coded alert system devised by the US Homeland Security Administration in 2003 was intended to keep the public informed about the potential threat of terroristic attacks. At the same time, one wonders about the extent to which the shifts from Red (for severe) through Orange (for high), to Yellow (elevated), etc., were utilised for keeping people afraid and hence hesitant to question governmental surveillance of private lives.
7. Amusement park rides, especially roller coasters with sudden and sharp drops and turns, also gratify some of these impulses.
8. The fact is that some people do get traumatised by seeing horror movies. Relatively widespread traumatisation after the release of the movie, *Jaws*, was evident in a large number of people's avoiding swimming at the shores.
9. My observations are limited to working with adults. Not having experience of working with children, I am not comfortable commenting upon the vicissitudes of clinical praxis in that realm.
10. The first three of the five clinical vignettes provided in this chapter have also appeared elsewhere (Akhtar, 2013b) with a somewhat different slant. Some vignettes in other chapters have also been previously published. And, all the names given to the patients reported upon are fictitious.
11. Assessment of the risk of violence becomes a truly important measure in such work. For details on this, see Otto (2000), and Gellerman & Suddath (2005).

CHAPTER TWO

Greed

It is to the gifted Greek storyteller of ancient times, Aesop (circa 620 BC), that we owe the eternally impressive tale of greed. Among the numerous fables told by him is this story of the farmer who found a goose that laid a golden egg each day. Initially jubilant at his good fortune, the farmer soon felt unable to wait twenty-four hours for the next egg to arrive. He imagined that the goose had hundreds of eggs inside her but was stingy in doling out the wealth. The farmer grew restless and wanted all the gold immediately. He cut the goose open but found no gold inside it. All that happened was that the goose died and the farmer lost the daily nugget of riches that was assured to him.

In this brief tale, Aesop elegantly addressed the coexistence of enormous hunger, impatience, inconsolability, a defective sense of empathy, and ingratitude towards one's benefactors. It is this constellation of descriptive and dynamic features that are subsumed under the rubric of greed. Since greed—along with narcissism, paranoia, and discontent—constitutes an important feature of severe personality disorders and has an unmistakable impact upon their treatment, it is surprising that psychoanalytic literature has given inadequate attention to it.

My contribution here aims to fill this gap in our literature. In it, I will discuss the nature of greed and highlight its phenomenological components. I will describe its primary and secondary manifestations and also the defences that are frequently deployed against it. Following this, I will address the origins of greed in the crucible of early childhood experiences and the consolidation as well as regressive activation of greed at crucial junctures during adulthood. Then, I will make a brief foray into the sociocultural realm and attempt to demonstrate its corrosive impact upon the quality of human life at large. Returning to the clinical chamber, I will delineate the various ways in which issues pertaining to greed impact upon the process of interactive psychotherapy and/or psychoanalysis. That being said, allow me to begin with the well-recognised and less-than-optimally recognised manifestations of greed.

Descriptive aspects

Webster's dictionary defines greed as "excessive and reprehensible acquisitiveness" (Mish, 1998, p. 511). The meaning of this phrase seems self-evident. However, a careful look reveals its ambiguous, even though textured, nature. The first qualifier ("excessive") suggests that acquisitiveness is to be termed greed only after it exceeds a certain threshold but does not specify what that threshold is and how and by whom it has been set up. The second qualifier ("reprehensible") posits that greed lacks dignity, is vulgar, perhaps even immoral, and something to be looked down upon but does not reveal why does greed deserve such derision. Left in a phenomenological morass, we open our eyes wider, search for more clues, and look deeper and farther. Now it dawns upon us that what we call "greed" is actually a complex set of affects, attitudes, and fantasies lumped together. For didactic ease and to create epistemic order out of chaos, I divide the phenomena pertaining to greed into three categories: (i) primary manifestation, (ii) secondary manifestations, and (iii) defensive distortions.

Primary manifestations

The best-recognised aspect of greed—to the extent that it is considered the crux of the matter—is an excessive and unrelenting desire to acquire and possess goods. Its "excessive" nature is revealed by the fact that the quantity of goods desired far surpasses actual need as well as by its exaggerated quality when compared to the desires of others. Its "unrelenting" nature is revealed by the fact that the individual afflicted by it is momentarily pleased with the attainment of supplies and then becomes unsatisfied, empty, and inconsolable. "Greed, in its nature, is inherently insatiable, and so can not be satisfied. It wants everything, nothing less will do" (Kaplan, 1991, p. 508). While out of proportion with realistic need, desires associated with greed are subjectively experienced as a "need". And, since psychic "needs" (as opposed to "wishes") do not carry the burden of intentionality,[1] experiencing greedy desires as needs confers upon them an aura of justifiability and a guilt-free status. Thus, entitlement comes to be a third feature of greed, along with excessive desire and inconsolability.

The realms in which greed can manifest itself vary greatly. Food and money are the most prominent of these. Overeating that leaves one physically bloated but psychically unsatisfied is a telltale sign of greed. Similarly, an insatiable desire to amass wealth, regardless of its instinctual origins in oral acquisitiveness or, as Fenichel (1938) declared, in anal retentiveness, gives evidence of greed as a character trait. Pathological gambling, too, emanates, at least in part, from greed. Writing about this elsewhere (Akhtar, 2009), I observed that, in pathological gambling,

> ... the disproportion between the amount spent (e.g., on lottery tickets, roulette, off-track betting) and the desired reward (in thousands and millions of dollars) creates the illusion that what one is about to receive is free of charge. This constitutes a powerful allure since it secretly gratifies the infantile wish of getting something for nothing. After all, it is only in infancy and childhood that one actually gets free supplies (tangible or emotional); once that period of life has passed, all material acquisition and even all love and respect has to be earned. Gambling, by "promising" a windfall and a generous gift from the "mother nature", as it were, creates the possibility of being a carefree child again. At the same time, ignoring the fact that the probability of winning is miniscule (a fact that *is* pre-consciously known), prepares the ground for masochistic self-punishment; the guilt over resorting to unfair and effortless path to success (unconsciously equated with transgression of the oedipal barrier which demands respect for generational boundaries and therefore of time) is thus relieved. (p. 75, italics in the original)

Money and food are, however, not the only realms in which greed makes its appearance. Sex is another area where the operation of greed is frequently discernible. In the setting of narcissistic character structure especially, the desire for sexual encounters gets out of control. "Here, eternally youthful bodies are needed compulsively, regardless of the face, the person, and the attitudes with which such bodies relate to the narcissistic individual" (Kernberg, 1980, p. 144). Sexual promiscuity, like other addictions, is often orally derived and betrays an intensification of sensual desire due to chronic childhood frustrations. Hunger and greed of such proportions end up cannibalising whatever goodness might exist in the relationship and leave the narcissistic individual empty all over again.[2]

Secondary manifestations

Alongside the three "primary" features of greed (i.e., excessive desire, inconsolability, entitlement) exist certain other manifestations. Prominent among these are a constant sense of hurry, ingratitude, defects of empathy, and corruption of superego functions. Hurrying, on which there is a lamentable lack of psychoanalytic musing, is a frequent accompaniment of greed, since to be able to wait means tolerating "less-than-full" states of body and mind. Waiting for supplies also implies taking turns, sharing with others, and believing in a less than magical regeneration of goods. The greedy individual insists upon sustained fullness and cannot tolerate temporal gaps in the appearance of supplies; impatience is the twin sister of avarice.

Ingratitude is also a frequent accompaniment of greed. Called the "marble-hearted fiend" by Shakespeare (*King Lear*, 1606, I, iv, p. 283), ingratitude is, in essence, a refusal to acknowledge that one has received goodness, love, and material supplies from others. No amount of indulgence appears enough to the one incapable of gratitude. Inwardly measuring every favour against the "debt" owed to him due to childhood deprivation, such an individual becomes incapable of enjoying what is offered and remains thankless to his benefactors. He gobbles up what is given, does not acknowledge others' generosity, and keeps craving for more (Akhtar, 2012; Bergler, 1945).

Constant yearning for supplies leads to pushing others aside and losing contact with their needs and rights. Driven self-interest causes blindness to others' place in the market of libidinal supplies. This indifference to fellow human beings is most likely the reason that greed is deemed "reprehensible" in its dictionary definitions (see above). Moreover, such defective empathy has a boomerang effect insofar as others gradually begin to avoid the greedy person. He or she loses the respect of family members and peers, is ostracised. The resulting loneliness increases his insatiable need for love and material goods. The defects in empathy associated with greed also have a cause-and-effect relationship with superego corruption; lack of concern permits exploitation and cutting ethical corners gives rise to the unconscious sense of being bad which, in turn, propels one to seek more love, more praise, and more reassurance from others. A vicious cycle of excessive need, exploitative taking, and unconscious guilt is thus established.

Nikelly (2006) has pooled together the studies of individuals driven to have more and more money and yet remaining unsatisfied (Berglas, 1986; Rohrlich, 1987; Shames, 1989) and offered the following portrayal of the greed-driven "pleonexic personality":[3]

- No concern for the effects of unlimited accumulation, such as the depletion of natural resources or the fomenting of social conflict, deprivation, and suffering.
- Acquisitions are considered worthy in themselves and for private luxury but poverty and the public good are ignored.
- The hunger for increasing wealth has no logical purpose; having everything is not enough, and the desire for more is like a race without a finish.
- Living for the here and now, as if life will soon come to an end, feeds the urge to grasp and to hold as much as possible.
- Confusion of means with ends and the distortion of priorities in life; failure to grasp the "big picture" and to acknowledge important human values.
- Failure to recognise ethical obligations and their impact on society; insensitivity to the unmet basic needs of others.
- Possessions become synonymous with self-worth, freedom, and privilege along with a sense of superiority and self-righteousness.
- Social interactions become impersonal and perfunctory, lacking warmth and not letting others come close; personal encounters are limited to those that enhance personal gain.
- Disdain and contempt towards those who do not take advantage of opportunities to compete and to surpass others in wealth. (p. 72)

Such overtly greedy characters stand in sharp contrast to those who suppress/repress their greed and develop firm characterological defences against it.

Defensive distortions

Greed can be rendered unconscious by defensive operations of the ego due to moral condemnation from within and/or due to the need to safeguard a lofty self-image. Four common defences deployed against greed are repression, reaction formation, splitting, and projective identification. By the use of repression, all temptations and longings felt to be "greedy" are sent into psychic exile. However, since "[T]he repressed exercises a continuous pressure in the direction of the conscious" (Freud, 1915d, p. 151), hints of greed continue to appear in parapraxes and dreams. Moreover, the individual who has repressed his own greed feels exquisitely uncomfortable at encountering the attitude in others and might even equate their healthy appetites with avarice. A not infrequent accompaniment is pretended contempt for money in real life (Jones, 1913) and "moral narcissism" (Green, 1986), that is, yearning to be pure, free of attachment, and above ordinary human needs.[4] Disenchantment with food to the extent of developing anorexia nervosa is often the consequence of such narcissism and repressed greed (Davies, 2004).

Reaction formation against greed can give rise to "unrelenting generosity" (Akhtar, 2013a), which involves excessive and incessant giving to others. The individual feels helpless in the face of an inward command to provide and be helpful; such giving exceeds realistic limits both of what one has and what others need. It cloaks and defends against greed, envy, and the need to control the object (Seelig & Rosof, 2001).

Another distortion occurs when self-representations tinged with greed are held in abeyance via the mechanism of vertical splitting. A "mirror complimentarity of the self" (Bach, 1977) then develops whereby the individual consciously experiences and alternately acts out the contradictory attitudes of being greedy and being not greedy. He seems rational and well regulated in his appetites and then, to everyone's surprise, suddenly turns greedy. Sequestered avarice of this sort can also undergo projective identification and lead to the perception of others being greedy. When this happens, desires and demands of others are looked at with suspicion, even if those wishes are, in fact, realistic.

At times, others (especially the spouse and children) are unconsciously manipulated to "live out" one's own repudiated greed. Scorn and contempt can then be directed at them. The deposition of one's greedy self-representation into others can also result in uncanny empathy with their acquisitiveness and fear of being devoured by them. Guntrip (1969), long ago, discerned this mechanism in the fluctuating closeness-distance patterns of schizoid personalities. More recently, Kernberg (1995) has found that often it is the projection of greed onto the desired love object that creates dread of relatedness in narcissistic personalities. According to him, in such individuals:

> Unconscious greed and envy tend to be projected onto the desired sexual object and, as a consequence, fear of the possessive greed and potential exploitation by the sexual object becomes a threat, reinforcing the need to escape into "freedom." For the narcissistic patient, all relations are between exploiters and exploited, and "freedom" is simply an escape from a fantasied devouring possessiveness. (p. 16)

The mention of dread and anxiety in the setting of hungry desire to devour brings up the relationship of greed to hope and envy on the one hand and to pain and despair on the other hand. To grasp such nuances, we must turn to the developmental origins of greed.

Developmental origins

The word "greed" appears only six times in the complete corpus of Freud's work (Guttman, Jones & Parrish, 1980). Five of these usages are colloquial and of little theoretical significance. The sixth, though set in the context of his ironic view of human nature, does reveal where he thought greed originated in the course of psychic development. Freud stated the following:

> Among the majority even of what are called "respectable" people traces of divided behavior can easily be observed where money and property are concerned. It may perhaps be generally true that the primitive greed of the suckling, who wants to take possession of every object (in order to put it into his mouth), has only been incompletely overcome by civilization and upbringing. (1901b, p. 158)

This unmistakable link to orality was, however, nowhere to be found when he returned to discussing greed sixteen years later. At that time, Freud (1917c) stated that "[A]varice, pedantry, and obstinacy spring from anal-erotic sources" (p. 127). A careful look, however, reveals that "avarice" was not the prime designation Freud used for the obsessional's interest in money in this paper. His preferred term for the anally fixated attitude towards money was "parsimony". The shift from "parsimony" to "avarice", however, creates the possibility of viewing greed as a two-sided phenomenon. One side pertains to excessive acquisitiveness (of oral determination), and the other to inordinate retentiveness (of anal determination).

Freud's early followers, especially Abraham (1924) and Fenichel (1945), continued to trace the development of greed to oral phases of psychosexual development. Fenichel's (1938) paper on the compulsion to amass wealth did rest upon the formulation of anal fixation and constitutes an exception in this regard. By and large, though, greed became firmly associated with early oral fixation in post-Freudian literature. Abraham (1924) emphasised that the instinctual derivatives of the oral phase did not require as much disguise via reaction formation and sublimation as did those of the anal phase. He linked oral greed with clinging dependency and aggression-tinged patterns of speaking.

> In their social behavior these people always seem to be asking for something, either in the form of a modest request or of an aggressive demand. The manner in which they put forward their wishes has something in the nature of a persistent sucking about it; they are as little to be put off by hard facts as by reasonable arguments but continue to plead and insist. One might almost say that they "cling like leeches" to other people. They particularly dislike being alone even for a short time. Impatience is a marked characteristic with them. In some cases, those in which psychoanalytic investigation reveals a regression from the oral-sadistic to the sucking stage, their behavior has an element of cruelty in it as well, which makes them something like vampires to other people. (pp. 158–159)

Fenichel (1945) declared that the appearance of "... intense greed, either manifest or, after its repression, in the form of derivatives, is always traceable to oral eroticism" (p. 63). It was, however, Abraham's analysand, Melanie Klein, who elucidated the development and metabolism of greed in early infantile object relations to its fullest extent. Deftly linking the operation of instinctual drives and the evolution of object relations, Klein (1952) traced the earliest appearance of greed to the bedrock of intensified oral aggression. Although she acknowledged that "deprivation increases greed" (1957, p. 183), her emphasis remained upon the complex interplay of actual deprivation and innate intensity of drives. She stated the following.

> It could be conceived that in periods of freedom from hunger and tension there is an optimal balance between libidinal and aggressive impulses. This equilibrium is disturbed whenever, owing to privations from internal or external sources, aggressive impulses are reinforced. I suggest that such an alternation of balance between libido and aggression gives rise to the emotion called greed, which is first and foremost of an oral nature. Any increase in greed strengthens feelings of frustration and in turn the aggressive impulse. In those children in whom the innate aggressive component is strong, persecutory anxiety, frustration and greed are easily aroused and this contributes to the infant's difficulty in tolerating privation and in dealing with anxiety. Accordingly, the strength of the destructive impulses in their interaction with libidinal impulses would provide the constitutional basis for the intensity of greed. (p. 62)

In this formulation, the origin of greed lies in the linkage between constitutionally determined intensity of aggressive drive and actual frustrations during early infancy. At a later occasion, Klein (1959) went a step further and spoke of "innate greed" that, once aroused, refuses to be mitigated by gratification.

> Some babies experience strong resentment about any frustration and show this by being unable to accept gratification when it follows on deprivation. I would suggest that such children have a stronger innate aggressiveness and greed than those infants whose occasional outbursts of rage are soon over. (p. 249)

Klein posited that under such circumstances only hallucinatory wish-fulfilment brings satisfaction, since the conjured breast is inexhaustible. A pathway from greed to idealisation is thus opened up; restless search for "all-good" objects (e.g., a perfect mate, an exquisitely attuned employer, a profoundly grateful child) then becomes a lifelong pattern. Conversely, under the influence of a harsh superego, greed is repressed and denied, leading to false self-reliance, stifling of love, and turning away from dependence upon others. Klein (1957) also elucidated the relationship between greed and envy. The former aims at sucking the object dry. The latter does that as well but additionally strives to put bad parts of the self into the object. In Klein's own words, "[G]reed is mainly bound up with introjection and envy with projection" (1959, p. 181). However, both envy and greed diminish if hatred is renounced; the latter step can be taken if love from others is accepted and internalised.

Klein saw greed as the opposite of gratitude. If loving feelings predominate within the infant-mother dyad and in the former's intrapsychic economy, then receiving libidinal supplies leads to a feeling of gratitude towards the giver. In contrast, if the libido-aggression balance within the dyad (and in the infant's intrapsychic world) is tilted towards aggression, then receiving supplies stirs up more hunger and more anger; this angry hunger constitutes greed. In explicating this dynamic, Roth (2008) stated the following.

> The appeasement of greed, Klein insisted, cannot bring gratification. It can bring satiation, a feeling of lack of hunger, an absence of appetite. But gratification, according to Klein, concerns experiences beyond the satisfaction of hunger: pleasure and delight from smell and from touch, from gazing and being gazed at, from being held comfortably and safely. It contains all the budding sensory and psychological experiences that will gradually become what we know as love. If greed can be understood to be about getting all the goodness for oneself, then gratification can be seen to be about an experience of closeness and intimacy. (pp. 15–16)

In contrast to these Kleinian ideas is Winnicott's (1968) proposal that the infant's appetite has an inherently aggressive component which, in its original intent, is actually a vehicle of powerful love. Winnicott acknowledged that the infant has a vast capacity for destructiveness but emphasised that the mindless robustness of his taking (breast, milk, love) from the mother must not be mistaken for hostility. He noted that:

> ... the important thing to note about this instinctual aggressiveness is that although it soon becomes something that can be mobilized in the service of hate, it is originally a part of appetite,

> or of some other form of instinctual love. It is something that increases during excitement, and the exercise of it is highly pleasurable. Perhaps the word "greed" conveys more easily than any other the idea of infantile fusion of love and aggression, though the love here is confined to mother-love. (pp. 82–83)

While proposing such "primary greed" (in my phraseology), Winnicott (1956a) also came to describe a "secondary" sort of greed in his paper on "antisocial tendency". There, Winnicott observed that childhood deprivation (especially if it follows some experience with gratification) leaves the child hungry and perpetually in search of rectifying this lack. The child then pushes the envelope of supplies, takes a lot, steals from his caregivers, and behaves in outrageous ways. Stealing is intended not only to compensate himself for the earlier deprivation but also to hurt the benefactor who has come to stand for depriving primary objects. Outrageousness is a sign of hope and a method to compel the environment to respond (see also Casement, 1991, in this regard). The greedy taking associated with such "antisocial" tendency is what I have termed here as Winnicott's concept of "secondary greed" in opposition to "primary greed" by which he meant the inherent ruthlessness of early infantile love.

Winnicott's follower and exponent, Guntrip (1969) took up the "secondary greed" hypothesis with full force. He underplayed the constitutional element in the genesis of greed and emphasised that greed was healthy appetite gone awry due to the depriving and tantalising attitudes of primary caregivers. This intensified hunger frightened one since it could lead to cannibalistic destruction of the object or rejection by the object which felt threatened. Consequently, one suppressed the greed for objects and, in a protective move towards them, adopted a solitary life style.

Putting this formulation (appetite turning into greed) upside down on its head, Boris (1986) proposed that greed antedates appetite in the course of development. Greed is the primary attitude from which appetite might or might not emerge. In this view, the fact that the mother has two breasts leaves the infant with having no contact with one breast no matter how gratifying the other breast seems at the moment of nursing. Inability to bear the "loss" of the other breast is what underlies greed. In other words, greed reflects an unevolved state of mind in which the infant wishes to suck on both breasts simultaneously. With acceptance of reality and consistent if alternate availability of both breasts, so to speak, greed can evolve into appetite. Appetite makes actual (and not wished-for) experience for the first time a player in the developmental process. The fact is that actual experience not only plays a role during the formative years of childhood, when it contributes to the genesis of greed, but also during adult life where it sustains greed and/or causes its reactive flare-ups. This "actual experience" comes both from home and from the society-at-large.

Sociocultural aspects

The topic of greed and culture is vast and can hardly be dealt with comprehensively in this largely clinical essay. Nonetheless, it is important to be addressed since neither do our children grow up in a cultural void nor our patients remain unaffected by the societal currents around them. In innumerable ways, sociocultural institutions and practices interact with, and are affected by, the human propensity towards greed. Such interplay is more marked in societies dominated by capitalistic ideology and the free market economy. The monetary ambition of producers of goods forcefully impacts on individual subjectivity and seeks to turn the general population into mere "consumers.[5] The following scenarios highlight the interplay of capitalism and human greed.

- *Induction of false needs*: Even though all human beings have the same psychological needs (e.g., needs for safety, freedom, identity, affirmation, love, causality, temporal continuity, and generativity), those living in capitalist economies are vulnerable to experiencing their wishes also as needs (Akhtar, 1999a). For instance, food is a need but the variety of pizza toppings offered can create a wish for them which under the mesmerising juggernaut of advertising can be experienced as an urgent *need*. Respite from the daily humdrum of work and turning to moments of leisure is certainly an emotional need but the alluring luxuries of today's resorts and retreats can delude one into thinking that such accoutrements are truly *needed* for relaxation. Induction of such "false needs" lies at the core of a consumer-driven economy; the more one can make people buy things, the better off the state of the nation, declares this mentality. Hypnotised by seductive television commercials, the vulnerable person begins to feel needy and, over time, turns greedy.

- *Distortion of the parameters of success*: In capitalist societies, the notion of personal success is linked with financial status. As a result, the bar for contentment is very high (Wachtel, 2003). How big a house is big enough? What imported car delivers greater social prestige? Or, conversely, what would happen if one does not wear brand-name clothing, drives an "ordinary" car, lives in a modest home? Such preoccupations are created, sustained, and fuelled by the corporations that produce goods and these pied pipers of materialism recruit masses to relentlessly pursue the "good life" by purchasing more things. Satisfaction felt at every new purchase soon evaporates. Hunger for acquisition returns and greed sets in.
- *Eclipse of child care and communal bonds*: The free market economy tantalises, offers betterment of life through acquisition, and makes people buy more and more things. It thrives on people remaining in a state of want. A frequent result of all this is that the length of maternal care of infants is abbreviated since the households "need" two incomes. Employers, responding to their own financial "needs", curtail the length of maternity leave.[6] Children are sent to "pre-school" nurseries, and even "pre-nurseries" at an extremely young age (often at a few weeks or months) and, not surprisingly, grow up to be driven and ambitious adults. Another deleterious effect of the forever escalating consumption is that people's energy is spent on earning, buying, and paying back loans. This leaves little actual or mental space for communal bonds. One does little community service and the idea of social sacrifice becomes foreign. On a local level, the sense of neighbourhood declines; instead of being companions, neighbours become competitors for standards of living. On a global level, one fails to gain (or repudiates) awareness of how vast numbers of people across this world are living in poverty and deprivation. "Capitalist greed" (Sievers, 2012) activates ferocious competitiveness that seeks to annihilate competitors. Pursuit of money and the things it can buy fuels a narcissistic orientation to life.

Two caveats must be entered here. The first pertains to whether some nations are more greed-driven than others and whether the East and the West differ in the extent and nature of greed. The second pertains to our selective use of the word "greed" vis-à-vis certain pursuits in life. Regarding the first matter, it should be noted that such generalisations are prone to error and fail to take into account that all sorts of human beings exist in all sorts of societies. At the same time, it is possible that some cultures might be less money-driven than others. A comparison, for instance, of the over $60,000 annual fees for medical school tuition in the United States with Germany, where such education is free for the students pointedly brings this point home. Another illustration comes in the form of socialised medicine. Nations that provide universal access to health care create an ambiance of safety and fuel material pursuits to a lesser extent. Less greed is in the air people breathe in such lands.

The second matter, namely, our applying the term "greedy" to some pursuits and not to others, also reveals some interesting points for consideration. For instance, if an investment banker makes a lot of money and has little sense of civic responsibility or if a real estate mogul keeps building one high rise tower after another, we are quick to call them greedy. But if a fiction writer churns out novel after novel or if a psychoanalyst publishes paper after paper, we do not look upon them as "greedy". We readily discern greed in overeating but are reluctant to see it in voracious reading. Why? Is all this a knee-jerk response to our exposure to corrupt and scandalous entrepreneurs like Bernie Madoff? Is this a moral recoil from Gordon Gekko's[7] celebrated declaration that "greed is good"? Or does it express an idealised preference for aim-inhibited discharge of instincts on our part? Have we inherited this legacy from Freud's stoic ethics? If that is indeed so, are we not ignoring that some creative activities are actually "pseudo-sublimatory" (Kernberg, 1975), that is, done in the pursuit of glory, fame, and immortality? And, worse, by harshly judging rich businessmen, are we not overlooking that their work itself might be about making money (sublimation in the direction of what we deride as instinctual) and require great devotion and intellectual prowess? To be sure, no clear-cut solutions exist for such conceptual conundrums but we must acknowledge their existence. Humility of this sort might preclude moralising and enhance curiosity. It might even become a stepping stone for developing poignant empathy and "respect" for what is or seems to be greed in others. This applies to sociopolitical views as well as to clinical work with patients.

Back to the clinical realm

Greed makes its appearance in the clinical situation in myriad ways. The patient might bring greed within himself or herself, in a "one-person psychology" manner. Or, the patient's greed might have been stirred up by the analyst's overly depriving attitude. And, the analyst might have his own struggles with greed. While the two types of greed (the patient's, the analyst's) are often related to each other in a dialectical fashion and tearing them apart is difficult, it is didactically prudent to consider them separately.

The patient's greed

Manifestations of the patient's greed can be crude or subtle. Included in the former category are struggles over the payment of fees, sensitivity to the slightest lateness of the analyst, wishes for longer and more frequent sessions, tenacious withholding of associative material, and frequent contact-seeking between appointments (e.g., by phone, email). "Malignant erotic transference" (Akhtar, 1994), with its typical coercive quality, also is a manifestation of greed. To be sure, factors other than greed (e.g., anxiety, mental pain, unbearable amounts of loneliness) can play an aetiologic role in such developments but greed is often at their centre. The same is true of the patient's hatred of the analyst's other patients: the analytic breast is not allowed to feed anyone else. Needless to say that such gross manifestations of the patient's greed extract a heavy toll on the analyst's poise and patience. The risks of moral judgment become great under such circumstances (Kaplan, 1991). This risk can only be avoided if the analyst holds on to the fact that lurking behind the patient's inconsolable hunger is the void of desperation and feeling utterly unlovable. Waska (2002) eloquently describes the tense ambiance of clinical work with "greedy" patients.

> Patients want desperately to change and find relief from their chronic and often debilitating anxiety. At the same time, they cling to their demands for unrealistic change and ignore, devalue, and attack the true potential they have. To accept the strides they do make, within the less-than-perfect analytic relationship and the intimacy and progress capable outside of the analytic relationship, brings on a sense of loss too deep to bear and too confining, confusing, and persecutory to allow. As one patient put it, "I want more in life. It has to be more or nothing." This seals their fate into an endless and exhausting hunt for better, ideal, and impossible states of union with fantastic, idealized versions of the self and of the object. (p. 508)

Waska (2003a) notes that greed destroys insights gained in analysis. The hunger for more coupled with intense oral aggression makes internalisation and retention of good objects (including the analyst) difficult. Prognosis is far better, in my experience, for patients who are consciously aware of their greed and can even muster a bit of self-reflective humour about their malady.

Clinical vignette: 6

> Phil Robertson, a highly successful businessman in his late thirties, had sought analysis for being unable to establish a sustained romantic relationship with a woman. He was tall, handsome, wealthy, well mannered, and, generally speaking, a very likeable person. As a result, he had no difficulty in finding women to date. He was constantly "fixed" with women by his peers and relatives; others sought him out spontaneously. The problem, though, was that he could not tolerate them beyond three or four dates. Their slightest "blemish" would lead him to become totally disenchanted, even hateful. One had a coarse laughter. Another came to the date wearing sandals. A third one did not know who Chaucer was. And, a fourth one hated Boston (which Phil liked very much). And so on. Soon each became history. Phil's restless search for a "good" woman (he was smart and avoided the word "perfect") began to appear endless.
>
> Soon after starting analysis, Phil said, with wry laughter, "Doc, I am the sort of guy who is never satisfied by ninety per cent of anything." Elaborating upon this, he said, "If you put all my favourite food items on a boat in amounts that would last for a hundred years and then have me sail away, I would still be worried about the potential of scarcity. What if I wanted something and it was not on the boat? What if it had fallen out of the boat? What will I then do?" As this material unfolded, a childhood memory emerged. Phil recalled that, on more than one occasion, when a dish was being passed around during the family's dinner, his mother reversed the direction of the dish's movement as it was about to reach him. Consequently, he was unable to take that food item. The "screen memory" (Freud, 1899a) nature of this account did not preclude my empathy with his sense of chronic deprivation during childhood. Somehow, though, he had maintained a sense of humour,

> too, about this pain. For instance, once he laughed and said, "Doc, wouldn't you say that life with a woman who has a big mole on her back would be tough?"

In contrast to such self-reflective irony is the attitude of sadomasochistic oblivion to one's greed and its destructive impact upon clinical work.

Clinical vignette: 7

> Amira Hashmi, a Pakistani-American student of clinical social work, was bored with her studies and wanted to drop out of the university. However, she had no alternative plan. Nothing excited her. She felt depressed, adrift, and utterly anhedonic. Referred by a fellow analyst, she came to see me having tried psychotherapy as well as antidepressant medications to no avail.
>
> A polite, soft-spoken woman of extraordinary intelligence and keen empathy for her "clients", Amira filled the sessions with what Warren Poland has called "militant hopelessness" (cited in Jordan, 2002, p. 989). She cried endlessly, declared incessantly that her treatment with me was bound to fail. "Nothing will change, I can tell you. Ten years will pass and I will be suffering in the same way and to the same extent."
>
> The omnipotence that underlay such a seemingly hopeless (but darkly triumphant) rant was beyond her awareness. Calling herself weak, mindless, lifeless, inept, and stupid, Amina nonetheless displayed great eloquence, impressive debating capacity, and stunning certainty regarding her dire predictions. More strikingly, she would beseech me to speak, comment, and comfort her, but would instantaneously turn anything I said as meaningless; she either told me that I was flat-out wrong or repeated my interventions in an exaggerated and mocking manner. Nothing I could say or do brought her any comfort. She told me so and yet she came to her sessions with saintly devotion and asked me to speak with greater frequency during sessions. She was intolerant of my silence and rejecting of my words. I was an emptied out, defiled breast from which she nonetheless demanded the milk of therapeutic optimism.

Here the patient seems utterly incapable of accepting the feeding by the analyst-mother due to the powerful infantile greed, destructive intentions towards one's "dead mother" (Green, 1980), and unconscious guilt over such sadism. Analytic work in such cases has to continually oscillate between affirmative and interpretive interventions (see Killingmo, 1989, and more specifically, Waska, 2003b). On the former front, the analyst must empathise with and validate the patient's agony and desperation. On the latter front, the analyst must point out the sadomasochistic destructiveness in the patient's reducing his interventions to "shit": inert, offensive, and useless. Both manoeuvres are ultimately aimed at helping the patient transform his greed into appetite. However, this work is not easy. The patient often misconstrues overtures of validation and alliance as throwing "crumbs" and mercilessly devalues the analyst's efforts. Silence is found unbearable and speaking useless. In such an environment, the potential for "negative therapeutic reaction" (Freud, 1923b) is great and the analyst might be better off focusing upon what did not happen (in the course of the patient's development) than what did take place.

Discussing the technical dilemmas that clinical situations of this sort present, Klein (1957) states:

> It makes great demands (both) on the analyst and on the patient to analyse splitting processes and the underlying hate and envy in both the positive and negative transference. One consequence of this difficulty is the tendency of some analysts to reinforce the positive and avoid the negative transference, and to attempt to strengthen feelings of love by taking over the role of the good object which the patient had not been able to establish securely in the past. This procedure differs essentially from the technique which, by helping the patient to achieve a better integration of his self, aims at a mitigation of hatred by love ... We find that ... the patient's strong desire to receive evidence of love and appreciation from the analyst ... is never completely given up ... In identification with his patient, the early need for reassurance may strongly influence his [the analyst's] counter-transference and therefore his technique. This identification may also easily tempt the analyst to take the mother's place and give in to the urge immediately to alleviate his child's (the patient's) anxieties. (pp. 225–226)

Powerful and accurate though this statement is, it does not take into account that the patient is not alone in bringing the hues of greed into the clinical situation. The analyst contributes to it, too. An excessively austere style of intervening on the analyst's part can stoke the fires of greed in the patient. Such "co-creation" needs to be acknowledged, rectified, and only then handled in the customary interpretive manner. And, then there are more "personal" struggles with greed that the analyst often faces.

The analyst's greed

On a gross level, the analyst's greed becomes evident via an exorbitant fee, ostentatiously decorated office, overly packed clinical schedule, and refusal to consider retirement even on becoming old and infirm.[8] Sadly, none of these attributes are rare among psychoanalysts and seem to have become more pervasive as analytic patients become scarce, insurance companies shirk reimbursements, and the monetary wellspring of academia dries up.

On a subtler level, the analyst's greed is stirred up in response to the patient's seduction, and the idealisation of interpretive prowess. The former can tax the countertransference experience heavily and, at times, can lead to the breakdown of treatment.

Clinical vignette: 8

> Pamela Kasinetz, an elderly woman of extreme wealth, sought psychotherapy for depression and anxiety of recent origin. The apparent trigger for this was the worsening relationship with her husband of over three decades. With their children no longer at home, the two had become quite alienated; he was engrossed in his business and she with her social commitments and philanthropic work. Matters became worse when Pamela ran into an "adorable" seven- or eight-year-old Cambodian boy in a shopping mall and "fell in love with him". She took it upon herself to help him and his financially strained family. The boy gradually became her constant companion. Paying huge sums of money to his parents, Pamela pretty much took over his life. She would pick him up from school, bring him home, shower him with lavish gifts, and indulge all his whims and desires; his friends also were welcome at her house and were treated with similar indulgence. While numerous examples can be given, one instance should suffice, where she spent in excess of thirty thousand dollars over a weekend entertaining her little "friend" and his four playmates. All this led to frequent arguments between Pamela and her husband, who insisted on putting limits

> on her expenses. Seeking symptomatic relief, Pamela appeared unprepared to look into the deeper meanings of her fascination with this little boy. Raised in a family of means, she readily dismissed any enquiry into a childhood sense of feeling deprived and thus blocked the therapist's efforts at linking her runaway altruism with potential unconscious issues pertaining to early trauma. It was all "real" and rationalised in terms of kindness and generosity towards the underprivileged, as far as she was concerned. Soon after starting treatment, she expressed a desire to pay a much greater fee for her sessions, quoting what appeared to be truly an exorbitant amount. The situation was complicated by parallel problems in the therapist's countertransference to her and to the financial glitter of the situation. Having suffered a childhood parental loss at about the same age as the Cambodian boy Pamela so adored, and being financially strapped himself owing to a recent personal crisis, the therapist was made terribly uncomfortable by Pamela's financial seductions. Reacting defensively, he not only made premature transference interpretations but also sternly rejected her offers. He failed to explicate and explore them in a peaceful manner. Pamela soon dropped out of treatment.

This adverse outcome seems to have been the result of a number of factors in the therapist: (i) current financial distress made it hard for him to listen peacefully to his patient's extravagance; it stirred up too much greed, (ii) childhood trauma made it difficult for him to hear about his patient's indulgence in a little boy; it stirred up too much envy; and (iii) not seeking a consultation in what was obviously a difficult clinical situation for him, it led to defensive recoil and over-interpretation. Flying solo under these circumstances was an inappropriate clinical choice.

In contrast to the vignette above is the following case where the analyst was able to manage his greed (with helpful consultation from a colleague) and, in the process, deepen his work with the patient.

Clinical vignette: 9

> In the process of writing her will, Kathleen Roberts, a wealthy widow in her late seventies, became anxious and sought consultation with me. Intellectually gifted, artistic, and good looking,

Kathleen was nonetheless in considerable distress. She felt torn about how to leave her estate in an equitable manner. She had two children and wanted to leave more money to the one with lesser financial resources. But she felt guilty at such "unfairness"; dividing the money and property on a fifty-fifty basis also appeared unjust to her. She did not know what to do.

Expectedly, this contemporary scenario of fair-unfair dealing contained echoes from her past. Kathleen was the younger of two sisters and had been known to be "her mother's child". This, however, did not mean that she received more love than her sister did from their mother. It meant that she was trapped, controlled, and possessed by the mother. With further exploration, a history of childhood sexual abuse by the mother came to the surface. With great anxiety and shame, Kathleen recounted being asked to take off all her clothes, spread her legs, and then undergo a "test". This consisted of her mother rubbing her genitals to make sure that there was "no weakness there, no eczema, or anything". This masturbatory ritual went on from the age of four to five till thirteen or fourteen years of age. After that, its place was taken by the mother's asking Kathleen to describe her imaginary encounters with boys and, as the years went on, by the mother's insistence on hearing each and every detail of Kathleen's sexual life with her boyfriend. But why was Kathleen and not her older sister chosen to serve the mother's perverse aims? Was this fair that one child was abused and the other escaped the violation, Kathleen wondered.

As our work deepened and with Kathleen's work in sorting out her enormous estate getting into full swing, material began to appear which suggested that she wanted to leave me a huge amount of money. At times, this appeared in derivative forms, as in parapraxes and dreams. At other times, it was explicitly verbalised. Kathleen was genuinely grateful to me for helping her gather the sequestered parts of her psychic life and feel deeper and more meaningful as a person. Her wish to give me something emanated from gratitude. She wanted my work to be available to more women in her situation; there was thus an altruistic streak to her generosity as well.

However, it was my countertransference experience that told the deeper story. I felt split. At one time, I would feel omnipotent, powerful, and entitled to millions of dollars for my work. At other times, I felt that I was being corrupt, unethical, and greedy in my temptation to seduce her to leave me a huge sum of money. Upon brutally honest self-reflection and a consultation with a senior analytic colleague, I was able to connect my vulgar desire to grab her money with an identification with her sexually abusive mother who grabbed her genitals and my recoil from it with my becoming a mother that she needed but did not have. It was such countertransference vigilance and working-through that allowed me to interpret her oscillation between putting herself in a potentially abusive situation and hoping that such exploitation would not happen.

Such "gross" and money-related scenarios do not exhaust the ways an analyst has to struggle with the forces of greed. A subtler pressure comes from what I call "interpretive greed". Dedicated to analytic work and idealising of interpretation as the centrepiece of his clinical enterprise, the analyst might interpret excessively, too deeply, or prematurely.

Clinical vignette: 10

Judith Conahan, a highly intelligent lawyer with narcissistic personality disorder, was in analysis with me. For the first year or so, all she talked about was how she felt unloved by her husband and, during her childhood, by her mother. She never made a comment about me and in effect treated me with an indifference that was quite like what she had received from her mother. Then, in the eighteenth month of her analysis, I announced that I had to take a few days off at rather short notice. The patient responded to the news with immediate acceptance and the usual lack of associations. The next day, however, she began her session by telling me that one of her clients had cancelled an appointment that morning. During that hour, she went through her desk drawers and found her home insurance policy. Judith went on to tell me that she got quite upset upon reading parts of that policy. There were too many loopholes, too little coverage! Discerning unmistakable allusions to my impending absence (e.g., "cancelled appointment", "too little coverage") in her associations, I said: "Perhaps, you find it easier to talk about an insurance policy with loopholes than an analysis with interruptions." After a long pause, she responded in a pained voice:

> "I can see how you arrived at what you said but it hurt my feelings because I was really worried about the policy and it seems that you are not paying attention to my concern about it."

Clearly, in too rapidly pointing out the deflected transference implications of her overt concern, I had succumbed to "interpretive greed". Issacharoff (1979), who has elucidated "the analyst's unconscious greed", and Epstein (1979), who has talked about the analyst's "compulsion to interpret", propose that withholding patients and verbally fascinating patients elicit the analyst's greed with remarkable intensity. Both authors warn about the risks of over-interpretation which I was guilty of in the preceding illustration. The following two clinical vignettes, however, show greater restraint on my part.

Clinical vignette: 11

> Stephanie Brooks, an analysand with known psychosomatic sensitivity to fresh paint, started to sneeze and cough badly during her second session in my office in a brand new building. Knowing that the hallway water fountains were not yet functional, she asked me where she could get some water to drink. I told her that she could step out and I would instruct my secretary, on the intercom, to give her a paper cup, which she could take to the ladies' room to get some water. The patient went out and returned within a few minutes. She mumbled "Thanks" and resumed the chain of thought she was pursuing earlier. I listened to the material carefully, wondering if any overt or covert reference to my intervention would appear. None did. During the next couple of sessions, I silently looked for any reference to my intervention but did not find it.

Clinical vignette: 12

> In the throes of a regressive transference, Jill Schwartz entered my office enraged and waving a finger. Approaching the couch, she said, "I have a lot on my mind today and I want to do all the talking. I don't want you to speak even a single word!" A little taken aback, I mumbled, "Okay." Jill shouted, "I said, 'not one word' and you have already fucked up this session!" Now sitting on my chair behind her, I was rattled. "Did I do wrong by speaking at all?"

> I asked myself. As she lay on the couch, angrily silent and stiff, I started to think. Perhaps she is so inconsolable today, so intent upon forcing me into the role of a depriving person, that she found a way to see even the gratification of her desire as its frustration. I was, however, not entirely satisfied with this explanation and therefore decided to wait, and think further. It then occurred to me that maybe she was rightly angered by my saying 'Okay'. In my agreeing to let her have omnipotent control over me, I had asserted my will and thus paradoxically deprived her of the omnipotence she seemed to need. I was about to make an interpretation along these lines, when it occurred to me that by sharing this understanding, I would be repeating my mistake: making my autonomous psychic functioning too obvious. As a result, I decided to only say, "I am sorry," and left the remaining thought unspoken. Jill relaxed and the tension in the room began to lessen. After ten minutes of further silence, she said, "Well, this session has been messed up. I had so many things to say." After a further pause, she said, "Among the various things on my mind …" and thus the session gradually "started". By the time we ended, things were going pretty smoothly.

In both these cases, I chose not to explore and not to interpret what was overtly an "attractive" piece of clinical material. In the first vignette, I did not ask what, if any, fantasies the patient had about stepping out of my office, getting a cup from the secretary, drinking water, and coming back. In the second case, I did not ask the patient what the patient had been thinking during the long silence before she resumed talking. Interestingly, upon hearing the presentation of both vignettes, some analytic colleagues expressed the opinion that I had missed important data by my lack of investigation. While I am able to see their point and even have some "old" empathy[9] with such a perspective, I believe that not analysing or letting go of some aspects of these sessions was preferable. To do otherwise would unnecessarily "pathologise" iatrogenic events and betray analytic greed.

Similar restraint is needed when faced with moments of "mutual silence" (Akhtar, 2013b) during the clinical session. Such silences feel peaceful. The analyst and the analysand are attuned to each other but experience little need to speak (Elson, 2001). Take a look at the following vignette.

Clinical vignette: 13

> Marcy Schectman begins the last session of her nearly ten year long analysis by saying that on her way to my office, she felt as if she were coming to a funeral. She describes her experience of there being an air of finality, solemnity, and loss to the afternoon. As I remain silent, Marcy goes on to recount her experiences at a couple of funerals she has attended. She sobs. I too feel sad, but do not say anything. Gradually, her associations shift to her getting a doctorate soon and then to graduation dinners, commencement ceremonies, etc. She begins to be animated. Soon, however, she catches herself and observes that this talk of happy endings (graduations) is defensive against her sadness (funerals). Significantly, she adds that while this might be the case, the two sides most likely represent the two sides of her feelings regarding parting from me for good: "happy and sad, sad and happy". I now say, "Yes, it does seem like that," and, after a momentary pause, add "but you know, all well-timed funerals are graduations of a sort and all graduations contain funeral-like elements." Marcy nods in agreement. She remains silent and so do I for the next couple of minutes. The sense of our being together in each other's apartness is evident as the end of the session approaches.

Here, like in the two preceding vignettes, it would have been greedy to insist upon a verbal exploration of the patient's silence, especially as it occurred during the last few minutes of a long analysis. A better technical choice was to allow the non-verbal relatedness to remain intact, and avoid succumbing to "interpretive greed". Even outside the drama that the very last session of an analysis presents, non-intrusive handling of silences can form an extremely important "intervention" and a demonstration that the analyst has mastered his interpretive greed.

Clinical vignette: 14

> Marilyn McDonough, a very attractive architect in her fifties, had sought help following an emotional crisis with one of her children. Once the acute matter was settled and the treatment began to deepen, the centrality of her own mother's death when Marilyn was barely five years old came to the surface. A talented

and industrious woman, Marilyn had devoted all her energies to raising her kids (after a tumultuous marriage ended in divorce) and to advancing in the profession she loved. She excelled at both these endeavours and, all along, the pain of her early maternal loss remained psychically sequestered—never repressed but not entirely worked through either. Later, she got married again and had since then maintained a reasonably satisfactory marital life.

Her analysis remained focused upon the lifelong effects of early loss; it coloured transference anxieties, sensitivities to separation, and fear of getting retraumatised by losing me. Provision of ample psychic space, empathic validations, gentle uncovering of defences against the awareness of the pervasive impact of the childhood tragedy, and interpretive handling of "survivor guilt" (Niederland, 1968) and the resulting inhibition of healthy entitlement led to great improvement in her capacity to mourn. Energy thus freed up was then directed to deepening ties with her family and newer sublimations.

One phenomenon during this middle phase of Marilyn's analysis was outstanding. It began around the late second or early third year of her treatment and lasted off and on for a very long time, though with changing hues and increasing insight into its nature on the part of both her and myself. The phenomenon consisted of her stopping talking some five or six minutes before the end of each session and then remaining quiet until we parted for that day.

Reflexively, I wondered whether I should interrupt Marilyn's silence and explore what was going on in her mind. Something, however, told me not to do so. Then, an association occurred to me. This pertained to the diminished pressure under which gasoline gets pumped into the car just before the paid-for amount is to be reached. The gas continues to go in the car but now under less pressure. This cognitive allusion reflected a growing certainty in my inner experience that Marilyn and I were not only deeply related but still "in analysis" during those last silent minutes of each hour. The fact that neither she nor I felt restless, dammed up, inhibited, or in need of talking confirmed the correctness of my therapeutic stance. Further reflection reminded me of the concept of a young child's "low-keyedness" (Mahler Pine & Bergman, 1975), whereby his or her diminished interest in external reality, lesser motility, and sombreness of mood reflect the effort to inwardly hold

> on to the image of a mother who, at that particular moment, is unavailable. I surmised that, during these end-of-session silences, Marilyn was keeping me inside her while simultaneously separating from me. The work of mourning (her actual mother) was as evident in her silence as was the preparatory effort at separating from me (in transference). I remained "non-interpretive" but emotionally attuned to her throughout these moments.
>
> Confirmation of such insights came from Marilyn, who—after about a year or so after the beginning of these silences—one day said, "Do you know what I am feeling and thinking during the times we are silent towards the end of the session? I feel very peaceful and in no need to talk. I feel I have talked enough and now I can be with you without speaking. And, you know, sometimes when I am silent, I see an image of the sign infinity which is pulsating." Contrary to my usual practice of waiting for further associations and/or asking for clarification, I felt the comfort to intervene immediately. I said, "Infinity—like forever, pulsating—as fully alive. There, yes, there is the mother who's gone forever and yet fully alive within you!" Marilyn nodded in agreement.

Restraining interpretive greed at the first few end-of-session silences led to my ability to connect with the patient on a deeper level. Whether it gratified an unspoken transference wish or simply acted as "holding" (Winnicott, 1960) is open to debate. The fact that the patient became able to talk about the potential meanings of what was going on in her mind (and this became more developed still later in the course of her analysis) leads me to believe that the "permission" to let her "lie fallow" (Khan, 1983) and to be "alone in the presence of the other" (Winnicott, 1958) advanced her treatment.

In contrast to such "non-interpretation" over a length of time, there are sudden and sharp decisions that an analyst has to make to curtail his interpretive greed. An example of such restraint is evident in the following case.

Clinical vignette: 15

> Laura Klafter, a blond sixty-year-old widowed attorney, was in psychotherapy with me for interpersonal difficulties that had plagued her for a very long time. Estranged from her son, she felt bereft

> and painfully alone. As our work progressed, a disastrous event occurred. Laura was diagnosed with an especially lethal form of intestinal malignancy. The day she learned of this diagnosis, she had a scheduled appointment with me. As she sat on her usual chair and talked about the tragedy amid sobs and tears, I noticed that she had picked up a trinket from the nearby occasional table and was caressing it, absent-mindedly, with her hand. I wondered if I should bring this to her attention but decided not to; I restrained my analytic greed in favour of remaining available, affirmative, and attuned to her distress.

What all these clinical examples show is that the analyst has to make choices of not only what to address in a session but also of what to leave untouched. Such titration of dosage, timing, and even the very offer of interpretation is what makes analytic work forever challenging. Limentani's (1989) quip that "Psychoanalysis is an art and for this reason it needs discipline" (p. 260) is pertinent in this context. Needless to say that the "art" consists of both interpreting and not interpreting. Interpretive appetite is good, analytic greed is not.

Concluding remarks

In this chapter, I have delineated the phenomenological aspects of greed, clarifying its manifestations into three categories: (i) primary, (ii) secondary, and (iii) defensively altered. Following this, I have elucidated diverse perspectives on the ontogenetic origins of greed and included the concepts of constitutionally innate greed, developmentally-inevitable greed, and greed as an angry intensification of appetite. After taking a brief foray into the sociocultural realm, I returned to the clinical realm and discussed how conscious and unconscious greed operate in the matrix of transference-countertransference relatedness.

Two areas remain to be addressed: variations in nature and intensity of greed that are lifespan dependent and/or gender based. As far as the impact of the unfolding epigenetic sequence of development is concerned, only one thing is certain, that greed originates in infancy and early childhood. What remains unclear is whether massive deprivations during late childhood (e.g., death of a parent when the child is six or seven) can "activate" or even "cause" greed for the first time.

In either case—whether greed is coming from early infancy or late childhood—manifestations of greed might vary in accordance with developmental phases. These might include hoarding of toys and video games during latency, inconsolable hunger for peer approval and sexual contact during adolescence, pressured pursuit of home furnishings, automobiles, and other status-rending accoutrements during young adulthood, unending accumulation of awards and honours during midlife, and extraordinary zeal for leaving behind a glittering "post-self" (Shneidman, 2008), that is, an embellished and thoroughly crafted legacy during old age. The encounter with limit that occurs during middle age (Erikson, 1950; Kernberg, 1980) certainly triggers a greed-asceticism dilemma. Facing limits of time and becoming aware of one's mortality, one gets regressively pulled towards brooding withdrawal and cynical anhedonia on the one hand and pseudo-youthfulness and dramatic changes in vocation and marriage on the other hand. Reworking the freshly aroused greed during this time can lead to deeper contact with reality and an enhanced capacity to enjoy what one possesses and what one has become.

The second question, pertaining to greed and gender, is more difficult to answer. From an overt and behavioural perspective, the fact that women are less prone than men to gambling, promiscuity, and addiction (Grant, Chamberlain, Schreiber & Odlaug, 2012; Potenza et al., 2001; Robertson, 2013; Seedat et al., 2009) can be taken to mean that they are less "greedy" or, at least, more content and consolable. Support for this conclusion also comes from the developmental variable of the female child venturing less far away from the mother (Akhtar, 1992b; Mahler, Pine & Bergman, 1975) and the intrapsychic variable of women's strong identification and intuitive closeness with their mothers. Unlike boys who must undergo a developmentally necessary "dis-identification with the mother" (Greenson, 1968), girls retain an ongoing internal contact with their mothers; this, in turn, might dampen their mother-hunger and diminish their vulnerability to greed.

In the end, though, such lifespan related and gender based speculations pale in front of direct clinical evidence. Our interest as psychoanalysts remains in one individual at a time and that, too, in accordance with the ebb and flow of drives, affects, fantasy, and levels of cognition. We remain open to the possibility that greed might fluctuate in intensity, get eclipsed by defences, drive the ego's acquisitive ambitions, or become a source of self-hatred, remorse, and guilt.

Notes

1. For a detailed discussion of the need-wish distinction and its implications for psychoanalytic technique, see Akhtar (1999a).
2. Hoarding of things and animals appears to be a consequence of greed on the surface. At its depth, though, hoarding is mostly a result of fear of loss, inability to let go, and profound feelings of insecurity. Forever needing the warmth of closeness to his objects, a hoarder is an ocnophile (Balint, 1959) *par excellence.*
3. The term "pleonexic personality" was coined by Nikelly (1992) to describe a character constellation dominated by pathological greed. In his view, such preoccupation can be traced to fixation at the anal stage, with money and faeces being symbolically connected. It may also be attributed to loss of gratification.
4. Green (1986) distinguishes the resulting asceticism from masochism on two grounds. First, the moral narcissist suffers from shame over his needs, while the moral masochist suffers from guilt over his wishes. Second, the moral narcissist seeks to impoverish his object relations in order to restore his infantile megalomania of self sufficiency, while the moral masochist retains a tormented but rich tie to his objects. An illustration of moral narcissism comes from Gandhi (1940) who, in attempting to become passion-free, concluded: "I must reduce myself to zero" (pp. 504-505).
5. This is clearly not true for many societies. To begin with, the sheer fact of poverty keeps people "uninvolved" with money matters. And, on top of it, the values of stoicism, asceticism, and spirituality uphold disinterest in monetary affairs. It is therefore not infrequent to find men and women, especially of older age, with pretty much no contact with money and little desire to purchase things. This can come as a huge surprise to those living in capitalistic societies. No wonder the publication of *The Man Who Quit Money* (Sundeen, 2012), an account of a Utah man who has survived without spending a penny since 2000, in the United States, was received with great scepticism and curiosity.
6. The provision of maternity leave for twelve weeks (with highly variable salary support) in the United States compares poorly to the thirty-six weeks in Norway and twenty weeks in Estonia, Poland, and Russia (all with 100 per cent of the salary).

7. The investment banker protagonist of the successful movie, *Wall Street* (1987), Gordon Gekko gave a spellbinding speech on the virtues of avarice to a hushed audience of businessmen.
8. An analytic colleague and a good friend, Ira Brenner, told me that early on in his career, he marvelled at senior analysts who kept working well into their eighties, and sometimes even in their nineties. With greater maturity, he has tempered this idealisation and thinks that a combination of love of psychoanalysis, anxiety about aging, and greed for prestige and money drives such professional longevity (personal communication, November 6, 2013). This latter dynamic became especially apparent to me during a recent visit to a North American psychoanalytic institute where younger training analysts confided their dismay at their seniors' (who were far along in their eighties) grabbing all the attractive and well-paying applicants for training analyses.
9. I was trained in a very strict classical tradition, which put premium upon clarification and interpretation at the cost of tactful and "permissive" silences. As a result, I am able to empathise with colleagues who express reservations about my not exploring the material that presumably underlay these patients' reticence.

CHAPTER THREE

Guilt

"I am sorry" is perhaps the most versatile combination of three words in the English language. Compared to its lexical rival, "I love you," the expression "I am sorry" is used far more often and in much more varied contexts. It can carry the hues of emotions that vary from flimsy courtesy through considerable remorse to soul-wrenching contrition. It can therefore be spoken with comparable ease at spilling coffee on the tablecloth, forgetting to turn the cell phone off during a play, hurting a lover's feelings, and hearing the news of someone's passing away. It can also be used by a child molester seeking a lesser punishment in a court of law, a politician caught embezzling party funds, and even a head of state expressing "regret" for policies that led to abuses of an ethnic minority or for a weak response to a natural disaster.

All these instances involve the experience of guilt, be it real or pretended, mild or severe, fleeting or sustained. The utterance of "I am sorry" is always motivated by guilt. But what is guilt? What gives rise to it? How does it affect us? And, why do some people feel so much guilt, others so little? Certainly the emotion does not result solely from committing "bad" (i.e., hurtful) acts. If that were the case, hardened criminals and psychopaths would be enormously guilt-ridden and law-abiding citizens would be devoid of the inner naggings of conscience. Actually the opposite is true. The one who commits crimes and breaks the law is often free of remorse while the one who avoids moral and ethical transgressions frequently suffers from the pangs of guilt. The relationship between "bad" actions and guilt seems highly tenuous. It seems best, therefore, to start our investigation by defining the terms involved in it.

Definition

According to *Webster's* dictionary, the word "guilt" stands for: "1. The fact of having committed a breach of conduct, especially violating law and involving a penalty; 2a. The state of one who has committed an offense, especially consciously, and, 2b. Feelings of culpability, especially from imagined offenses or from a sense of inadequacy" (Mish, 1998, p. 517). The scope of this definition is broad. It includes (i) an act of breaking rules, (ii) the possibility that such act only took place in the imagination, and (iii) the emotional state of the one who has committed the transgression. Additionally, by mentioning culpability from a "sense of inadequacy", the dictionary definition acknowledges that acts of omission can also underlie feelings of guilt. This is pure and simple English.

Now let us turn to five prominent psychoanalytic glossaries. Surprisingly, two of these (Eidelberg, 1968; Laplanche & Pontalis, 1973) do not have entries on "guilt". The other three (Akhtar, 2009; Moore & Fine, 1990; Rycroft, 1968) do but end up with definitions of guilt that are of variable quality. Rycroft (1968) regards it to be "the emotion which follows infringement of a moral injunction" (p. 59). He adds that guilt differs from anxiety insofar as

> (a) anxiety is experienced in relation a feared future occurrence, while guilt is experienced in relation to an act already committed, and (b) the capacity to experience guilt is contingent on the capacity to internalize objects whereas the capacity to experience anxiety is not; animals and infants may feel anxious, but only human beings with some awareness of time and of others can feel guilty. (p. 60)

Moore and Fine (1990) offer the following passage by way of defining guilt.

> Refers, like shame to a group of affects, including fear of retribution both from outside and within the self, feelings of remorse, contrition, and penitence. Its core is a form of anxiety with the underlying ideational content: "If I hurt somebody else, I shall be hurt in turn." In addition to this outer or inner retaliation for one's sexual or aggressive acts or wishes, one may hold the depressive connection that one has already hurt the other and is being punished for it; therewith goes the hope that, by atonement through mental or physical suffering, one can attain forgiveness, that is, regain love and acceptance. (p. 83)

Though impressive at first glance, these definitions are replete with problems. Both make inadequate distinction between guilt and remorse. Rycroft overlooks that guilt *is* a form of anxiety. Freud (1926d) explicitly stated that "The fear of castration at [the father's] hands becomes transformed into an undefined social or *moral anxiety*" (p. 128, italics added). And, in a footnote to this passage, Strachey translated guilt as "conscience anxiety", noting that "[O]ften in Freud, as in the present passage, stress is laid on the factor of anxiety in the concept" (p. 128). Rycroft's insistence on differentiating guilt from anxiety overlooks all this. Moore and Fine do recognise that guilt is a form of anxiety but lump too many phenomena (e.g., remorse, atonement, search for forgiveness) under the rubric of guilt. Moreover, Rycroft leaves no space for imaginary crimes and Moore and Fine equate guilt with the fear of punishment (which is a consequence of guilt). The latter also do not make it explicit that the "sexual or aggressive acts" stirring up guilt are only those prohibited by the particular society within which they take place (and its internal representative, the superego) and not of any and all varieties. Avoiding the excessive zeal of Moore and Fine's definition, I opted in my own *Comprehensive Dictionary of Psychoanalysis* (2009) for a more modest approach and described guilt as: "a dysphoric experience felt at breaking rules (familial, religious, national, etc.) or even at the thought of committing such a transgression" (p. 126). By restricting the use of the word "guilt" to the gnawing unease felt at a real or imaginary infraction, I prepared the ground for demarcating the boundaries of guilt from phenomena that are often lumped together with it.

Relationship to shame, remorse, and regret

It is commonplace to come across discussions of guilt—psychoanalytic or otherwise—that belabour the distinctions between guilt and shame, but pay little attention to the ways in which guilt differs from remorse and regret. In the following passages, I will attempt to rectify this omission and address the overlap of guilt with all three emotions.

Guilt and shame

The literature on the shame-guilt overlap is voluminous (e.g., Abrams, 1990; Grinker, 1955; Kilbourne, 2005; Levin, 1967; Morrison, 1989; Spero, 1984; Wurmser, 1994) and can hardly be summarised here. It might suffice to say that the contributors to this literature have variable emphases, separate theoretical perspectives, and different descriptive nuances. However, most contributors seem to agree upon certain similarities and certain differences between the two phenomena. As far as the similarities are concerned, both affects are regarded as dysphoric. Both are seen to lower self-esteem. And, both work as brakes on inner temptations and guarantors of "appropriate" behaviour. As far as differences are concerned, the following are frequently mentioned: (i) shame is predominantly visual while guilt is predominantly auditory; shame stirs up fears of being seen and found unseemly whereas guilt makes one hear inner voices of condemnation; (ii) the experience of shame is often accompanied by physiological markers (e.g., blushing, palpitation) while the experience of guilt is not; (iii) shame results from the rupture of self-continuity consequent upon psychomotor or social clumsiness or loss of control (e.g., belching or farting in public, mispronouncing a word); guilt results from actual or imaginary breaking of societal and, internalised rules (e.g., going through a red light, wanting to steal); (iv) shame, owing to its narcissistic underpinnings, is often felt for the loved ones' behaviour as well (e.g., when one's children act inappropriately in public) while guilt is experienced almost solely regarding one's own actions or inactions; (v) in structural terms, shame results from falling behind one's wished-for self-image and betraying one's ego ideal, while guilt results from violating or wanting to violate the dictates of one's superego; (vi) shame pushes for hiding, guilt pushes for confession; (vii) shame is diminished by "quiet" acceptance by others and guilt is reduced by "loud" forgiveness by others; (viii) shame is developmentally earlier than guilt; the latter, in its true meaning only evolves after the post-Oedipal consolidation of the superego,[1] and (ix) defences against shame include narcissistic self-inflation, withdrawal, or turning passive into active by shaming others; defences against guilt include blaming others, fearing external punishment, and masochistic self-laceration.

Guilt and remorse

Guilt is a nagging unpleasant feeling of being morally questionable. It arises from harbouring conscious or unconscious impulses to commit acts that are prohibited by one's religion, family traditions, local law, and, in the internalised form of all these, by the superego. In the end, guilt is about breaking rules, regardless of whether such transgressions actually take place or remain confined to the imagination. Remorse is an unpleasant and burdensome affect as well. It, too, makes one feel "bad". However, there are important differences between guilt and remorse. Guilt is about breaking rules and remorse about hurting others. Guilt is diminished by confession, remorse by making reparation. Guilt can be about past, present, or future; one can feel reprehensible for having broken rules, in the midst of breaking rules, and at wanting to break rules. Remorse is always about the past. It is a dysphoria that arises after one realises (and truly acknowledges) that one has hurt someone innocent, or worse, a loved one. Guilt is the sister of anxiety, remorse a cousin of regret.

The psychoanalyst whose work is of greatest significance to the experience of remorse is Melanie Klein. While using the terms "guilt" and "remorse" interchangeably, Klein (1937) described the childhood origins of the latter emotion in eloquent detail.

> When a baby feels frustrated at the breast, in his phantasies, he attacks this breast; but if he is being gratified by the breast, he loves it and has phantasies of a pleasant kind in relation to it. In his aggressive phantasies he wishes to bite up and tear up his mother and her breasts, and to destroy her also in other ways. A most important feature of these destructive phantasies, which are tantamount to death wishes, is that the baby feels that what he desires in his phantasies has really taken place; that is to say he feels that he *has really destroyed* the object of his destructive impulses ... in the

> baby's mind the conflicts between love and hate then arise, and the fears of losing the loved one become active. These feelings of guilt and distress now enter as a new element into the emotion of love … Side-by-side with the destructive impulses in the unconscious both of the child and of the adult, there exists a profound urge to make sacrifices, in order to help and put right loved people who in phantasy have been harmed or destroyed. (pp. 308, 311, italics in the original)

As this passage demonstrates, Klein's views deftly portray the genesis of destructive impulses, phantasies of having destroyed the love object, subsequent feelings of remorse, and the impulses of reparation emanating from these.

Winnicott (1954) proposed the term 'the state of concern' for such developments and saw their beginnings to be around six months of the child's age. In a paper titled "'Psychoanalysis and the Sense of Guilt", Winnicott (1956b) declared that

> … this important phase of development is composed of innumerable repetitions spread over time. There is a benign circle of (i) instinctual experience, (ii) acceptance of responsibility which is called guilt, (iii) a working-through, and (iv) a true restitutive gesture. (p. 24)

Winnicott emphasised that maternal tolerance of the infant's "ruthless love" and robust instinctual hunger lays the groundwork for the capacity for guilt, concern, and reparation in the child. While immensely valuable, Winnicott's ideas failed to distinguish between guilt and remorse; indeed, "remorse" is not even listed in the index of *The Language of Winnicott* (Abram, 2007), a painstakingly meticulous dictionary of his use of words.

Guilt and regret

Guilt due to having broken rules (established by family, religion, law, and society) is often accompanied by wistfulness. One yearns to undo the act, desperately wishes that one had not done it. And, it is at this phenomenological juncture that guilt begins to have similarities with regret. Guilt about past transgressions and regret are both about events that have already taken place. Seen this way, regret is even closer to remorse since the latter is always about something in the (remote or near) past. Commenting upon this, I have elsewhere noted that both regret and remorse

> ... are about the past. Both are about one's own actions. Both can involve acts of commission or omission. Both lead to a wistful rumination to somehow erase or undo the events of the past. Both can, therefore, underlie the "if only ... fantasy" (Akhtar, 1996). This fantasy assumes that, in the absence of this or that "calamity", everything would have turned out all right. Both "regret" and "remorse" can impoverish the ego and contribute to anhedonia, depression, and suicidal tendencies. Finally, both "regret" and "remorse" can serve screen functions and both can be put to secondary (e.g., sadomasochistic) uses. However, there is one very important difference between the two emotions: "remorse" involves feelings about how one's actions have affected others, while "regret" involves feelings about how one's actions affected oneself. In other words, "remorse" is more object related, "regret" more narcissistic. (Akhtar, 2009, p. 244)

Two caveats must be attached to the foregoing portrayal of guilt: (i) the description focuses upon the conscious manifestations of guilt. The fact is that clinically significant guilt generally exists on an unconscious level. It is discerned through various derivative phenomena including self-denigration, self-destructive behaviour, inhibitions of assertiveness and sexuality, inability to accept compliments, provocative actions to incite punishment, and the phenomenon of "success neurosis" (Freud, 1916d; Holmes, 2006); and (ii) in real life, distinctions between shame, guilt, remorse, and regret often get blurred (see Table 2). This is because the four can coexist. Guilt might cause inhibitions of ego functions and the consequent failure to act appropriately in a given situation might lead to shame. Vulnerability to shame might preclude helping someone in distress and, in this way, result in feelings of guilt. Breaking a rule ordinarily gives rise to guilt but if it leads to a loved one getting hurt, remorse may also follow. Remorse over hurting others might be associated with regret over one's characterological proclivities. And, so on.

Table 2. Shame, guilt, remorse, and regret.

Variables	*Shame*	*Guilt*	*Remorse*	*Regret*
Trigger	Social or physical clumsiness or failure	Wish to break rules, to do prohibited acts	Having hurt someone by an act of commission or omission	Having complicated one's own life by an act of commission or omission
Source	Ego ideal	Superego	Object relations	Narcissism
Modality	Visual	Auditory	Auditory	Unclear
Physiological concomitants	Marked	Some	Absent	Absent
Reflexive response	Hiding	Confessing	Rationalising	Denying
Relief provided by	Acceptance	Restraint	Forgiveness	Compensation

Origins of guilt

The search for the *font origio* of guilt leads us to two registers of experience and fantasy. One is made up of ubiquitous events and experiences of childhood. The other is constituted by occurrences that might be common enough but by no means are ubiquitous. The first category leads to (i) annihilation guilt, (ii) epistemic guilt, and (iii) Oedipal guilt. The second category leads to (i) separation guilt, (ii) induced guilt, (iii) borrowed guilt, (iv) deposited guilt, and (v) survivor guilt. Needless to add that the latter four types of guilt, while originating from idiosyncratic and serendipitous occurrences, can readily exploit the ubiquitous roots of moral unease; in other words, the two broad categories of guilt (i.e., ubiquitous and serendipitous) can get condensed with each other. Waelder's (1936) "principle of multiple function" applies to guilt as much as it does to any other psychic phenomenon.

Annihilation guilt

During childhood, our desires are simple, direct, and intolerant of delay in their gratification. We want what we want; we despise realities and people who come in the way of the fulfilment of our wishes. We wish such "enemies" gone, vanished, even dead. We wish to annihilate them. Given the limited circumference of our childhood interpersonal world, it is our parents and siblings who usually constitute such "enemies".[2] They are the ones who seem to come in the way of the immediate gratification of our wishes. No wonder we hate them from time to time and, in the typical childhood mode of absolutism, wish them dead. And, it is the persistence of these death wishes towards others that becomes the bedrock of the human experience of guilt. Unlike "annihilation anxiety" (for a formidable survey of literature on this topic, see Hurvich, 2003), which is the distress felt due to the anticipated disintegration of the self, "annihilation guilt" is the distress felt at the self-caused destruction of one's love objects.

A particularly nuanced manifestation of such guilt is seen in those brought up by parents who wish them dead, on a chronic basis, but did not have the physical and moral courage to actually do the deed. The child thus raised is unconsciously aware of the parental death wishes (Ferenczi, 1929) and, if he or she is fortunate enough to achieve a coherent sense of selfhood and agency, feels guilt at harbouring hateful feelings towards the parents.

Epistemic guilt

An additional source of guilt is formed by our childhood curiosities and their uninhibited expression. As children, we ask questions that seem natural to us (e.g., "Why does grandpa smell of pee all the time?", "Wouldn't Aunt Jenny die if she smokes?") but make adults around us uncomfortable. At other times, even mundane questions of ours (e.g., "Dad, what time are we going out?") are responded to by our parents (especially if they are tired, hung over, sick, worried, etc.) with annoyance and disapproval. In either case, we are silenced. But the questions—and the wish to ask them aloud—remain alive within us. And since we have internalised the adult injunctions, it makes us feel bad. This is "epistemic guilt".[3]

Curiously, development of such guilt is more marked in bright children. Delineating the multifaceted contribution of superior intelligence to neurosogenesis, Keiser (1969) wrote the following:

> Repeatedly it was observed that the child felt guilty for being more highly endowed than his parents or siblings. Areas of conflict are often created because the avenues of expression that a child

> of superior intelligence may have to seek are completely foreign to the values of his family. His ambitions for an intellectual life must frequently be kept secret until late adolescence or even into adulthood. During the analysis, it became manifest that the wish for an intellectual life was felt as an expression of hostility toward the parents. Not only did these patients have the feeling that they were rejecting their parents because they chose a professional life commensurate with their ability, but they felt rejected by their parents because of this choice. This was felt with particular force if they were the only member of the family with intellectual ambitions. (p. 458)

Another special form of epistemic guilt pertains to our sexual curiosities and all sorts of "naughty" prying into our parents' privacy caused by them. Remember how, as children, we fearfully but fervently tried to figure out the mysteries of sexuality? How do babies come into a mother's "tummy"? What are the penis and vagina actually meant to do? What is this thing called "sex"? Is it pleasurable or painful? Do our parents really "do it"? Such questions and the accompanying sense—caused by the parental reaction of disapproval—that there is something wrong about entertaining them, preoccupied us. This, too, forms an important layer to the bedrock of guilt in all of us.

Immigration is another context that can intensify the ordinary epistemic guilt of childhood. Children of parents who have migrated from repressive and collective cultures to expressive and individualistic cultures are especially vulnerable to this. They openly ask questions (regarding authority, rules, career trajectories, their rights, or even about factual matters such as the history of "their" country) which their parents are ill-equipped to answer. The parents, if already compromised in their psychosocial functioning, can then retaliate by making the child feel bad for their enquiries.

Oedipal guilt

When the "annihilation guilt" and "epistemic guilt" occur in the context of early triadic relations within the family, the resulting phenomenon is called "Oedipal guilt". Here, the importance of Freud's (1912–13, 1916d, 1917e, 1924b) observations is paramount. He emphasised that "[P]arricide and incest with the mother are the two great human crimes"

(1916d, p. 333) and that the sense of guilt derived from the Oedipus complex was a reaction to "the criminal intentions of killing the father and having sexual relations with the mother" (ibid., p. 333). The gender bias implicit in these pronouncements (i.e., matricide and incest with the father being overlooked) was more or less corrected in some of his other writings. For instance, Freud (1916–17) stated that:

> As you see, I have only described the relation of a *boy* to his father and mother. Things happen in just the same way with little girls, with the necessary changes: an affectionate attachment to her father, a need to get rid of her mother as superfluous and to take her place, a coquetry which already employs the methods of later womanhood—these offer a charming picture, especially in small girls, which makes us forget the possible grave consequences lying behind this infantile situation. We must not omit to add that the parents themselves often exercise a determining influence on the awakening of a child's Oedipus attitude by themselves obeying the pull of sexual attraction, and that where there are several children, the father will give the plainest evidence of his greater affection for his little daughter and the mother for her son. ("The Introductory Lectures", Vol. 16, p. 333, italics in the original)

Freud's main point, however, remained that the erotically driven wishes to woo the opposite sex parent and eliminate the same sex parent form the essence of the Oedipus complex,[4] and the persistence of such wishes in the unconscious (despite their overt renunciation due to parental disapproval and, later, superego threat) forms a source of lifelong vulnerability to guilt. The greater the strength of such unconscious wishes, the greater the amount of guilt. Success in life's pursuits then gets equated with Oedipal victory and mobilises guilt. Indeed, some individuals are "wrecked by success" (Freud, 1916d, p. 316) and often engineer their own failures. A few others become "criminal from a sense of guilt" (ibid., p. 332), that is, they arrange to be punished by conscious misdeeds as an expiation for transgressive impulses in the unconscious. Freud's earlier (1912–13) proposal of an actual, even if "pre-historic", murder of the primal father having saddled man with ancestral "badness" had a similar Oedipal ring to it.

Regardless of its specific colouration and context, Oedipal guilt invariably results in a compromised love life. Rescue fantasies towards the "suffering mother" (in the primal scene) lead men to repeatedly seek needy women as their love objects (Freud, 1910h), a scenario that often ends up in frustration once the "rescue" operation is over. In women, Oedipal guilt frequently leads to frigidity, inability to achieve orgasm or bursting into tears at the moment of orgasm, and a compulsion to get involved with abusive and betraying partners. Prostitution fantasies often colour sexuality (in both men and women) when Oedipal guilt plays a prominent role in psychic life.

Separation guilt

The feelings of "wrongdoing" that narcissistic and needy parents inculcate in their children when the latter begin to take steps towards psychic autonomy and independence is termed "separation guilt" by Modell (1965). Here the child's ego advances are age-specific and maturationally appropriate but are rendered doubt-ridden and "bad" by the parental response to them. Pine's (1997) useful distinction between "separation anxiety" and "separateness anxiety"[5] is, however, important to keep in mind; the former refers to the mobilisation of anxiety due to actual separation from love objects, the latter refers to the anxiety that results from experiencing oneself as an autonomous source of agency, thought, feeling, morality, and action. In light of this, it is better to call the bad feeling aroused by parental rejection of the growing child's autonomy as "separateness guilt". Regardless of which label one uses, this sort of guilt is seen more often in children raised by self-centred, sickly, lonely, and otherwise needy parents.

One situation which can contribute to such guilt with particular ferocity is that of immigration. Children of immigrant parents often experience an "acculturation gap" (Prathikanti, 1997) between their parents and themselves. This has the potential of causing role reversal between them. As a result, children can be placed in a position where they have to "translate" (literally or metaphorically) the ways of the culture-at-large for their parents. This may range from innocuous advice on how to operate a VCR or a computer to the more serious interventions of advocacy in medical and legal settings that are beyond the full comprehension of immigrant parents; clearly, this is more likely to occur if the older generation is less educated, non-optimally acculturated, and not proficient in English. Lan Cao (1997), a Vietnamese American writer, described such role reversal in poignant terms:

> The dreadful truth was simply: we were going through life in reverse, and I was the one who would help my mother through the hard scrutiny of ordinary suburban life. I would have to forego the luxury of adolescent experiment and temper tantrums, so that I could scoop my mother out of harm's way and give her sanctuary. Now, when we stepped into the exterior world, I was the one who told my mother what was acceptable and inacceptable behavior. And even though I hesitated to take on the responsibility, I had no choice. (p. 35)

The consequences of such role reversal are that the child comes to know the family's financial, medical, and legal secrets somewhat prematurely. This can burden his ego. More importantly, the parental dependence makes the child's developmentally appropriate movement toward separation and autonomy guilt-ridden.

Induced guilt

A related phenomenon is "induced guilt". This refers to the feeling of "badness" that arises in a child when the parents vociferously announce the suffering they have undergone in raising him. For instance, mothers who repeatedly tell their child about the difficulties in her pregnancy and labour ("You know, when you were born, I bled so much that I nearly died") end up burdening him with profound guilt (Asch, 1976). Similarly, immigrant parents who parade their culturally dislocated lives as a sacrifice for their offspring ("We came to this country so that you can have a better life") cause the latter to suffer enormous amounts of guilt (Akhtar, 2011a). Espiritu (2009) notes that "We did it for the children" is a common refrain among Filipino immigrants. However, this might also apply to many other groups, including those from India, Pakistan, Mexico, and African and Central American countries. The refrain has a more nefarious twin: "We stayed in this country because of you guys." This conveys to the child that the parents are suffering on a daily basis and are tolerating it only for the sake of their children. Such declarations on the parents' part can saddle their offspring with much guilt.

Children of Holocaust survivors are also vulnerable to induction of guilt by their parents. Having undergone extreme suffering, the latter often fail to recognise their children's age-specific doubts and apprehensions (Brenner, 2004; Kestenberg, 1980). To a child complaining about his or her day-to-day angst, such parents tend to respond by saying: "You do not know what being in trouble means!" Or, "You call *this* a problem? You have no idea what I have gone through," and so on. The child exposed to such retorts feels badly about voicing his problems and becomes guilt-ridden.

More frequent than such dramatic inductions of guilt are instances where parents discourage a child's authentic strivings and make him feel guilty for being unique and different from them. Highlighting such dynamics, Frattaroli (2013) states that:

> ... highly narcissistic parents who induce this kind of soul-crushing guilt cannot tolerate, let alone appreciate, their child's unique individuality. They systematically violate the sacred play space between parent and child, invalidating or punishing any spontaneous gesture of the child's True Self, making them feel guilty and ashamed about what is most alive in them, as if any genuine self-expression is an offense punishable by death or shunning. (p. 90)

Borrowed guilt

A counterpart to parentally induced guilt is what, for the lack of a better term, might be called "borrowed guilt". This consists of a growing child taking the blame for parental mistreatment upon himself and exonerating them altogether. Such development, designated "moral defence" by Fairbairn (1940) has two origins: (i) the child's ego-centric perception which precludes an awareness of independent motivation on the parents' part, and (ii) the child's attempt to preserve some hope of things getting better. In other words, if the child allows himself to feel that his parents are "bad", then the situation becomes unbearable since he has no other place to go and no one to seek love from. But, if he feels that it is he who is "bad", then, by behaving better, he can hope that his parents might treat him kindly and stop abusing him.

Deposited guilt

This type of guilt results from the child's succumbing to the "projective identification" (Kernberg, 1975; Klein, 1935) of their parents' guilt. In other words, parents feel guilty about something and cannot bear it. They split their guilt-ridden self-representations off and deposit them in their child. Then they subtly manipulate him to live these attributes out. An illustration is formed by a father who feels guilty about harbouring hostility towards his own father; he can ward off this intrapsychic burden by harshly criticising his son for every little transgression of family rules. Repeated over a long period of time, especially during the formative years of childhood, such "depositing" (Volkan, 1987) results in a son who is chronically guilt-ridden due to no fault of his own.

Once again, children of Holocaust survivors are vulnerable to such guilt. Parents who might hold themselves responsible (rightly or wrongly) for the death of relatives in concentration camps, might project their guilt and "deposit" it in their offspring. The latter then feel strangely guilty and remorseful, without knowing what is the crime they are supposed to have committed. Immigration also constitutes a particularly fertile ground for such developments. Elsewhere, I have elucidated this phenomenon in some detail.

> Children of immigrants can become the "containers" (Bion, 1967[a]) of the parental guilt that is deposited into them. Though idiosyncratic and highly personal variables can lie at its roots, such parental guilt is usually the result of their having left family members and friends behind in the country of origin, becoming more affluent than them, and living in a new country with less than complete loyalty to it. Such guilt is greater if the move has been from less affluent and politically unstable countries. And, if the grief over leaving one's country and the associated guilt are not adequately "mentalized" (Fonagy & Target, 1997) and mitigated by the means of reparative measures, it can be passed on to the next generation, neatly gift-wrapped in cultural rationalizations. (Akhtar, 2011a, p. 173)

While true, this statement does not mean that "deposited guilt" is restricted to the children of immigrants. Parents who are carrying a heavy load of guilt due to *any* reason (e.g., corruption at work, cheating in their marriage) can shift the burden of their remorse and make their children feel guilty. The latter then develop a proclivity for masochism in a phenomenon that is best termed "self-punishment by proxy".

Survivor guilt

This type of guilt is seen among individuals who suffer from lifelong anguish over their escaping the fatal blow that fell upon their friends and family members. Niederland (1968), who originally described such guilt in the context of Holocaust survivors, states:

> In order to understand more fully the pathogenesis of the survivor syndrome, I repeatedly stressed the need for a sharper focus on the all-pervasive guilt of the victim as well as the need for a sort of hyperacusis to guilt on the part of the analyst who has to be aware of the difficulties because of repression, elaborate defenses, and denials that tend to obscure the guilt. The patients' guilt-ridden fear of emotional closeness, their frequent attempts to assuage guilt, their repetitive guilt-ridden fantasies and dreams about death, violence, destruction, and their lost love objects, not only demonstrate the marked ambivalence toward the latter but also resort from the sadistic and incorporative fantasies leading directly to guilt in orally-regressed personalities and situations. (p. 314)

It is also seen in those who have outlived comrades killed in combat and loved ones in accidents. Individuals whose parents died during their childhood and individuals raised with a grossly impaired sibling are vulnerable to "survivor guilt" as well. The death of a child almost invariably leaves a residue of such guilt in his or her parents. One variable that might determine the intensity of guilt in such situations is whether the escape from ill fortune is the result of an active decision made by the survivor or due to mere happenstance (Mark Moore, personal communication, 3 April, 2008). A teenager who defies a parental curfew and upon his return home finds a parent killed due to a house fire feels more guilty than one who is unscathed in a car accident which kills the driver-parent.

Extending Niederland's ideas further, Modell (1965) proposed that a sense of guilt can be precipitated by "… the awareness that one has something more than someone else. This sense of guilt is invariably accompanied by a thought, which may remain unconscious, that what one has obtained is at the expense of taking something away from somebody else" (p. 328). This sort of guilt might get condensed with other sources of pre-Oedipal or Oedipal guilt but remains a dynamic entity unto itself. The guilt Western tourists experience while visiting the poor nations of Africa and Asia is the type that Modell has delineated. It is based upon the awareness of being more fortunate than others; to be sure, unconscious childhood wishes of robbing one's siblings (of mother's love) and feelings of contempt towards the less fortunate also play a role in the genesis of such guilt.

Having elucidated the various origins of guilt, we can move on to the consequences of guilt. The question, "What causes guilt?" has a counterpoint in "What does guilt cause?"

Adverse consequences of guilt

Feelings of guilt—and remorse—can exert considerable influence upon the course of an individual's life. The impact is greater if the guilt is excessive, the ego is weak, and access to receiving forgiveness (for guilt) and making reparation (for remorse) is blocked. Moreover, bearable amounts of guilt and remorse, especially when existing on a conscious level, are more amenable to productive outcomes. Unconscious guilt, in contrast, is vulnerable to defensive distortions that, in turn, lead to maladaptive behaviour patterns. In clinical practice such outcomes appear to result from (i) projection of blame, (ii) externalisation of persecutor, and (iii) libidinisation of suffering, leading to masochism and self-punishment.

Projection of blame

Guilt is often warded off by attributing blame to others. By irritable nitpicking, the guilty individual shifts the burden of contrition to someone else. Finding faults in others relieves him of self-criticism. Paranoia thus becomes a useful defence against depressive anxieties. In his elucidation of the relationship between guilt and hate, Jones (1929) made the following astute observation.

> Hatred for someone implies that the other person, through his cruelty or unkindness, is the cause of one's sufferings, that the latter are not self-imposed or in any way one's own fault. All the responsibility for the misery produced by unconscious guilt is thus displaced on to the other, supposedly cruel person, who is therefore heartily hated. The mechanism is, of course, very familiar in the

> transference situation. We know that behind it there always lies guilt, but further analysis still shows, in my opinion always, that the guilt itself is dependent on a still deeper and quite unconscious layer of hate, one that differs strikingly from the top layer in not being ego-syntonic. (p. 384)

Clinically, this is evident in patients who chronically complain about others' behaviour while overlooking their own role in provoking such mistreatment. Many "injustice collectors" (Bergler, 1961) carry a heavy burden of guilt over their own aggression underneath their persistent portrayals of others as wrong and blameworthy. Societally, this mechanism is responsible for political leaders blaming "outsiders" for problems of their people while ignoring the ways in which they themselves have contributed to these problems. The Osama bin Laden–George Bush diatribe is a case in point. Osama bin Laden held Western, particularly North American, cultural imperialism and political hegemony responsible for the turmoil in the Islamic world, taking little notice of how the corrupt and autocratic leaders of Muslim nations were equally, if not more responsible for the crises there. George Bush, a pro at externalisation himself, put the blame of America's problems on Muslims "out there" who simply did not like "our way of life" and were out to destroy it;[6] he closed his eyes to how the policies of the US government themselves were corroding the fabric of education, health care, and employment opportunities in the nation. Bin Laden blamed the West, Bush blamed the Middle East. Neither were willing (or able) to look at their own dismal records.

Externalisation of the persecutor

Another pathological consequence of unconscious guilt is that it undergoes externalisation and gives rise to undue fears of adverse occurrences (Jones, 1929). The dread might remain diffuse and create all sorts of doom and gloom scenarios in the mind. Or, it might be focused upon authority figures. Employers, policemen, and other individuals in positions of power then begin to appear too intimidating. One lives a life of fear and avoidance, though unconscious hostility towards authority figures (the original cause of guilt) often breaks through and serves as an agent provocateur of punishment. Locating this dynamic within the Oedipal context, Jones (ibid.) observed that:

> If the self-punishing tendencies are at all highly developed, we may expect to find that the patient will provoke the outer world, i.e. father-substitutes, to inflict punishments on him, and it is easy to see that this is done in order to diminish the sense of guilt; by provoking external punishment the patient saves himself from some of the severity of internal (self-) punishment. We get three layers very alike to the other sets of three mentioned above: first dread of external punishment (e.g., by the father); then guilt and self-punishment to protect the personality from the outer one, the method of religious penance; and finally, the evoking of external punishment, a disguised form of the original one, so as to protect the personality from the severity of the self-punishing tendencies. (p. 386)

That externalisation of the source of persecution wards off repressive anxieties is evident at the large-group level as well. The ubiquitous human "need for enemies" (Volkan, 1988)—evident at both individual and group levels—is often determined by this very pathway. By constructing others at threatening, an individual forecloses enquiry into the unacceptable parts of his own mind. By designating the other partner as selfish, unempathic, and even sociopathic, warring spouses avoid looking into how they themselves might have contributed to the marital unhappiness. By locating the source of its problems outside its geographical boundaries, a nation precludes the scrutiny of how its own domestic policies contribute to the distress of its people.

Libidinisation of suffering

This is perhaps the most common manifestation of guilt in clinical practice. Guilt gives rise to a need for punishment and to masochism which satisfies this need. Since this is a realm of great clinical importance, it might not be bad to look into the "need for punishment" and "masochism" concepts a bit more carefully.

Sigmund Freud's ideas about what he called the "need for punishment" evolved in four steps: (i) In "Notes upon a Case of Obsessional Neurosis" (1909d), he noted that the self-reproaches of the obsessional neurotic were forms of self-punishment; (ii) In "Some Character Types Met with in Psycho-Analytic Work" (1916d), he described a character type called "criminal from a sense of guilt"; this constellation involved committing outrageous and socially unacceptable, even criminal, acts in order to elicit punishment and relieve unconscious guilt; (iii) In *The Ego and the Id* (1923b), he described the phenomenon of "negative therapeutic reaction" whereby the analysand responds adversely to a correct interpretation, thus betraying his difficulty with improvement; this, too, is an evidence of unconscious guilt; and (iv) In "Neurosis and Psychosis" (1924b), he talked about how the "need for punishment" can become sexualised. What was an attempt to seek superego retribution now turns into an instinctual gratification itself.

Such gratification is subsumed under the concept of "masochism". A term coined by von Krafft-Ebing (1892) as a generalisation for the erotic role of pain and humiliation in the novels of Von Sacher Masoch; "masochism" consists of being dominated, controlled, hurt, and humiliated by a person of the opposite sex for the purpose of erotic gratification. This narrow definition led to Freud's (1905a, 1915c, 1919h, 1920g, 1924c) wide-ranging ideas about masochism. The trajectory of these speculations dovetails the evolution of his instinct theory in general and the Oedipal situation in particular. To begin with, Freud (1905a) regarded sadism and masochism as component instincts of sexuality and declared that they invariably coexisted; it was thus heuristically better to speak of sadomasochism than of sadism and masochism alone. In his first dual instinct theory, Freud (1905a, 1915c) regarded sadism—a pleasurable infliction of pain upon others—as primary and masochism as secondary (being a deflection of sadism upon the self). In his second dual instinct theory, Freud (1920g) proposed that masochism was a manifestation of the death instinct; it was primary, and sadism, its outward deflection, was secondary. In these and other papers (e.g., 1919h, 1924c), Freud related masochism to the fantasy of being beaten by the father and saw it as providing both sexual satisfaction and punishment for one's forbidden wishes. He thus introduced the intricate relationship masochism has with guilt and divided masochism into three types: (i) *primary*, which was the somatic substrate of the death instinct bound with the libido of the life instinct; the pleasure in pain came from the latter source; (ii) *erotic* or *feminine*, which was the attitude underlying sexually exciting fantasies in men of being bound, beaten, and humiliated,[7] and (iii) *moral*, which emanated from an unconscious sense of guilt and led to chronic self-depreciation and self-punishment. Analytic investigators following Freud (e.g., Bergler, 1961; Berliner, 1958; Brenner, 1959) elaborated, elucidated, and expanded the meanings of the term "masochism". This led, on the one hand, to increasing sophistication of understanding, and on the other hand, to the term "masochism" acquiring "a confusing array of meanings and connotations drawn from varied levels of abstraction ... [which] may falsely suggest underlying similarity between fundamentally different phenomena" (Maleson, 1984, p. 325).

A natural corollary of the evolving psychoanalytic ideas on masochism was the concept of "masochistic character". While a large number of analysts have contributed to its understanding, the views of the following seem most prominent. Reich (1933) proposed that "masochistic character" arose out of severe childhood frustrations; much aggression was mobilised, but, instead of being discharged on frustrating others, was defensively directed at oneself; individuals with a "masochistic character" were passive–aggressive, guilt-inducing, and coercive in their demand for love. Berliner (1958) sidelined the instinctual basis of masochism and emphasised its object-relational value. Masochism, for him, was a child's way to cope with his sadistic parents. The masochist mistreated himself and sought mistreatment by others because his superego was patterned after his cruel parents; love of suffering was an adaptive response to an abnormal childhood environment. Brenner (1959), in contrast, declared that masochism represented the acceptance of a painful penalty for forbidden sexual pleasures associated with Oedipal fantasies. Bergler (1961) saw masochism as "a desperate attempt to maintain infantile megalomania" (p. 18). The masochist unconsciously provokes and enjoys rejection but consciously reacts with righteous indignation. This helps him deny his responsibility in the rejection and his unconscious pleasure in it. After the outburst of pseudo-aggression, he indulges in self-pity and unconsciously enjoys the wound-licking. Cooper (1988), who highlighted the coexistence of narcissism and masochism, proposed the concept of "narcissistic-masochistic character" (see Chapter Five on betrayal for further details on this personality constellation). Individuals with such psychopathology seek suffering for their instinctual excesses and find justification for these excesses in their suffering.

Salutary outcomes of guilt and remorse

Guilt and remorse are, in themselves, neither "good" nor "bad". It is their underlying causes and, more importantly, their psychic handling and, after that, their behavioural management which determine whether matters have turned out to be "good" or "bad". To be sure, healthier ways of handling guilt and remorse exist than the mechanisms of projection, externalisation, and masochistic libidinisation described above.

Permitting oneself to be aware of unease at wanting to break rules—"signal guilt" in Fenichel's (1945, p. 136) terms—can stop one from giving in to unruly temptations. Recognising that one also harbours impulses to commit social infractions (e.g., stealing, sexually licentious behaviour, violence) can curtail the tendency to harshly judge others. Seeing that just across the abyss of guilt is the terrain of one's corrupt and immoral self can result in humility. Confessing one's real and/or imaginary "crimes" can serve as a stepping-stone for deeper self-scrutiny, including seeking psychotherapy or psychoanalysis. Taking account of all this, it is instructive to note that William Menninger, who raised many millions of dollars to finance the Menninger Clinic's educational and research programmes, often spoke of "the constructive power of guilt" (quoted in Rosen, 2009, p. 372).

Experiencing remorse, too, can have positive consequences. It cuts through the "manic defense" (Klein, 1935) of regarding oneself as blemish-free and diminishes the need for denial and rationalisation. This, in turn, improves reality-testing. Apologising to the individual one has hurt, neglected, or betrayed might follow. The possibility of being forgiven is thus enhanced. Acknowledgment of one's "bad" behaviour and expressing contrition raise the self-esteem of the victim and therefore go a long way in repairing the damaged relationship between the victim and the perpetrator.[8] Offering reparation as a subsequent step further diminishes the perpetrator's remorse and the victim's sense of hurt and violation. However, it should be noted that material reparation in the absence of acknowledgement of wrong-doing and apology can further humiliate the victim and deepen his or her psychic wound.

The application of these ideas to the justice system at large merits further enquiry. Not unaware of the limitations of restorative justice, Harding (1999) proposes that it is important that opportunities be provided to the offender to understand the significance of the victim's experience and to make appropriate gestures of remorse and atonement. Chase (2000) reports upon the "victim-offender conferencing program" (developed in the United States during the mid-1970s) in which the court brings offenders and their victims together with a neutral facilitator. During the meeting, the offender is offered an opportunity to apologise to his victim, an action that is often met with relief on the part of both parties.

The principle of "doing good" to undo the "bad" undergirds the rehabilitative dimension of the justice system as well. Guilt and remorse are washed away by years of good conduct (even if it is done behind bars) and the damaged internal objects can be more or less restored by acknowledgement of wrongdoing, apology, reparation, and reformed behaviour. Often matters do not need to go this far and a guilty individual is able to "balance" his inner sense of unworthiness by devotion to civic service and philanthropy.

Technical implications

Freud's (1912e) injunction that the psychoanalytic attitude involves "not directing one's notice to anything in particular" (p. 111) has been tempered by later technical innovations which speak not only of sharply focused attention (Brenner, 2000; Gray, 1994) but also of therapeutic "strategy" (Levy, 1987) that dictates measured and deliberate tracks of interventions. The comments I am about to make upon working issues of guilt and remorse in the clinical situation are in this latter spirit. However, to my mind, the "free-floating responsiveness" (Sandler & Sandler, 1998) and strategic confrontations and clarifications are not opposed to each other. Good psychoanalytic work fluctuates between these two polarities. It is quiet and lambent at one moment and forceful and direct at another.

Having stated that, I propose that technical handling of guilt and remorse involves a multi-pronged strategy which takes the following six factors into account: (i) interpretation of the defences against the awareness of guilt, (ii) interpretation of the defences against the awareness of the masochistic pleasure drawn from guilt, (iii) interpretation of the unconscious sadistic aspects of chronic self-blaming, especially in the context of transference, (iv) reconstruction of the sources of guilt, (v) interpretation of defensive functions of guilt (e.g., against lack of omnipotence in those who have lost parents as children), and (vi) help with bearing some guilt and finding productive ways of dealing with it. A brief explication of each of these follows.

Interpretation of defences against the awareness of guilt

Overt self-accusation is infrequently encountered in clinical practice. Derivative forms of guilt and remorse are, however, common, and present in myriad ways. For instance, the patient cannot tolerate happiness and success. Or, he cannot acknowledge receiving love. He chronically blames others and fills up each session by old and new anecdotes of having been treated unjustly. If the patient is lonely and has few love objects, he keeps the analyst "safe" from such blame and restricts the "injustice collecting" (Bergler, 1961) to the extra-clinical realm. If the patient does have a well-populated interpersonal life, the analyst is dragged into his paranoid defences faster. In either case, the forceful projection of the patient's harsh superego has to be interpreted. By continually constructing himself as a victim of others, the patient is warding off the awareness of the fact that, above all, he is a victim of his own self-hatred and guilt. This needs to be pointed out and made into a topic for consideration. The anxiety in the path to recognising this and the consequent squeamishness need to be empathised with and the unmasking of the unconscious guilt should be done in a piecemeal manner.

Interpretation of defences against the awareness of masochistic pleasure drawn from guilt and remorse

Masochism involves drawing pleasure from pain. Guilt and remorse constitute its powerful catalysts and triggers. As an analyst and psychotherapist, one frequently comes across patients with ferocious superegos and severe masochistic inclinations. They curse themselves, call themselves names (e.g., "fatso", "monster") and, in one form or another, indulge in endless self-condemnation. These are their ways of paying back their conscience without really intending to actually do anything different. They are *mea culpas*. Such patients are often unaware of the fact that they are drawing a certain kind of pride and joy from their proclamations. This masochistic pleasure has to be brought to their attention though there is always the risk that they will regard such an interpretation as yet another assault. Nonetheless, gently pointing out that their pain might have "additional" aspects often constitutes the first step. This might be followed by bringing to their attention the zeal and near-excitement with which they report occurrences of shabby treatment. Still later, a question might be raised if they "like" unpleasant affects aroused in them. If none of this brings resolution, the analyst might be forced to "refuse to listen" (Akhtar, 2011c) to endless masochistic tales and thus block the instinctual discharge (and pleasure) in the repeated recounting (see also Sharpe, 1940, in this context).

Interpretation of the unconscious sadism in self-blaming

Patients who constantly curse themselves, call themselves names, declare themselves incurable (while coming with striking loyalty to all their sessions), seem to manifest what Procci (1987) has called "mockery through caricature". Using this mechanism, an individual emulates a harsh parent to the extreme. This allows him or her to maintain an ongoing tie with the primary object. However, the limit of success in patterning one's behaviour after the cruel parent exposes to the world the unfairness and absurdity of the parent. Pseudo-compliance with the anti-instinctual attitudes to the extent of caricature ends up mocking the parent and thus covertly discharging the repressed regression towards him or her.

Within the transference-countertransference realm, such tenacious self-castigation and "militant hopelessness" (Poland, cited in Mathias, 2008) have a devastating impact upon the analyst's sense of aliveness, usefulness, and creativity. That the patient is suffering must never be overlooked. However, sooner or later in the course of treatment and with "affirmative interventions" (Killingmo, 1989) firmly in place, the sadistic dimension of the patient's masochism has to be brought up for consideration. If this stirs up further self-condemnation (which reflects a combination of genuine remorse vis-à-vis the analyst *and* an intensification of masochistic sadism), then that has to be handled firmly with interpretation.

Interpretation of the defensive function of guilt

Alongside the interpretation of the sadomasochistic discharge via guilt self-recrimination, the defensive functions of guilt need to be uncovered. It should be remembered that guilt and remorse can themselves acquire manic aims in order to ward off genuine sadness at what has happened and what one has done. Moreover, constantly feeling guilty can serve as a shield against competitive and acquisitive desires that, despite having been caught in conflict, might be developmentally appropriate. Guilt can also mask the dread of weakness. Remorsefully holding oneself responsible for the death of a parent during childhood, for instance, protects one from the horror of realising that it happened despite one's goodness and there was utterly no recourse to an alternative outcome in this scenario. Finally, guilt and remorse can also serve as defences against one's goodness and robust capacity for pleasure especially if these elements have become ego-dystonic due to the discouraging and disparaging treatment by early caregivers (and their later internalisation).

Reconstruction of the sources of guilt

This is a matter fraught with difficulty. Too early an attempt at reconstruction runs the risk of oversimplification of the patient's problems and fuelling the patient's tendency to project and externalise. At the same time, validation of early trauma (especially if it was gross, sustained, and severe) is essential. The analyst therefore has to oscillate between the broad strokes of such validation and finer brush painting of moment-to-moment analysis of associations. Space must be left for surprises to surface and for the patient's "personal myth" (Kris, 1956)—a rationalised but incomplete autobiographical narrative—to gradually dissolve. Vectors of the patient's own agency and even selectivity in establishing internal objects (Corradi-Fiumara, 2009) must be assimilated into finer reconstructions during the later periods of treatment.

Help with bearing guilt and finding productive ways of dealing with it

The analyst has to make sure that the result of his patient's diminishing guilt and masochism is not the emergence of narcissism and sadism but that of humility and concern. The analyst

> [...] must convey to the patient not only the direction he wants the patient to move in, but also confidence that the movement is inherent in the patient, which means that what the uncured patient wants is indeed a representation, however distorted, of what the cured patient will get. (Friedman, 1969, p. 150)

Such movement is facilitated if the analyst retains faith in the patient's healthy capacities for growth, a proposition reflecting Loewald's (1960) outlining of the childhood need to identify with one's growth potential as seen in the eyes of one's parents.

Concluding remarks

In this chapter, I have described the subjective experience of guilt and distinguished it from the related phenomena of shame, remorse, and regret. I have traced the origins of guilt to infantile and childhood aggressive and hostile impulses, both outside and within the Oedipal context. I have tried to show that Klein's work is more pertinent to pre-Oedipal remorse and the consequent drive of reparation while Freud's work is more pertinent to Oedipal guilt and the consequent need for punishment. In addition, I have noted that seeds of lifelong guilt can be sown by parental proclamations of suffering and sacrifice on behalf of their children, by parental depositing of their own unresolved guilt into the children's psyche, by parental intolerance of their children's developmentally appropriate strivings for autonomy, and by accidents of nature and random occurrences that leave the individual in a more fortunate position than his loved ones. Finally, I have delineated three pathological outcomes (projection, externalisation, and libidinisation) and one healthy (apology and reparation) outcome of guilt.

Despite casting a wide net, I have not been able to address two important issues, namely, the impact of gender and of culture upon the experience of guilt. Both variables demand attention but the burgeoning literature on these topics defies a quick summary here. Suffice it to say that (i) it is conceivable that some cultures (e.g., Japan) are more driven by shame (Kitayama, 1997) and others by guilt, (ii) the earlier report of a high rate of suicide in Germany, Austria, Japan, and Switzerland and the low rate of suicide in Holland, Italy, Brazil, and Spain (Weiss, 1974), as well as the more recent assertion (Nock, Borges & Ono, 2012) that rates are highest in Eastern Europe and lowest in Latin American countries make one wonder about the culturally determined vulnerability to guilt and self-punishment,[9] and (iii) in a sharp rebuttal to Freud's (1923b, 1925j) denigration of women's morality, recent studies (e.g., Bernstein, 1983; Gilligan, 1982) have found differences in the nature, not in the strength, of the female superego when compared to its male counterpart. The relevance of such culture-based and gender-specific insights to the understanding of guilt in its clinical and non-clinical dimensions is indeed great and needs to be pursued further.

Notes

1. This traditional viewpoint is called into question by the concepts of "deposited" and "induced" guilt; these are discussed later in this chapter. Moreover, the long-held position that the capacity for genuine guilt is a post-Oedipal development has been called into question by the epigenetic scenarios postulated by Klein (1937, 1940) and Winnicott (1954, 1956b). These theorists place the origin of guilt in the child's early dyadic relationship with mother, though their use of the term "guilt" differs in important ways from that of Freud's (1912–13, 1916d, 1924a). This difference is taken up in the later parts of this chapter.
2. Freud (1916–17) notes that while murderous impulses are a regular component of the childhood Oedipal experience, such wishes are even more strongly felt and verbalised in the context of the sibling relationship.
3. The biblical tale of Adam and Eve is an illustration *par excellence* of such "epistemic guilt".
4. Clearly, the opposite is the case in the context of homosexuality; for literature pertaining to this matter, see Akhtar, *Comprehensive Dictionary of Psychoanalysis* (2009, pp. 131–132).
5. Pine emphasises that all anxiety at separation is not "separation anxiety". For instance, a patient who feels anxious upon learning of his analyst's vacation may be responding to a drive upsurge consequent upon the removal of an externalised superego. Or, he may be responding to an anticipated disorganisation of the self. The former anxiety, while precipitated by separation, is not true "separation anxiety", since the separation in question is from a well-differentiated object. True "separation anxiety" involves a relationship with an undifferentiated other and is therefore an "anxiety over the sense of separateness" (1997, p. 230). This is better termed "separateness anxiety".
6. Such anti-Islamic xenophobia led to the emergence of the "good Muslim, bad Muslim" dichotomy in the public mind. Mamdani's (2004) penetrating analysis of this issue details the unfortunate consequences and politico-economic antecedents of this development.
7. The fact that all the cases from which Freud drew the idea of "feminine" masochism were males betrays a certain rigid preconception of theorising.
8. Sexual abuse literature pays special attention to this issue, with some family therapists (e.g., Madanes, 1990) requiring the perpetrator to actually, even ritualistically, apologise to the victim in front of other family members.
9. Clearly, more than guilty self-punishment contributes to suicide *and* the rates cited here might not be entirely reliable since the reporting patterns of suicide vary from country to country.

PART II

SUFFERING INFLICTED

CHAPTER FOUR

Deception

While overtly destructive acts derived from rage and hatred draw sharp clinical and public attention, far more damage is done to human relations by the quieter evils of lying, cheating, and deceit. In myriad forms that range from pretentious decorum at official events to pseudo-cordiality among political adversaries, from socially convenient bending of truth to outright lying for monetary gain, and from laborious inflation of the self to deliberate fraud for seducing others, deception corrodes trust that is the glue of attachment and interpersonal bonds. Regardless of its form, deception arises from trauma and causes suffering to self and others. A common denominator in various types of deception (e.g., mendacity, forgery, betrayal) is the existence of a lie.

It is this central feature that I will address in this contribution. I will begin with elucidating the formal characteristics of lies and the motivations that propel individuals to distort the truth. In the passages that follow, I will take up the developmental achievements necessary for the capacity for lying to emerge. Then I will make a brief sociocultural foray into the worlds of art and entertainment, politics, propaganda, advertising, forgery, and counterfeit. Following this digression, I will return to the clinical realm and address the implications of lying for conducting psychotherapy and psychoanalysis. I will conclude with a few synthesising remarks.

About lying in general

Borrowing a phrase from the former vice-president of the United States and Nobel Prize winner, Al Gore, I wish to begin this discourse on lying with some "inconvenient truths". Here they are:

- Everyone lies.
- Anyone who claims to be forever truthful is telling a lie.
- It is undesirable to be truthful under all circumstances.
- Lying is essential for smooth social dialogue and interpersonal politeness.
- Different forms and varying extents of lying are integral to many socially useful lines of work.
- Lying can at times save lives.
- Since all sorts of grey areas exist between what constitutes a lie and what constitutes a truth, it is not always easy to separate the two.
- The inherent "truth bias" (Feldman, 2009) of human beings makes them prone to believe what they are told and compromises their capacity to discern lies.
- Even in forensic settings where distinguishing between truth and lies is of paramount importance, there is no foolproof method to detect deception (Watson, 2009).
- Lies come in many shapes and forms even though they share certain common features.

In order to grasp the various formal characteristics of a lie, it might not be out of place to begin with a simple dictionary definition. A lie, according to *Webster's Ninth Collegiate Dictionary* (1987) is "an untrue statement with intent to deceive" (p. 689). Also included in the explanatory comments that follow the initial crisp definition are phrases like "an assertion of something known or believed by the speaker to be untrue" and the deliberate creation of a "false or misleading impression" (p. 689). Pooling these titbits with the notion of lying implicit in the well-known judicial instruction to tell "the truth, the whole truth, and nothing but the truth" leads one to the idea that a lie can be told in many ways. Lying is a multifaceted sport with diverse moves available to the deft player. Some prominent forms of lying are:

- Not telling the truth. Remaining silent while being asked to respond to a question, the answer to which one actually knows, constitutes a lie.
- Replacing the facts one knows to be true by false and misleading information.
- Telling the truth but not the "whole truth" and, by such withholding of parts of relevant information, altering the inference to be drawn from one's report.
- Telling the truth but embellishing it in a way that results in a caricature and thus puts its veracity in question. The mechanism of "denial by exaggeration" (Fenichel, 1945) belongs in this category.
- Flatly and forcefully questioning and even repudiating an established truth. The phenomenon of "gaslighting" (Barton & Whitehead, 1969) where one individual seeks to drive someone crazy by stirring up doubts about the latter's perception is an example of this type of lying. Instances of "soul murder" (Shengold, 1989) where a child's perception is ruthlessly erased by a cruel and abusive parent, and the denial of Holocaust, are other examples from individual and collective arenas, respectively, of this very type of lie.
- Acknowledging the truth about a certain matter but retrospectively imputing motives to it that were not in operation earlier. The ego operation of "sliding of meanings" (Horowitz, 1975) seen in narcissistic personalities is an example par excellence of such a strategy.

What all this demonstrates is that lies come in many forms.[1] From baldfaced assertions of falsehood to subtle distortions or reality, lies elude simplistic nosological traps. To discern them, one is not only required to pay close attention to what is being said and why but also to what is not being said, what is being exaggerated, what is being minimised, and what is being painted with a revisionist brush. One also has to take into consideration the intrapsychic and interpersonal context in which a lie is being constructed and conveyed; lying invariably involves a self-object scenario, however deeply buried under narcissistic grounds that might be. And this brings up the consideration of the motivational dynamics behind lying.

Like all human behaviour, lying is multiply determined (Waelder, 1936). Each lie involves instinctual pressures, narcissistic interests, superego defects, and ego loopholes. Each lie is a cavern of a wishful fantasy and an attempt to ward off a dreaded imaginary scenario. Each lie constitutes a psychic manoeuvre to alter the self-object relations; the object involved might be a specific human being or a diffuse world of people and institutions. Each lie has origins and consequences both within the subject's psyche and his or her interpersonal surrounds. Each lie creates something and destroys something. Being opposed to truth, each lie, to a greater or lesser extent, attacks, or at least bypasses, the great realities of separateness, finiteness, and the ubiquitous nature of aggression, genital differences, and the incest barrier.[2]

The foregoing constitutes a description of the diverse rock-bottom elements in lying. However, in a particular instance of lying, one or the other variable might play a more central role. This necessitates the distinction of motivationally different types of lies though not at the cost of overlooking their shared psychic ancestry. The following six categories readily present themselves though clearly they are not tightly exclusive and overlap each other in many ways.

- *Social lies* which involve the innocuous excuses and pretences of daily life.
- *Narcissistic lies* which include omissions and exaggerations for avoiding shame.
- *Psychopathic lies* or deliberate misrepresentations aimed at obtaining material or sensual gratification.
- *Pathological lies* which betray a pervasive inability to tell the truth arising out of an early and fundamental hatred of reality.
- *Life-saving lies* which have to be spoken in situations of being held hostage or tortured.
- *Occupational lies* or deceits are integral to being a spy or undercover agent.

Within psychoanalysis, Bion (1970) has given most thought to this topic, looking at the pathological as well as creative aspects of lying. Bion concluded that truth, being self-evident, does not require a thinker but a lie, being a manufactured thought, does. Moreover, the distinction that Bion (1957) made between psychotic and non-psychotic personalities—or, to put it more accurately, between psychotic and non-psychotic parts of personality—centres the former's hatred of reality;

the category of "pathological lies" mentioned above is quite often a manifestation of such hostile destructiveness towards reality and one's perception and knowledge of it.

Lemma (2005) has also made a significant contribution to the psychoanalytic understanding of lying. According to her, there are three psychic and relational configurations associated with lying: (i) *sadistic lying*, where the object is duped in an effort to reverse earlier humiliations of the self, (ii) *self-preservative lying*, where an embellished picture of the self is offered in order to seduce someone perceived to be disinterested, and (iii) a different form of self-preservative lying which could be called *self-protective lying* (though Lemma herself does not employ this expression), and is intended to protect oneself from an intrusive object.[3] Clearly, the dynamic constellations of the self-object representations in these forms of lying are quite different.

> In the first scenario, the self experiences the object as emotionally unavailable or inscrutable. In the second scenario, the self experiences the object as intrusive and omniscient. Unlike sadistic lying, the primary anxiety in self-preservative [and self-protective] lying is not about castration. Rather, in the first scenario, the anxiety relates primarily to the loss of, or uncertainty about, the primary object's love and concern. In the second scenario, claustro-agoraphobic anxieties are primary in response to an intrusive object. (p. 744)

Two other issues need mention. The first pertains to the collapse of motivation and consequence in lying (e.g., shame leading to lying and this resulting in a deceived other party). Sometimes, this conflation is obvious. At other times, there occur consequences that were not motivationally sought (e.g., shame leading to lying resulting in an awful feeling of guilt at having misled someone). In other words, the consequences of lying are both the desired one and the undesired ones and both types of consequences might involve the self and other. A parallel concern is the psychology of one who is lied to. While unconscious collusion might exist between him and the liar, the individual who is fooled brings his own dynamics to the situation. He might be unduly gullible and believe all that is told to him though not without feeling deceived and hurt later on. Curiously, some paranoid personalities—while contemptuous of others' naivety—are themselves remarkably, though latently, gullible (Stanton, 1978).

The second issue pertains to the distinction between lying and "negation" (Freud, 1925h). Negation involves *unconscious* sequestering of the emotional validity of the psychic truth; even the intellectual awareness of that truth is limited to its inverted form. Lying, in contrast, involves *conscious* sequestering of what is known and felt to be true. When an individual using negation says "I never thought of such and such," he is speaking the truth; indeed, he has never consciously thought of such and such. However, when a liar says "I never thought of such and such," he is not speaking the truth; he has consciously thought of it and he knows that he has. Negation involves deceiving oneself. Lying involves deceiving others.

Developmental origins of the capacity to lie

The capacity to tell lies is not hard-wired.[4] It evolves, becomes refined, and gets consolidated over the course of development. There is evidence that children as young as three can lie and sometimes even two year olds can do so (Feldman, 2009). The first lies, which are in the nature of "I did not do it", gradually evolve into the more advanced form of "I did not do it; he did it". Denial of culpability thus finds an ally in displacement of responsibility. The "countless extravagant lies" that Freud (1909b, p. 129) said Little Hans spoke in describing the addition of a younger sibling to his family were even more complex in their forms and motivations.

Before going into what propels children to lie, however, it is important to consider the capacities that are required for the child to become able to lie in the first place. Fischer (2009) has painstakingly mapped out this territory. She counts a secure attachment that allows for both a sense of oneness and separateness *and* the demarcation between self and others as two prime benchmarks for the capacity to lie. Also of great importance in this context is the child's attainment of reflective functioning, which implies the renunciation of equating psychic and physical reality. The consequent "pretend mode" (Fonagy & Target, 1997) permits playing out different schema, trying out different roles, and experiencing things from an imaginary perspective while retaining contact with reality. The child in the "pretend mode" (e.g., playing he is Superman) is not lying; he not only knows that he is not Superman but recognises that others know that as well. And yet, he enjoys the act and enjoys others' indulgent attention towards his play. Fischer (2009) concludes that achievement of an Oedipal organisation is the

> ... ultimate requirement for full-fledged lying. It is only then the child can pull together fantasy, reality, conflict, and compromise, develop a narrative, know the difference between reality and pretense, feel the pressure of the prohibiting superego, and attempt to mislead or deceive the other. (pp. 27–28)

Blum (2009) concurs that the development, during the second year of life, of symbolic, cognitive, and linguistic capacities for pretence and play and for anticipation of consequences foreshadows the appearance of intentional lying. According to him, children begin to lie around three years of age and do so largely to avoid blame. The list of motivations to lie grows as development proceeds further.

> Lies are frequently related to avoiding, restoring, and repairing narcissistic injury, to raising self-esteem, to avoid punishment, or to unconsciously seek punishment. The child who invents or exaggerates abilities and accomplishments wishes to be the idealized adults, to become the ideal aggrandized self—the hero or heroine of a family romance. Wishful thinking, magically undoing disappointments, narcissistic injuries and traumas, and the greater reliance of children on defenses of denial, splitting, and role reversal sets the stage for magical tricks of pretense, deception, guile, and lies. The child who has experienced parental lying may seek revenge for having been deceived. (p. 52)

This last part cannot be over-emphasised. The development of "basic trust" (Erikson, 1950) in children is dependent not only upon repetitive satisfactory outcomes of the infantile appeal cycle but also upon experiencing parents as honest. Even those children who are fortunate in this regard can find the situation puzzling at times. For instance, a child is punished for telling the truth that his grandmother's cooking stinks and rewarded for appearing thankful for a gift that he does not like. In imparting the etiquette of social civility, parents can (and often do) confuse the child. However, such minor miscarriages of truth do not lead the child to become a liar. It is chronic betrayal of his trust by parents and their explicit hypocrisy and dishonesty that lays the groundwork for lying. At times, however, the parents appear quite moral, even moralistic, and yet the child turns out to be habitually deceitful. More often than not, such parents have unconsciously encouraged the child's delinquency and have vicariously enjoyed it. This transgenerational duplicity leads to what Johnson and Szurek (1952) have termed "superego lacunae" in the offspring.

Addititional to these psychoanalytic ideas are empirical studies of lying children. An important one pertains to the "peeking game" research (Talwar & Lee, 2002) whereby a child is given a chance to commit a transgression (e.g., by looking at a forbidden object) and then fib about his action. Three year olds can do so but they lack "semantic leakage control", that is, maintaining consistency of verbal statements and not letting the fact out that they have peeked. By the age of about six or seven, some 50 per cent of children can maintain feigned ignorance. Edelsohn (2009), who has recently reviewed research studies on children's lying from elementary school through adolescence, concludes that while young children lie to avoid punishment and buttress self-esteem, adolescents lie for protecting their privacy and enhancing their autonomy and individuation. Both honesty and lying are learned in the home and reflect not only the child's cognitive and moral development but also the texture of the child's relationship with his or her parents. Predominance of love between the two parties strengthens the capacity for honesty. Predominance of hate tilts the balance towards lying.

Pertinent psychiatric syndromes

While antisocial personality disorder is readily associated with mendacity and deception, the fact is that other severe personality disorders (i.e., narcissistic, paranoid, hypomanic, borderline, schizoid, "as-if", and schizotypal) are also prone to lying (Stone, 2009). Such vulnerability to distorting facts in external reality is overdetermined.[5] The prevalence of "manic defenses" (Klein, 1935)—the trio of idealisation, denial, and omnipotence—makes remaining loyal to "facts" difficult. Narratives get slanted and accounts of what-happened-when get exaggerated in this or that direction. The unrelenting search for "all-good" objects leads to compromises of perception and registration; aspects of reality that do not fit with the desired experience (at a given moment or on a sustained basis) are repudiated. Consequently, their recall bears little resemblance to facts. Yet another factor that propels individuals with severe character pathology to lie is the intolerance of weaknesses or blemishes in their own selves. Dreading shame, they give in to the temptation of narcissistic self-inflation and, in the process, resort to lying about their accomplishments and their status in life.

The foregoing statements need to be tempered by recognising the quantitative and qualitative variations of lying between specific types of character pathology. Individuals with antisocial personality disorder, for instance, manifest sustained "deceitfulness, as indicated by repeated lying, use of aliases, or conning others for personal profit or pleasure" (*DSM-V*, 2013, p. 659). Those with narcissistic personality disorder also show defects of ethics and morality. Their "readiness to shift values to gain favor" and "inordinate moral relativism" (Akhtar, 1992a, p. 69) is often accompanied by outright lying and deception. However, such behaviour on their part is less pervasive, less coldly manipulative, and less impulsive than that exhibited by antisocial individuals. Lying is also seen in association with schizoid and paranoid personality disorders. In the former, lying is deployed largely for social avoidance (e.g., to not attend a neighbourhood party). In the latter, the picture is more complex. The aggression-driven corruption of autonomous ego functions results in a biased, narrow, and rigid cognitive style. The "need" to overlook aspects of reality that do not accord with one's preconception is great and contributes to distortions of facts. Moreover, the moral self-righteousness of the paranoid individual often coexists with an expedient mendacity (Tobak, 1989) which can catch others by surprise.

Besides these explicit associations between lying and severe personality disorders, there are the instances of "secret lives". Here, a seemingly coherent personality organisation exists alongside a dissociated sector of fantasy, affect, and behaviour. Dissociation, in this context, does not necessarily imply a personified part of the self that is separated from the rest of the personality by an amnesic barrier, though that can also occur at times. More often the "sector disorders" referred to here emanate from a rigid and successful operation of splitting mechanisms (Akhtar & Byrne, 1983; Kernberg, 1975). The prominent and happily married politician who has secret out-of-town rendezvous with prostitutes, or the wealthy banker who adores his wife and children while having a hidden second family in another country, illustrate this type of psychopathology. Freud's (1924b) early description of perverse formations is along similar lines. He noted that the ego is pulled, often to a painful extent, in opposite directions by the demands of the id and external reality, and at times

> ... it will be possible for the ego to avoid a rupture in any direction by deforming itself, by submitting to encroachments on its own unity and even perhaps by effecting a cleavage or division of itself. In this way the inconsistencies, eccentricities, and follies of men would appear in a similar light to their sexual perversions. (pp. 152–153)

While the discovery of the resulting secret lives is fodder for newspaper headlines (especially when it involves celebrities and model citizens), the psychiatric clinics encounter a different type of syndrome associated with lying. This involves the spectrum of factitious disorder and malingering. Also known as Munchausen syndrome (Asher, 1951),[6] factitious disorder involves feigning physical or mental illness. Patients with this disorder simulate, induce, and exaggerate all sorts of symptoms, often to the extent of ingesting unsafe materials and inserting unsafe objects in their bodies. They might produce fake evidence of having bled and false documents of suffering this or that malady. They frequently seek hospitalisation and their goal is to be emotionally taken care of. While deceptive in the literal sense of the word, the behaviour of these individuals differs from malingering in an important way. In malingering, distress is feigned for material gain (e.g., monetary compensation, avoidance of work-related duties) whereas in factitious disorder, illnesses are faked in order to receive emotional care and attention (Sadock & Sadock, 2007). The boundaries between factitious disorder, malingering, and "genuine" hypochondriacal conviction are, however, not always easy to draw. The heightened susceptibility to auto-hypnotic suggestion might be so great that the individual succeeds in suppressing all knowledge of his or her desire to adopt a sick role (Davis & Weiss, 1974).

Lying and deception in culture at large

In delineating the concept of "false self", Winnicott (1960) acknowledged that, to a certain extent, reactive and even inauthentic behaviour is inevitable and might even be necessary for harmonious living with others. Politeness, good manners, and "white lies" that preclude ruptures of interpersonal fabric thus become integral to culture.[7] Harmless deceptions of such sort "grease the wheels of social discourse" (Feldman, 2009, p. 49). We take them for granted.

Then, we encounter the world of advertising. Here the whisper of deception grows more seductive. Ads in fashion magazines can be meticulously doctored. The curve of the waist of a beautiful model, who is wearing this or that lingerie item or supposedly wearing a perfume that a designer wants us to buy, is made more acute by the clever use of scissors. Her cleavage is brushed to appear more alluring. Even her legs are elongated by inventive photoshopping. Similar embellishment is evident in how expensive properties are portrayed in real estate brochures. All evidence of "ordinariness" (e.g., newspapers strewn about, shoes and socks, a wet umbrella, a half-empty bottle of ketchup) and lived human experience is excised. The interior of the house is presented as immaculate, undisturbed by those who inhabit it, ideal, and, in essence, as the domicile of a "purified pleasure ego" (Freud, 1915c). The lie mesmerises us.[8]

Lying and deception are also rampant in communication and journalism. Not restricted to the fakery on "reality" television shows (with those in dire circumstances staying in luxurious hotels between shoots) and sensationalism of checkout counter tabloids (e.g., "One-eyed aliens land in New Mexico"; "Woman gives birth to kittens"), manoeuvres of deceit find their way into respectable journalism as well. Feldman (2009), who has researched this matter, reports the following.

> The *New York Times* prides itself on its role as "the paper of record", printing corrections to stories sometimes decades after the fact to maintain its reputation of accuracy. Hence the sensation when it was revealed that Jayson Blair, a *Times* reporter, had fabricated or plagiarised material for dozens of national news stories. He'd offered reporting from places he had never been, he'd given quotes from people he'd never interviewed or met, he'd misstated facts, and he'd made up details. *USA Today* reported Jack Kelley was a finalist for the Pulitzer Prize before it revealed, in 2004, that he had invented material, including portions of the story that had earned him a Pulitzer nomination. In a front-page article, *USA Today* admitted that "Kelley fabricated substantial portions of at least eight major stories, lifted nearly two dozen quotes or other material from competing publications, lied in speeches he gave for the newspaper, and conspired to mislead those investigating his work." (pp. 197–198)

The fact that we respond to such revelations with dismay does not prevent us from marvelling at cold-hearted bluffs in a game of poker (Moore, 2009) and from enjoying depictions of scammers, impostors, and con artists on the big screen. Indeed, there has been a long genre of such movies that includes hits like *The Music Man* (1962), *The Sting* (1973), *Dirty Rotten Scoundrels* (1988), *The Grifters* (1990), *House of Cards* (1993), *Ocean's Eleven* (2001), and *Catch Me If You Can* (2002). Splitting-off their avowedly moral selves, the audience vicariously identifies with the slick protagonist's finesse while, at a still deeper level, partaking of the masochistic pleasure of the one who is duped.[9]

Stakes are raised when we encounter con artists in the real world. Running Ponzi schemes (e.g., the notorious Bernie Madoff) or glad-handing "liar loans" (Zibel, 2008)—home mortgages approved without checking the borrower's income or assets—they can lead us to financial ruin. Or they might sell us art and antiquities that turn out to be fake. One look at the exorbitant prices successful forgeries in the realm of art can fetch reveals that monetary benefit is a major motivation of lying here. The list of those who thrive in this business is indeed long. Two outstanding art forgers who made enormous money by their deceptive craft are Hans van Meegeren (1889–1947), the Dutch art dealer who painted many fake Vermeers, and Tom Keating (1917–1984), the British con artist who forged more than 2,000 paintings by more than 100 artists in his lifetime. The fact, however, is that the money made by these two master forgers constitutes a minuscule proportion of that made by art forgers all over the world. And art is not the only arena where fake products offer lucrative financial rewards. Collectors of autographs, rare manuscripts, old photographs, letters, and even stamps and coins know very well how widely inauthentic objects circulate in the bazaars of their passion. They can readily recount all sorts of tales involving someone being swindled by a forger who got away with a huge sum of money.

However, monetary profit is not the only motive for creating a forgery. Emotional factors also seem to play a role here. Prominent among these are the following:

- Creating a "successful" forgery affords one the wicked pleasure of fooling others. Compared to oneself, others now appear silly and stupid. Triumph over their innocence results in gleeful mocking on a secret basis. In talking of con artists, Blum (2009) emphasises

the "sadism behind their narcissistic charm and charisma" (p. 61). Deceiving others promises to undo the chronic feelings of inferiority and impotence the forger often carries within himself.
- Trading in fake products invariably involves a rebellion against ordinary morality. It involves breaking the law as well. Making and selling counterfeit objects can thus give vent to emotional conflicts with authority figures. The irreverence and bravado of an impostor is a slap in the face of the established order. The ever-present risk of being caught adds to the thrill of defiance.
- Fakery also fulfils strivings for magical powers. To produce a dollar bill in one's basement, for instance, gratifies our childish wishes for becoming "rich" pronto. To paint a Cezanne or a Picasso over a few days in downtown Cleveland is to reverse time, change location, and acquire creative genius at will. Just like that, with a snap of the fingers.

Such considerations of the forger's sentiments bring us to the other side of the equation, namely the emotional responses of the witness of a forgery. As victims of forgery, we feel an admixture of outrage and shame. We are hurt by the betrayal and embarrassed by our gullibility. Interestingly, even when we are mere witnesses or onlookers of a forgery, not its victim, our responses are not simple.

We are all familiar with the scorn we feel upon seeing poorly made Barbie dolls from the Persian Gulf, French perfumes concocted in the Philippines, faux-pearl necklaces offered on QVC, fake Rolex watches sold on a street corner, Coach handbags made in Guatemala, and designer-label clothing made in Bangladeshi sweatshops. We deride them. The scorn reflects our rejection of fraud in general. It helps us repudiate aspects of inauthenticity in our own personality make-up. It is as if by belittling fake products we are saying that we ourselves are entirely genuine in our day-to-day behaviour. Our dislike of counterfeit goods thus turns out to be rather self-serving. This is a sort of fakery itself.

More embarrassing is the possibility that forgeries and counterfeit products provide vicarious gratification of our hidden, less-than-noble impulses. The childhood intolerance for the labour of effort and for the helplessness of waiting to become adept at something finds a secret ally in the producer of artifice who fuels our suppressed longings for quick and swift results that are achieved without effort and practice. He tells us that the omnipotence we have reluctantly renounced can find gratification after all. He offers us a path that does not traverse through law-abiding territories of learning, practice, and hard work. And we gladly give in to his seductions. To put it bluntly, the clandestine pact between us and the forger goes like this: "If this guy in Texas can paint a Van Gogh, maybe we too can accomplish great and even impossible feats. If he can break rules and fool others, maybe we can also do that which is prohibited to us." No wonder we feel a mixture of barely suppressed thrill and a delicious wave of guilty fear upon encountering a fake product. Hold a counterfeit hundred dollar bill in your hands and you will immediately know what I am talking about.

Something even deeper about human nature is revealed by the observation that we admire a better fake more than a sloppy fake. The more devilishly fooled we are, the more delight we take in the impostor's product. Why is that? Is the pleasure offered us by a good fake merely aesthetic? In other words, do we like a better replica of Rodin's *The Thinker* or of the Leaning Tower of Pisa because they look good, that is, closer to the original thing? Or is it because the better executed fake shows more thoughtfulness and effort and, by implication, a greater amount of respect for the creator of the original? The answer to both of these questions is a resounding "Yes"! Overtly, our reasons for reacting more favourably to a good fake are aesthetic. A replica that closely approximates the original stimulates the admiration we feel towards the latter. We like the sensation. Covertly, witnessing a good fake provides us with a well-balanced compromise between our longings for magic on the one hand and the recognition of value of effort on the other. It also provides a simultaneous gratification of our childhood wishes to outsmart our parents as well as keep them on a higher level than us, and since all of us have the remnants of such childhood wishes in the basement of our minds, it is not surprising that we simply "love" a well-executed fake.

Far more sinister consequences are associated with the political spinmeister's rhetoric. Mario Cumo's (former governor of New York State) quip that campaigning is done in poetry and governing in prose pales in the face of the exhortative oratory by paranoid and narcissistic leaders. No tricks are left unused in them. Distortions, exaggerations, embellishments, and outright lies prevail. Hardly a reflection of contemporary moral relativism, deception has played an important, often devastating, role in politics since time immemorial. The infamous peace offering of the Trojan horse by ancient Greeks, the Dreyfus affair of late nineteenth-century France, the massive anti-Semitic propaganda by Nazis during the 1930s, the ideological witch-hunts of the 1950s McCarthy era in the United States are but a few examples of how wicked shenanigans pervade domestic and international politics. Notable in this context is Alterman's (2004) thorough account of lies told by the US presidents to Congress, the media, and the public at large. It is a painful saga of how moral values and the honourable covenant to uphold the truth at the highest level of a democratic government can be sacrificed at the altar of political convenience. While Bill Clinton's bald-faced denial ("I did not have sex with that woman, Miss Lewinsky") has its titillating impact, far more serious consequences have followed Lyndon Johnson's deceptive assurances regarding the second Tonkin Gulf incident, Richard Nixon's Watergate cover-up, Ronald Reagan's lies regarding the Iran-Contra deal, George Bush Senior's false promises ("Read my lips: no more taxes"), and the younger Bush's fabricated reasons to attack Iraq. Indeed hundreds of thousands of people have been killed due to the last mentioned deceit, to say nothing of its devastating impact upon the American economy and the nation's prestige in the eyes of the world.

Back to the clinical realm

Encounters with deceitful patients, especially those with prominent antisocial features, make one painfully aware of the limits of the applicability of psychoanalysis and even psychoanalytic psychotherapy (Stone, 2007). Freud's (1905b) declaration that in order to tolerate the rigours of psychoanalytic treatment, one must possess "a fairly reliable character" (p. 263) readily comes to mind in this context. Without honest self revelation, or at least the intent for it, the therapeutic alliance remains a sham. Gross psychopaths are therefore not suitable subjects for psychoanalytically derived therapies. Those with milder antisocial tendencies can, at times, benefit from such treatment especially when confrontational and cognitive-behavioural interventions are used in conjunction with it (Cloninger, 2005; Kernberg, 1984, 1992; Stone, 2007).

Such work might have to start from the very first session of the patient's evaluation. The discovery of an overt disregard for the basic conditions of treatment (e.g., refusing to tell one's real name or to give proper contact information) and outright lying needs to be immediately confronted. The prospect for future therapy is better if such confrontation leads to plausible explanations (e.g., the patient's need to conceal his identity because he is in a government witness protection programme) or anxiety and shame leading to a quick rectification of the earlier mis-statement. If, however, the patient responds to the confrontation by more lies, improbable rationaliszations, argumentativeness, and rage, the prognosis is guarded (Akhtar, 1992a). Under such circumstances it might not even be possible to begin a treatment. "Therapists who believe that with enough effort, they can make every patient stay the course are engaging in omnipotence" (Yeomans, Selzer & Clarkin, 1992, p. 9). Stone (2009), who has extensive experience in working with criminals and psychopaths, explicitly states that if the lying patient refuses to abide by the parameters of treatment, he or she needs to be discharged.

The discovery of deceitfulness might be made much later in the encounter with less psychopathic individuals. Lies, distortions of truth, and deliberate withholding of information might enter the treatment as a form of narcissistic resistance and a ploy to keep one's shame-laden aspects hidden from the therapist. Such self-protective motivations might extend to warding off castration anxiety by repudiating assertive authenticity (Gediman, 1985) and keeping in abeyance fears that one would not be liked for what one is in reality. On the other hand, lying may have greater discharge functions related to early object relations. Falsehood then itself becomes a form of transference relatedness. Analytic space, under such circumstances, becomes "a scripted, constrained space within which the therapist experiences the full impact of the enactment of an internalized relationship to an object with whom honest and direct communication is felt to be an impossibility" (Lemma, 2005, p. 752).

Here Kernberg's (1992) concept of *psychopathic transference* is pertinent. According to him, a patient in the throes of such transference consistently lies to the therapist, suppresses useful information, and, as a result of projecting his own corrupt tendencies, believes that the therapist is dishonest and untrustworthy. At times, the patient tries "unconsciously to provoke the therapist to deceptive or dishonest behaviour, or at least to inconsistencies in his behaviour that the patient may then interpret as dishonesty" (p. 223). Kernberg proposes that the proper approach under such circumstances is to confront the patient tactfully but directly and to explore the inherent transference relationship in detail and to resolve it interpretively before proceeding with other issues. Typically, the "psychopathic transference" gets transformed into "paranoid transference" before giving way to depressive reparative feelings and genuine self concern.

In extending Kernberg's work, Lafarge (1995) described three transferences characteristic of patients in whom deception and inauthenticity are organising themes: (1) *imposturous transference* in which the patient actively enjoys deceiving the analyst by his fabrications; (2) *psychopathic-paranoid transference* in which the patient is intensely involved with the analyst who he feels is lying to him and will betray him; and (3) the *psychopathic-unreal transference* in which the patient feels disconnected from the analyst and automaton-like in his own experience. Lafarge goes on to suggest that two kinds of splitting are evident in these patients. The first is a compartmentalisation of self- and object-representations along the libidinal and aggressive lines. The second is a schism in the experience of reality, with some self-and object-representations felt to be exaggeratedly and painfully real and others felt to be lifeless and devoid of meaning. Lafarge indicates that the two psychopathic configurations are dissociated halves of a single bad self- and object relations. Each half of this unit is used defensively against the full experience of complex but frustrated object relations. Moreover, each dissociated system incorporates a central fantasy of the parent–child relationship which comes to acquire determinants and functions from successive developmental levels.

The imposturous transference is at a somewhat higher level. It is derived from an identification, especially in male patients (who show it more often), with a grandiose representation of the father in order to patch over a defective body representation that is poorly differentiated from that of the mother. The imposturous transference can serve as a psychostructural umbrella for the psychopathic transferences and the latter can emerge as regressive defences when Oedipal guilt and castration anxiety render the imposturous tendency too risky.

Mention must also be made of O'Shaughnessy's (1990) elegant and thoughtful paper titled "Can a liar be psychoanalyzed?" Underscoring the fundamental antagonism between a liar and a psychoanalysis, O'Shaughnessy described two cases in detail which are quite similar to those included in the paper by Lafarge (1995) mentioned above. Both were males. Both lied with excitement initially and then turned paranoid. Both had "basic suspicions" (p. 190) instead of basic trust and both felt "cut off from their depths" (p. 191). Like Lafarge, O'Shaughnessy observed the impostor's tendency towards idealisation: "This lie about lying is at the center of the deterioration of his character" (p. 193). O'Shaughnessy delineated a characteristic "triad of a deficient primal object, a strong destructive instinct in the patient, and a general perverse overlay" (p. 193) and concluded that

> If the fundamental level of the lie can be understood, that a liar lies in identification with the lying object, and, at the same time, if the patient's hostile lying, his different perspective in regard to truth and also his perverse excitement at using the lie to communicate with his analyst can be analysed in all their concreteness, I am sure at least of this: a genuine analytic process can be set in train. (p. 194)

O'Shaughnessy's conclusion paralleled Kernberg's (1992) and Lafarge's (1995) proposals. Another commonality in their material is that their cases reflect the prevalence of males in instances of lying reported in psychoanalytic literature. This could be in part due to the greater prevalence of antisocial traits among men (Cloninger, Reich & Guze, 1975; DSM-IV, 1990). What is more curious, however, is that a disproportionate number of papers on lying are written by female analysts (Chasseguet-Smirgel, 1984; Deutsch, 1922; Greenacre, 1958; Lafarge, 1995; Lemma, 2005; Olden, 1941).[10] The reasons for this too are unclear. Could it be that female analysts are better at detecting lies told by analysands? Or, is it that deceitful men deliberately seek women analysts? The latter hypothesis finds support in Chasseguet-Smirgel's (1984) observation that male fraudulence grows out of maternal seduction and the resulting inability to fully experience the Oedipal situation. Perhaps imposturous men seek female analysts to avoid passive homosexual urges and unconscious guilt vis-à-vis the father whom they have bypassed and intrapsychically killed.

A special challenge is posed by patients who keep secrets. A secret is "an intrapsychic cul-de-sac which not only disrupts life's experiential continuity but also sets into motion defensive processes to guard its own existence" (Akhtar, 1985, p. 82). While psychoanalysts regularly hear material that their patients wish to keep secret from others and gradually discern the secrets of the child within these patients (Gross, 1951; Sulzberger, 1953), encountering patients who tenaciously withhold pockets of information is disconcerting to them. The risk of countertransference outrage and intrusiveness is great under such circumstances. While no hard and fast rule can be set, keeping the following guidelines might be helpful. When secrets betray split-off sectors of personality and secret keeping has instinctual discharge functions (e.g., teasing, exclusion, and sadism), then a confrontational-interpretive approach seems better. When secrets are kept predominantly as a defence (e.g., against shame) and the act of secret keeping has symbolic significance, the traditional, slow, step-by-step approach centring upon defence interpretation is more useful. Kernberg's (1984, 1992; Kernberg, Selzer, Koenigsberg, Carr & Applebaum, 1989) and Margolis's (1966, 1974) contributions are especially instructive in the former and latter regards, respectively.

Focusing specifically upon patients with severe character pathology, the approach of Kernberg, Selzer, Koenigsberg, Carr & Applebaum (1989) is direct, confrontational, and consistently centred upon interpretation. They emphasise that while it may take a long time to accomplish, deep exploration of the transference implications of the patient's lying takes precedence over all other material, except life-threatening acting out. The following passage illustrates the kind of clinical work recommended by the author.

- Lying as an expression of hostility towards the self: "You continually change your story about what happened. This makes it impossible for me to help you and thus ends up defeating you."
- Lying as an attack on the therapist: "You continue to tell me the same thing even after we have agreed that this is a made-up tale. You treat me, therefore, as if I'm not worthy of your respect."
- Lying as an expression of fear of retaliation: "You seem to fear telling me the truth about having taken my magazine from the waiting room because you think that if you told me, I would become angry and stop seeing you."
- Lying as an expression of disillusionment: "You act as if the only way you can save your skin is to create a fiction about what's happening. That means to me that you have no belief that were I really to know you, anything good could come of it." (p. 167)

Margolis (1966, 1974), dealing with somewhat healthier patients, states that the formation of neurosis during childhood involves keeping certain thoughts and feelings secret from parents. Later, the ego begins to keep the same (and similar psychic phenomena) hidden from the superego and even from portions of the ego itself. The provision of strict confidentiality and the adherence to non-participation in the patient's life outside analysis prepare the ground for growing trust in the clinical situation. With moment-to-moment interpretation of transference-based fears of criticism, some softening of superego occurs and the possibility of revealing secrets appears on the horizon. The process of defence analysis, in the hands of an abstinent and technically neutral analyst, encourages the patient to reveal the conscious secrets to the analyst and, later on, the unconscious secrets to his own ego and superego. In effect, in the psychoanalytic treatment of neuroses, the exact reversal of what happened during childhood occurs.

Regardless of its being incisive or painstakingly slow, the emphasis upon the interpretive approach must not overshadow the importance of the analysts "holding" (Winnicott, 1960) functions and of his capacity to discern unconscious hope (that the environment will tolerate the burden of deceit and yet continue to provide care) in the patient's cheating and outrageousness (Winnicott, 1956a).[11] Only with such a judicious and tactful admixture of holding and interpretive approaches and that too on a sustained and long-term basis can a liar be truly helped.

Concluding remarks

In this wide-ranging survey, I have delineated the formal characteristics of lies, phenomenological subtypes of lies, and psychodynamic motivations to distort the known truth. Utilising the scene of art forgery as a didactic scaffold, I have elucidated the dialectical configurations that intricately bind the liar and his victim. Such a "two-person" explanatory approach has, however, not stood in my way to recognise the truly "one-person" contributions to the phenomenon of lying. My emphasis has overall been on the multiply determined, multi-functional, object-related, and ubiquitous nature of lying. At the same time, I have emphasised that a concerted effort to be honest and seek psychic truth—to the extent any such striving can be fully successful—is a fundamental aspect of mental health and of intensive psychotherapy and psychoanalysis.[12] With this in mind, I have made brief comments on patients who misinform their therapists during the initial evaluation, the development of psychopathic transferences, and the special case of secret keeping that invariably complicates the progress of treatment.

In the emphasis on the fascinating, amusing, and even entertaining as well as sadomasochistic, harmful, and profoundly destructive effects of lying, it must not be overlooked that distortion of truth can, at times, be a loving act intended to protect others. Parens (2009), who makes this very important point, offers the following poignant vignette to illustrate his contention.

> May 1940, a Jewish mother and her eleven-year-old son, escaping the invading German army on a train from Belgium to southern France are traversing the region of Dunkirk. They hear explosions that are alarmingly near. Driven by the impulse to protect her son, eleven, but to her still "her child", the mother spontaneously says, "Don't be frightened, it's only thunder." Appreciating her motherly protectiveness, the son smiles at her. Ten minutes later, the train stops and they are told to immediately disembark; within moments of having done so and taken shelter behind dunes, fighter planes strafe the train, causing little damage. They re-embark when told to do so. In an unspoken *entente*, not a word was said about the mother's motherly effort to protect her son against too much fear. (p. 151)

Lying can therefore be a manifestation of kindness just as honesty can, at times, be an ally of sadism. Having entered this caveat, I would like to conclude this discourse on lying and deception with a parable drawn from *Panchatantra*, the ancient Indian book of folk tales (circa 1031 BCE). The tale goes like this. Once a woodsman was going through a jungle where he came across a lion trapped inside an iron cage. The lion is understandably upset and upon seeing the woodsman urges him to open the gate of the cage and release him. The woodsman does not appear keen on this since he feels afraid of the beast; indeed he fears that the lion will eat him up upon being released. However, when he voices his concern, the lion emphatically assures him that he would do no such thing. The lion says that he would be utterly grateful and could not conceive of attacking someone who saved his life. Finding the lion to be earnest, the woodsman opens the cage and the lion comes out. Moments later, the lion tells the woodsman that he wants to eat him up. The woodsman is dismayed and reminds the lion of his promise not to do so. The lion says that he was telling the truth when he promised but the procrastination on the woodsman's part to release him caused delay and this, in turn, made him hungry. He says that now he cannot help himself and has to eat the woodsman. Just as this discussion is going on, a jackal happens to pass by. He stops and asks the arguing duo as to what is going on. Upon being told the story, first by the woodsman and then by the lion, with their obvious mismatch, the jackal turns pensive. He thinks for a while and then says that he does not believe either of them. In fact, he calls both the woodsman and the lion liars. He says that he cannot believe that such a large and majestic animal like the lion could ever fit in that small iron cage. He mocks the woodsman and the lion for fabricating such an incredulous tale. Annoyed at this, the lion promptly decides to prove the jackal wrong and re-enters the cage. With lightning speed, the jackal locks the cage door and thus saves the woodsman's life.

As one encounters a fable of such richness, many questions present themselves.

- Was the lion telling the truth when he said to the woodsman that he would not attack him?
- Was the lion lying when he said that his hunger had grown because of the woodman's procrastination?
- Was the woodsman pathologically gullible (due perhaps to some unconscious masochism) in trusting the lion to begin with?
- Was the jackal truthful when he accused the lion and the woodsman of being liars?
- Was the lion pathologically gullible (due to his unconscious guilt at cheating the woodsman) to believe the jackal and re-enter the cage?
- Was the woodsman aware of the jackal's lying and in remaining silent about it, was he not lying himself?

Such questions—and I am certain that many more like these can be raised—underscore the grey areas between truth and lie, the importance of the perspective from which a particular statement is assessed, the moral dilemmas inherent in making judgments in this realm, and ultimately, the object relational and intersubjective context of lies and lying. These questions are therefore important. However, the richness of texture they provide should not be exploited in the service of moral scepticism. The existence of complexity in this realm does not mean that there is no such thing as objective truth. Indeed, there is. The fact that you are reading these words (regardless of your agreeing or disagreeing with them) is one such truth and to deny it would be a lie.

Notes

1. Any discussion of lies contains within itself implicit assumptions about truth. If it were not so and truth did not exist (or, was not known), how could anything be considered a lie? In other words, to know a lie is to know the truth behind its veil. This theorem might not fit well with the contemporary hermeneutic turn to psychoanalysis which lays emphasis upon co-constructed data, intersubjectivity, and "narrative truth" (Spence, 1982). Sass and Woolfolk (1988) have provided a thorough assessment of this tension and Hanly (1990, 1992) has elucidated the criteria (e.g., coherence, correspondence) for establishing "truth" in psychoanalysis.
2. Chasseguet-Smirgel's (1984) concept of regressive anal homogenisation in the perverse character and Grunberger's (1989) metapsychological discourse on the false notion of "purity" are especially pertinent in this context.
3. In the preoccupation with delineating different types of lies, it should not be overlooked that an inability to lie, when circumstances demand such a posture, might also reflect psychopathology. Such "compulsive honesty" (Rajnish Mago, personal communication, August 19, 2008) is often accompanied by self-glorification, moralistic exaltation of truth for its own sake, and a sadomasochistic bent to interpersonal relationships. In more severe cases, such driven desire to be "honest" is coupled with a split-off sector of personality that may be quite corrupt and perverse.
4. There is some evidence, however, that higher primates can "lie" to avoid blame and gain advantage over others (Byrne & Whiten, 1992; Fouts, 1997; Maynard-Smith & Szathmáry, 1999). Stone (2009) has recently provided a review of the evolutionary literature on the subject of lying.
5. Freud (1895) used the term "overdetermination" to denote the fact that psychic phenomena are caused by multiple factors operating in unison. Thus, forces of constitution and trauma, scenarios of past and present, and pressures by different psychic agencies converge into the final common pathway leading to a given phenomenon. Freud's later study of dreams (1900a) and parapraxes (1916–17) gave strong support to this idea. Still later, his delineation of a tripartite psychic structure (1923b) led to the conclusion that neurotic symptoms were not simply

breakthroughs of instinctual impulses but a compromise between the demands of id, ego, and superego. Eidelberg (1954) and Hartmann (1958) later added the aetiological vector of external reality, stating that not only neurotic symptoms but all psychic phenomena reflect a compromise between the demands of the id, ego, superego, and external reality.

6. The name of the syndrome is derived from the book of fanciful and absurd adventures and travels attributed to Baron Hieronymus Carl Friedrich Münchausen. Davis and Weiss (1974) provide a fascinating commentary on how this actually evolved: "The real Baron Munchausen (1720–1791) of Hanover, Germany, enjoyed an established reputation as a teller of exaggerated tales related to his experiences as a cavalry officer in the German-Turkish campaigns of 1737 to 1739. In 1785, Rudolph Eric Raspe published a book entitled *Singular Travels, Campaigns, and Adventures of Baron Munchausen*. The book, however, was a hoax derived from Raspe's imagination. He had met the Baron only briefly and did considerable elaboration upon his stories which rapidly established the Baron as a preposterous liar. It was because of the fanciful stories, which were both dramatic and untrue, that Asher decided to choose the name 'Munchausen' for the patients who traveled from hospital to hospital as described, although the original character never submitted to any surgical operation" (p. 280).
7. While true, this statement does not accommodate cross-cultural variation in the extent of social pretence and compliant avoidance of truth. Freeman (2009) provides a comparison of North American-Japanese cultures in this regard.
8. The idealised "someday … fantasy" evoked by such advertising has a counterpart in the "if only … fantasy" of nostalgic art and poetry; the former idealises the future and the latter glorifies the past, whitewashing the blemishes of lost places and times bygone (Akhtar, 1996).
9. See, in this context, my elucidation of gullibility and the unconscious need to be betrayed in Chapter Five of this book.
10. A few contributions by male analysts (Abraham, 1925; Blum, 1983; Kernberg, 1992) paradoxically support the female authorial dominance in this realm.
11. Abraham's (1925) psychoanalytically informed account of a chronic swindler's life with its unexpectedly good outcome underscores the potentially redeeming role of forbearance vis-à-vis such psychopathology.
12. The psychoanalytic emphasis upon truth, truthfulness, and truth-seeking should, however, not lead to idealising psychoanalysts. Knowledgeable though they might be about the matters of mind, psychoanalysts are nonetheless ordinary human beings. Like others,

they have character flaws and vulnerabilities. They are hardly immune to the temptations of lying. Sigmund Freud's signing "Dr Sigm Freud u Frau" (German for Dr Sigmund Freud and wife) when he checked into a hotel in Maloja, Switzerland on August 13, 1898, accompanied by his sister-in-law Minna Bernays (Blumenthal, 2006) is a recently unearthed piece of psychoanalytic history that supports this assertion. Other prominent examples are Wilhelm Stekel's fabricating clinical material for presentations at early gatherings at Freud's house (Bos & Groenendijk, 2006), Masud Khan's merrily declaring himself to be a "prince" (Akhtar, 2007b; Hopkins, 2006), and Heinz Kohut's (1979) report on the "two analyses of Mr Z" which in fact was an "appalling deception" (Giovacchini, 2000, p. 78) since Mr Z was most likely Kohut himself and there had been no second analysis (see also Strozier, 2004).

CHAPTER FIVE

Betrayal

The English word "betrayal" is derived from the old French *traïr* and the Latin *tradere*, both referring to "traitor". Indeed, the *Webster's* dictionary meaning of "betrayal" includes "to deliver to an enemy by treachery" (Mish, 1998, p. 109). Among other explications are "to lead astray, to fail or desert especially in time of need, to reveal unintentionally, [and] to disclose in violation of confidence" (ibid, p. 109). These phrases indicate that: (a) betrayal involves breaking someone's trust in one's reliability and availability, and (b) betrayal can be deliberate or unintentional. A third feature, though not explicit, can also be discerned. This involves the fact that (c) betrayal causes hurt. The Hindi word for betrayal, *vishwas-ghaat* (literally, wounded trust) captures the essence of this phenomenon.

Moving from the confines of the dictionary, I propose two other facets of betrayal: (d) the phenomenon comes in active and passive forms (i.e., betraying others and feeling betrayed), and (e) the affects connected with these forms are conscious or unconscious sadistic glee and sharp "mental pain" (Akhtar, 2000; Freud, 1926d; Weiss, 1934), respectively.[1] Yet another facet is that (f) betraying and being betrayed are not as aetiologically, dynamically, and phenomenologically apart as they initially appear. The drive to betray others and the need to be betrayed invariably coexist. The former is more evident in narcissistic characters and the latter in masochistic characters. However, the opposite wish is also present in each of them. Narcissistic individuals betray others while also arranging unconscious betrayals of themselves and masochistic individuals engineer being betrayed while betraying others themselves. Cooper's (1988) proposal of the "narcissistic-masochistic character", while addressing a somewhat different terrain of psychopathology is, in part, my heuristic ally in making this assertion.

This Janus-faced syndrome of betrayal, which has remained inadequately addressed in psychoanalytic literature,[2] forms the focus of my contribution. With the help of two detailed case reports, I will elucidate the unrelenting need to betray others and the comparably-driven, albeit unconscious, need to be betrayed. I will follow these case reports with comments on treating patients in whose lives themes of betrayal figure prominently and whose transferences are accordingly shaped and coloured. I will conclude by pulling this material together and pointing out areas that warrant further attention.

The compulsion to betray

In clinical practice and in life-at-large one often encounters people who are utterly unreliable. They promise to be somewhere, arrive at a certain time, bring something, and do some task but habitually fail to meet such expectations. Their behaviour hurts others who gradually begin to mistrust them and become wary of them. Behaviourally homogenous, such unreliability is actually of three different psychodynamic varieties:

a. *Diffuse ego-impairment*: These are hapless individuals who agree to others' demands because they lack the courage to say "no"; subsequently feeling burdened by what they might genuinely be unable to carry out, they end up disappointing those who are banking on them.
b. *Identification with over-promising parents*: These are adults who, as children, were repeatedly misled by their parents; the latter made all sorts of boastful declarations that never came true. Such dashing of hopes on a repeated basis deeply traumatised the children who, in an "identification with the aggressor" (A. Freud, 1946), unleash similar torment upon unsuspecting others once they grow up. Their

actions are often subtle and out of their conscious awareness. Their betrayals of others occur despite their good wishes and, at times, are a source of surprise and disappointment to themselves.

c. *Sadistic triumph over envied others*: Individuals who betray others with conscious sadistic glee usually display "malignant narcissism" (Kernberg, 1984), that is, a combination of pathological self-absorption, cruelty, and antisocial behaviour. They have experienced severe betrayal trauma during childhood and often view themselves as the most unfairly treated among the family's children. They envy other siblings and harbour intense envy and hatred over their privileged status. Their betrayals are enactments of their destructive impulses towards their siblings, though, at its base, their hostility is directed at their parents. Superego functioning is often compromised and an element of viciousness lurks underneath their overt seductiveness. The following case illustrates this sort of compulsion to betray others.

Clinical vignette: 16

Tall, big-boned, and bold in his gestures, sixty-year-old Paul Ruby sought psychotherapy reluctantly and pursued it in staccato fashion. He did accept my recommendation of twice-weekly sessions but took frequent and long leaves during the course of work which lasted nearly seven years. Paul had been forced to seek help by his daughter after his divorce when he had begun drinking excessively and missing work-related appointments. A prosecuting attorney of considerable repute, Paul had been a consummate womaniser and his divorce was precipitated by an affair which fizzled out once he was on his own. He could not tolerate his girlfriend's demands for deeper relatedness.

Over the course of time, I learned about two other affairs and a long series of one-night stands. Paul seemed embarrassed about some of these, while reporting others with a sense of triumph. Betrayal figured in all of them and curiously, the more conscious it was, the more it seemed to energise him. And, mind you, I am not referring to the betrayal of his wife—that was taken for granted. The betrayals in question were those of the various women he seduced. While the theme appeared again and again in the account of his life, two episodes struck him—and me—as paradigmatic of his driven need to betray, though from different vantage points and with different psychic consequences.

The first of these was "the story of Ellen McGuire" (he named his various escapades like chapters of a novel),[3] a stunningly beautiful woman whom Paul had known since their childhood. She came from a more sophisticated and elite family than Paul's, though they had grown up in the same affluent suburb of Pittsburgh as children. As a child and later as a teenager, Paul had been intimidated by her snobbish manner, her fine looks, and her elegant clothes. Then, decades later when he had become quite successful as a lawyer and had made a lot of money, Paul unexpectedly ran into Ellen who, in his words, "had not amounted to much". She was still beautiful, though. Paul "worked on her" for over a year, befriending her, showering her with gifts, and helping her obtain a decent-enough job. Soon, they became lovers. Paul had no shortage of money by this time. He rented a fine apartment and handed her the keys. A site of their amorous interludes, soon it became Ellen's place. Then after he had "fucked her and fucked her real hard and real good" many, many times, one day Paul arrived at the apartment and announced that he had terminated the lease and she had to vacate the place within a week. To a horrified Ellen, he now recanted with glee how this had been his plan all along and how this was his only way to overcome how intimidating he had found her during their childhood and adolescent years. What is more chilling here is that Paul was hardly regretful in telling me all this. On the contrary, he regarded his victory over Ellen as a sign of courage, determination, and manliness. Her pain at his profound betrayal was peripheral in his version of the story.

In contrast, Paul felt much shame and even a twinge of remorse in recounting "the story of the Yemeni woman". I could see that his betrayal of her had a less calculating and more "accidental" (i.e., more unconsciously driven) quality about it. Paul had much difficulty recounting what happened between them. Haltingly, he gave the following account. He had gone to London presumably for a business trip but actually to meet a woman whom he had been courting off and on for a while. With characteristic flair, he rented a high-end apartment for a week with tip-top amenities—concierge, chauffeur, cleaning service, and so on. The very first afternoon before his British lover-to-be could arrive at this fancy place, a poor Arab woman rang the doorbell. She was there to clean the apartment but, within twenty to twenty-five minutes, Paul had worked his magic and she was in his arms. They were interrupted by a call from the concierge, announcing the arrival of a "guest". The woman from Yemen went back to dusting and cleaning. Paul's British girlfriend entered the apartment and almost immediately he opened a bottle of champagne. As he went to the kitchen to fetch two glasses, he caught the hurt and accusing eyes of the cleaning woman. Paul claimed, and I believed him, that he never forgot that glance and he gets filled with remorse and shame each time he recalls it.

Though Paul's behaviour in the two scenarios differed—the first, deliberate and near sociopathic, the second, unmentalised and compulsive, the core sequence of seduction followed by betrayal was evident in both. (And, there were more "stories" like these in Paul's repertoire; only one was different since it pertained to *his* being betrayed by a young paramour.) But why was Paul acting this way and what connection did such behaviour have with his frequent dropping out from treatment (more marked in the earlier part of our work) and with his childhood background?

As we explored this, it became clear that Paul had himself suffered significant betrayals in his life. A first-born child and an "undisputed darling" (Freud, 1917b, p. 156) of his parents, Paul had been abruptly sent away to live with his out of town aunt when he was just two years old. He grew up with his aunt until he finished high school, visiting his parents only once or twice a year; the presumed reason for his exile was the birth of his younger sister who was a sickly baby and demanded a lot of attention from their parents.

In my estimation, Paul had been badly traumatised by this early betrayal. Then, the discovery that his father was having an affair when Paul was ten years old and of his uncle and aunt's enrolling their son into a private school while Paul attended a public school also were experienced as serious betrayals. He grew up determined to make loads of money, never depend upon anyone, and get even. His promiscuity was based upon his attempts to reverse the narcissistic injuries of his childhood, and his frequent withdrawals from me—just when I began to be optimistic about our work—embodied the all-too-familiar seduction-betrayal pattern.

An important aspect of Paul's transference was his sense that I was enjoying his dependence upon me. He suspected that I was gloating over my importance to him. This would anger him greatly: "Why should I be reliably present for you? Come here on fixed times, like a dog? What have you done to deserve such loyalty and obedience from me?" Painstakingly and in a piecemeal fashion, we sorted all this out to indicate that Paul wanted to be a reliable parent to me (in a reversal of his own anaclitic longings) but then would feel envious of my being the recipient of his reliability. I began appearing to him like his younger (and in his eyes, more fortunate) sister and he would have to rupture the treatment; the envy was simply intolerable. Then, after a few missed sessions, Paul would reappear with promises to be regular in attendance.

As these cycles were repeated, we reconstructed the pain he felt at having to separate again and again from his parents when he visited them during childhood. Turning passive into active, Paul had become "addicted" to betraying (instead of being betrayed). Working through the hurt, pain, and profound rage that were intermingled in this relational scenario gradually led to the emergence of genuine sadness about how his life had become messed up and remorse over how he had hurt so many women in his life. Paul's relationship with his sister improved. Though not entirely able to "forgive" her for having displaced him, he did become capable of seeing that is was hardly her fault. The rage at her was a displacement of the fury he felt towards his parents for having sent him away. We were also able to link the seduction-betrayal drama he had played out with Ellen to the amalgam of his feelings towards his sister and his mother. As the treatment approached its end, Paul was able to sustain a loving relationship with a woman. He was not free of impulses to cheat and to betray her but was able to handle them by suppression, by masturbating to fantasised sex with other women and, at times, by making fun of his greed and potential cruelty. Analysis had not "cured" him but had indeed made his life less driven, less sadomasochistic, and less complicated. For me, this exemplified what Freud (1933a) had meant by his statement that as a result of psychoanalysis, "Where id was there ego shall be". (p. 80)

This case poignantly illustrates the deleterious effects of pathological narcissism upon the capacity for object relations. Viewed within a long-term perspective of time,

> The grandiose self always has been, and remains, alone and in a strangely atemporal world of repeating cycles of wants, temporary idealizations, greedy incorporation, and disappearing of supplies by spoiling, disappointing, and devaluation. (Kernberg, 1980, p. 138)

Also pertinent here is Rosenfeld's (1964, 1971) observation that narcissistic object relations are characterised by omnipotence and defences against any recognition of separateness between self and the object. The narcissist's omnipotence is manifest in his ruthless use of others (see also Coen, 1992, in this regard) with concomitant denial of any dependence on them, since its recognition implies vulnerability to love, pain of separation, and envy of what others have to offer. A more malignant situation prevails when angry and destructive aspects of the self become idealised. Then the individual attempts to destroy whatever love is offered to him in order to maintain his superiority over others. In becoming totally identified with the omnipotent destructive aspects of himself, he kills off his sane, loving, and dependent self. At times, he remains wistfully aware of his inner imprisonment and feels that there is nothing anybody can do to change the situation. Avoiding the risk of being betrayed by anyone ever again, the narcissist isolates himself and thus ends up betraying his own needy self. Such was the case with Paul Ruby before he came to see me.

The need to be betrayed

In sharp contrast to him are persons who find themselves betrayed over and over again. Their employer fails to recognise their valuable contributions. Their friends do not reciprocate their parties. Their spouses rarely acknowledge their love and their offspring never celebrate their sacrifices. In Bergler's (1949) terminology, such individuals are "injustice collectors". Psychically bruised and embittered, they recount their woes with pained disbelief; it is as if they had hoped for better treatment from others but were jilted and rebuffed.

That the central problem in such individuals is that of masochism is clear.[4] Less evident is the reason *how* and *why* being betrayed (as against being beaten, being sexually abused, and so on) becomes the central feature of some masochistic individuals. The answer to *how* it happens is the following: the masochist possesses a remarkable, though latent, gullibility. He believes everything he is told and overlooks facts that contradict his rosy expectations. Isaacs, Alexander, and Haggard (1963) have eloquently described the genesis of such naiveté.

> When a parent misuses the faith and the developing trust of a child, a disillusionment occurs which is a great blow to the psyche. If the child has a strong enough ego, he will integrate the fact as a determinant of limitations and restrictions on the trustworthiness of parents and others. If he has a somewhat weaker ego, the disappointment may connote a loss of the illusion of ideal parents and thereby mean a resulting bereavement, loneliness, and depression. In such circumstances—anger over the loss of the illusion, and guilt over the anger—the distrust may be repressed and leave the child unprepared to discriminate between trustworthy and untrustworthy persons. He has thereby become gullible, for he can only indiscriminately trust. Gullibility has to do with a persistent need to be deceived. The fact of being repeatedly deceived may serve additionally as a reassurance that the parents are actually no less trustworthy than anyone else. (p. 464)

By such mechanisms, the masochist sets himself up for failure, injury, and feeling betrayed. In this aspect, he is like some paranoid personalities who, while contemptuous of other's naivety, themselves display a peculiar vulnerability to believing in what they hear from gossipmongers (Stanton, 1978). The next question—*why* being betrayed becomes the phenotypal expression of "moral masochism" (Freud, 1924c)—leads not only to diverse sources of unconscious guilt (Akhtar, 2013c; Asch, 1976; Modell, 1965; Niederland, 1968) but also to psychically felt betrayals in the form of *actual* losses during childhood. In the course of later development, these experiences tend to become libidinised and imbued with masochistic pleasure.

Clinical vignette: 17

> A diminutive and bespectacled middle-aged internist with a boy's face, Joel Lobner arrived at my office because he was considering divorce and wanted to be "really sure" about the correctness of

his decision. In the first session, he recounted in great detail how unappreciated he felt by his second wife, Nancy. He said that he had been of help to her in numerous ways, including bailing her out of serious financial mess during their courtship. With pained disbelief in his voice, Joel repeatedly talked about how hurt he felt at her ingratitude towards him. He had decided to divorce her but was afraid of becoming alone, not finding anyone to love and marry, and regretting his decision. That is why he had come to see me: to sort out his ambivalence over the decision he was about to make.

The subsequent sessions were filled with his providing more "proofs" of Nancy's thankless attitude towards him, her imperious stance, and her jealous rages. Joel repeatedly forgave her for such insults, began trusting her, but was betrayed over and over again. Just when he would relax and be spontaneous, she would throw a jealous temper tantrum, destroying his mental peace. Joel had shared some of these details with two of his friends and both had called him a "masochist" for staying in such a painful marriage. They urged him to get a divorce.

Further details gradually emerged. It turned out that even before their marriage, Joel had ample evidence of Nancy's narcissistic character structure and great sense of entitlement. He recalled that when they were dating and took their first vacation together, not only did he pay for all their travel expenses but the bills for all the ten to fifteen meals they ate together in the lovely West Coast town. Nancy never offered to share any costs of the trip and, in fact, never uttered "Thank you" upon his paying all the bills. Joel recalled that he had noted this with mild unease but rationalised it, thinking that she was just wanting to be pampered, was letting him run the show, helping him be a big man, and so on. But now, he considered her behaviour as entitled and, in retrospect, as a betrayal of his trust in her as a mutual and reciprocal adult.

Nancy was Joel's second wife. Joel had been married before and had felt severely betrayed by his first wife, Rosie, as well. She had misrepresented her social status, lied about her educational background, and misled Joel about her prior romantic and sexual history. In fact, Rosie was pregnant by someone else and only told this to Joel four days before their wedding. Joel was deeply hurt and, in a single exception to his all accepting and meek relational style, became physically violent towards Rosie. However, when, two days later, she offered to get an abortion, he readily forgave her and they got married. The details of lies about her social circumstances emerged later and each time Joel experienced the piercing and sharp pain of betrayal, but each time he forgave her and they carried on with their humdrum domestic life over the subsequent years. During this time, Joel had two extramarital affairs (i.e., he betrayed her); the second blew up in his face and resulted in the break-up of his marriage.

Joel remained single for nearly six years, during which he had many short-lasting relationships and one that felt deep and sustainable to him. According to him, he was able to truly love and have great sex as well. He was ecstatic. What he was ignoring was how narcissistic this woman, Angie, was. Sheepishly, he acknowledged that the first time he visited her apartment, he noted that the living room walls were adorned with her own photographs (twenty-one, to be precise). Madly in love, Joel "ignored" this. He also overlooked her intense ethnocentrism and her prejudice against ethnic and racial minorities. Joel "forgave" her self-willed nature which frequently caused him hurt. Soon after they would agree to a plan, Angie would come up with something else to do or would do something behind his back which derailed the course of action they had agreed upon. Joel felt betrayed and hurt but smitten by her beauty and, intoxicated by their glorious sex life, overlooked all this. Then one day, he felt greatly betrayed by her and, in a fit of rage, abruptly broke off with her. He was getting some kitchen remodelling done and had got her involved in it but she began interfering so much (often talking to the contractor behind his back) that he told her to stay away from the project. Angie promised to do so but then went ahead anyway, calling the contractor to do something this or that way. She did this without telling Joel, who was informed by the contractor. Livid with rage, Joel called the relationship off.

All three women in Joel's life (his ex-wife, his girlfriend between his two marriages, and his current wife) seemed to betray him in one way or the other. All three appeared to be phallic-narcissistic characters: proud, strong-willed, and self-centred. What became evident during the course of our work, though, was that not only had Joel too betrayed them (e.g., by occasional one-night stands, by two affairs, by inordinate absorption in his work), he had repeatedly overlooked the unsuitability of these women for him. Or, to put it correctly, he had overlooked their narcissism and their potential for entitlement, lying, and walking all over him. Joel *was* a masochist.

Joel's childhood background was characterised by many losses and many changes of residence. By the time he was five, he had lived in three different states. By the time he was eleven, he had lost four significant attachment figures to death (his beloved maternal aunt died when he was four, his mother died when he was six, his maternal uncle died when he was nine, and his maternal grandmother—who had been raising him after his mother's passing away—died when he was eleven). His mother's death had resulted from a protracted illness which required repeated hospitalisation, beginning at the time when Joel was merely two years old. Different babysitters took care of him each time. The impact of these ruptures was made worse by all the deaths he had to face as a little child.

Matters were made worse by the fact that Joel's father moved away to a distant city and kept promising to take Joel there but this never materialised. Joel's hopes were repeatedly dashed. His only sibling, an older brother to whom he was deeply attached, repeatedly stole from him, mocked him, beat him, and betrayed his trust by telling everyone things Joel had begged him to keep secret. As if this were not enough, Joel was sexually abused by a trusted and admired older cousin; in a household chronically burdened by grief, there was no one to protect this motherless child. Even Joel's grandfather (from whom Joel did receive support and guidance) sexually exposed himself to Joel repeatedly before passing away when Joel was eighteen years old.

All in all, Joel had grown up with betrayal as his constant companion. And, in a major disidentification with his unreliable caregivers, Joel had become a fiercely loyal and reliable friend to many individuals. He took great pride in the fact that some of these friendships went back as much as nearly fifty years. These friends were all men, however; with women, the scenario was entirely different. Like Limentani's (1989) "vagina man",[5] Joel had a tendency to find phallic-narcissistic women; they brought excitement and thrill to his otherwise depressive lifestyle and his latently effeminate character. Rosie buttressed his narcissism since he could easily project his inferiority-laden self-representations into her. Nancy and

> Angie enhanced his self esteem by their professional prominence. Parallel to such a narcissistic agenda of his own, Joel had a masochistic aim as well. He would cling to these self-absorbed women under the cloak of forgiveness and generosity while feeling repeatedly stabbed by their betrayals.
>
> In his treatment with me, Joel looked on the one hand for validation from me that he indeed was being betrayed, and that his current wife was (and previous women had been) treacherous and ungrateful to him. On the other hand, he repeatedly defended her, forgave her, and felt that if he left her, she would suffer greatly. He desperately sought my empathy but felt squeamish about receiving it. He seemed accustomed to his masochistic stance and could neither bear a challenge to it nor tolerate my attempts to unmask how he used his suffering as a justification for ignoring his wife's needs (betraying her, in a way). He seemed totally oblivious to the fact that he was betraying her on a daily basis by his "24/7" work addiction; they had not taken a vacation over the five-year course of their marriage. Fixed in this sadomasochistic equilibrium, Joel decided abruptly to terminate treatment, thanking me profusely, and saying that he would let the passage of time decide whether he should get divorced or not. He seemed to be ignoring the possibility that a few years down the road, he might regret his indecision (actually a "decision" to stay masochistic) and blame time as having betrayed him. Fascinatingly, one of his favourite novels was Louis Begley's *The Man Who Was Late* (1992), a wry account of a man unable to bear being loved and ending up committing suicide in late middle life. Joel left me sad, worried, and feeling betrayed.

This case—and the failure of treatment in this case—impels us to consider the pleasure and power of masochism. While an exhaustive review of such matters is beyond the scope of this chapter, some attention certainly needs to be paid to them here. In Brenner's (1959) perspective, masochism reflects the acceptance of a painful reality for guilt-ridden, Oedipal sexual impulses. This is often true. More pertinent to the case presented here, however, are the views of Bergler (1949) and Cooper (1988). Bergler posited that the preservation of infantile omnipotence is of prime importance to the reduction of anxiety and as a source of ego satisfaction. When the child faces excessive frustration, this omnipotence is threatened. The child feels humiliated and, as a result, furious. Being helpless to "get even" with his adult offenders, the child discharges the aggression upon himself. But, in order to maintain a semblance of omnipotence, he libidinises it and learns to extract pleasure from displeasure. Some inborn tendency made the occurrence of a pleasure-in-displeasure pattern possible.[6] These events later evolve into adult patterns of psychic masochism. Bergler delineated a three-step process as being paradigmatic in this context: (a) the masochist unconsciously incites disappointment and humiliation by his behaviour and equally unconsciously derives pleasure from it, (b) he replaces the knowledge of his own provocation and reacts to the insult with righteous indignation, and (c) after such "pseudo-aggression" creates further defeats, he indulges in conscious self-pity. Unconsciously, he enjoys the masochistic pleasure.

In elaborating upon Bergler's ideas, Cooper (ibid.) noted that the capacity to defensively alter the meaning of painful experiences of childhood is largely for maintaining an illusory self-control. He states that:

> Where the experience of early narcissistic humiliation is excessive for external or internal reasons, these mechanisms of repair miscarry. The object is perceived as excessively cruel and refusing; the self is perceived as incapable of genuine self-assertion in the pursuit of gratification; the gratification obtained from disappointment takes precedence over genuine but unavailable and unfamiliar libidinal, assertive, or ego-functional satisfactions. Being disappointed or refused becomes the *preferred* mode of narcissistic assertion to the extent that narcissistic and masochistic distortions dominate the character. (p. 128, italics in the original)

Cooper emphasised that the pleasure sought in such cases is not genital-sexual; it is pre-Oedipal and pertains to self-esteem and self-coherence. The coexistence of narcissism and masochism is central to Cooper's conceptualising. He declared that

> In any particular instance, the presenting clinical picture may seem more narcissistic or more masochistic ... However, only a short period of analysis will reveal that both types share the sense of deadened capacity to feel, muted pleasure, a hypersensitive self-esteem alternating between grandiosity and humiliation, an inability to sustain or derive satisfaction from their relationships or their

> work, a constant sense of envy, an unshakable conviction of being wronged and deprived by those who are supposed to care for them, and an infinite capacity for provocation. (p. 129)

Cooper's eloquence is humbling. It also serves as an exquisitely appropriate starting point for considering the problems in treating such patients.

Treatment considerations

Before elucidating the nuances and strategies of technique, two caveats must be entered. *First*, the suggestions I am making regarding the treatment of the betraying and betrayed patients are not to replace the customary work of empathic affirmation, transference interpretation, reconstruction, and countertransference vigilance,[7] Nor are these suggestions meant to interfere with the "trio of guideposts" (Pine, 1997, p. 13) of abstinence, neutrality, and anonymity that are a cornerstone of our approach. What follows are not rules to be respected in working with all such patients. Indeed, the more psychologically sophisticated and "analysable" the patient, the less attention needs to be paid to these guidelines. *Second*, even though I make separate suggestions for treating narcissistic-betraying patients and for treating masochistic-betrayed patients, the fact remains that hybrid forms of such psychopathology are common and shifting attention to narcissistic and masochistic aspects of the patient's functioning might be essential; this would call for the use of both types of technical interventions in one and the same patient.

Having entered these two caveats, we can move on to a consideration of treating narcissistic-betraying patients. The following sequence of interventions, though appearing overly schematic when put in writing, applies here. After ample psychic space has been provided for the analysand to present his version of events and a therapeutic alliance has evolved, the analyst needs to confront the patient with (a) the driven quality of his seducing and betraying others, (b) the contradiction between his seeking love and security while not providing those very experiences to people he is involved with, (c) the denial of his hostile and destructive aims towards others who are puppets in an inner theatre of vindictiveness, and (d) the active jettisoning of moments when empathy towards a victim is experienced and of similar affective-cognitive movements in the transference experience. The analyst also needs to help the patient (e) become aware of the pleasure he derives from betraying others, thus seeking to render that pleasure ego-dystonic; (f) mourn the lost opportunities for love, and (g) bear the newly emergent remorse over his cruelties towards others.

Throughout such work, the twin dangers of a moralising countertransference and of causing injury to the patient's self-esteem should be avoided. This would necessitate a coupling of interpretive unmasking with empathic-reconstructive remarks (consistently indicating the traumatic origin of the patient's behaviour). The defensive functions of betraying others (e.g., turning passive into active, warding off dependent longings) and the felt need for such defences must also be underscored.

Just as the treatment of narcissistic patients who betray others is difficult, so is working with masochistic patients who keep bringing the same tale of being betrayed in various guises again and again. Such work requires enormous patience. The analyst must not rush the process even though the material might appear eminently "interpretable". Although made in a different context, the following comment by Amati-Mehler and Argentieri (1989) is pertinent here.

> The patient ought to experience for a sufficient length of time and at different levels of the soundness of the therapeutic rapport, the security of being understood, the benefit of a careful and thorough working-through of the transference, and a relational structure that enables him or her to contain the comprehension and the elaboration of the disruption of the transference play. (p. 303)

Such disruption of the patient's masochistic proclivity, though long in coming, is ultimately essential. The analyst must (a) understand that there is a sort of "success" in all the failures reported by the patient; (b) recognise that "… wreckage may represent more than painful defeat or punishment. For example, it may also represent the triumph of archaic moral aims over infantile libidinal aims" (Schafer, 1988, p. 83), or it may be a way to avoid separateness and aloneness by clinging to a hurtful "inconstant object" (Blum, 1981); (c) "point out to the analysand how, when, and why he or she tries to bring about failure or to experience failure, or dwells on failure in the analytic situation" (Schafer, 1988, p. 89), especially when good things are about to happen and happiness seems to be just around the corner;[8] (d) help the patient see how and how often he dismisses or minimises the presence of reliable people in his life, that is, people (including the analyst) who do not betray him; (e) unmask and interpret the patient's envy of the analyst's reliability (Kernberg, 1992) and, in a paradoxical turn of perspective, of their own reliability in keeping the analytic appointments; and (f) manage, control, and learn from the countertransference feelings of exasperation and hostility as well as defences against these burdensome affects (Asch, 1988; Maltsberger & Buie, 1974).

A note of caution is needed here.[9] In focusing upon the betrayer's sadism and the betrayed's masochism, one ought not to overlook that the former is continually depriving himself of genuine love and affection (i.e., he is being masochistic) and that the latter in harping about his suffering is displaying his moral superiority and a condescending attitude towards others (i.e., he is being sadistic). Remembering Freud's (1905a) declaration that sadism and masochism invariably coexist helps the analyst retain a complex and multifaceted perspective on patients' associations and transferences.

Concluding remarks

In this contribution, I have delineated some phenomenological and metapsychological aspects of betrayal. Utilising two case reports, I have attempted to show the lived and transference experience of betraying others and of feeling betrayed by others.[10] I have emphasised that these narcissistic and masochistic scenarios often coexist even if one is more overt and the other covert in a given case. Following the discussion of these cases, I have outlined some guidelines for the treatment of betraying narcissistic and betrayed masochistic patients, while reminding the reader that the suggestions I have made are neither essential nor applicable in all cases. Moreover, they are not intended to replace our usual ways of conducting analytic treatment.

While I have cast a wide net, a few questions remain unanswered. First, since both the betraying and the betrayed types seem to have suffered severe betrayal trauma in their childhood, what accounts for their phenotypical difference? In other words, why do some victims of childhood betrayal become narcissistic betrayers and others masochistic seekers of betrayal? Such "choice of neurosis" (Freud, 1913c) is most likely dependent upon some difference in constitutional endowment with the more inherently aggressive child "opting" for the narcissistic route and the inherently less aggressive (or less outwardly aggressive) child succumbing to masochism. Perhaps the age and the degree of ego maturity when the childhood betrayal occurred and the qualitative difference in helplessness it produced (e.g., by broken promises *vs.* actual death of a parent) also play a role here. Putting all these possibilities together gives rise to the following speculations. Betrayed children who were constitutionally less aggressive, traumatised earlier, repeatedly, and had no recourse but to cling to their betrayers while growing up, most likely turn out to be masochists. Betrayed children who were constitutionally more aggressive, traumatised somewhat later, less frequently, and had recourse to caregivers other than their betrayers most likely turn out to be narcissists. However, more data and more thought are needed about these issues for one to be certain about these hypotheses.

Another area that needs further exploration is why some narcissistic and some masochistic patients improve with analytic treatment whereas others do not. While patient-based variables (e.g., honesty, psychological mindedness, absence of substance abuse, work-related sources of efficacy and pleasure) contribute much to the prognosis, quality of the "fit" between the patient and analyst might also matter; this less than optimally explored realm merits more investigation. And so does the potential impact of gender and culture upon which pole of the betrayer-betrayed scenario will predominate in the final psychopathological picture in those exposed to the trauma of severe betrayal during childhood.

While answers to such questions are awaited, one thing remains clear. Betrayal is both a specific form of trauma and a constituent of all psychic trauma. Sexual abuse, physical maltreatment, profound neglect, mockery, and bullying all include an element of betrayal. All involve breaking someone's trust and putting someone's faith and hope in question. As a result, the dynamic and technical observations contained in this chapter might apply—in small or large measure—to all traumatised individuals while maintaining their specificity for those who have been betrayed and hurt by their caregivers.

Notes

1. Having unintentionally betrayed others, however, leads to remorse, and realising that one has been unintentionally betrayed diminishes mental pain.

2. The word "betrayal" appears only eighteen times in the entire corpus of Freud's writings (Guttman, Jones & Parrish, 1980, pp. 272–273). Five of these usages are colloquial and carry little scientific significance. Nine pertain to "psychic self-betrayal" via slips of the tongue (Freud, 1901b), clumsy testimony during a court trial (Freud, 1906c), or bodily fidgetiness in a failed attempt to suppress a secret (Freud, 1905e). The remaining four usages are in the context of compulsive rituals (e.g., keeping scraps of paper) to control a fear of betrayal (Freud, 1896b), the mass paranoia of a nation defeated in war defensively evolving a collective "delusion of betrayal" (Freud, 1950a), and the masochistic tendency of certain individuals who find themselves repeatedly betrayed by friends (Freud, 1920g).
3. Besides his calling these relationships "stories", Paul always referred to various women by both their first and last names. I have encountered this phenomenon in another narcissistic patient and believe that it is an unwitting fetishistic ploy to turn women into caricatures.
4. While the term "masochism" has been used in many ways (see Maleson, 1984, for a comprehensive review), Brenner's (1959) definition remains authoritative. Masochism, for him, is "the seeking of unpleasure, by which is meant physical or mental pain, discomfort or wretchedness, for the sake of sexual pleasure, with the qualification that either the seeking or the pleasure or both may often be unconscious rather than conscious" (p. 197).
5. Limentani coined this term for an individual who harbours a powerful wish to be a woman and has deep envy of everything female. He also has a secret fantasy of possessing a vagina. Intelligent, charming, and friendly, the "vagina man" reads voraciously, looks at things intently, and insatiably seeks the company of others, especially women. He is feminine but his femininity is hidden behind his attentiveness towards women. Owing to this attentiveness, his sexual performance is better than average. According to Limentani, such a person has been raised by a mother who was somewhat masculine, while also treating her child as her phallus. The "vagina man" constellation results from an identification with such a mother. It serves as a defence against homosexuality. Moreover, the fantasy of belonging to the other sex helps avoid the fear of castration.
6. The binding of the death instinct by the libido lays down the ground for such "primary masochism" (Freud, 1924c). While many psychoanalysts have reservations about such a formulation, poets have subscribed to this view wholeheartedly. A recent illustration is evident in the line *Ghum ke sehnay mein bhi qudrat ne mazaa rakhha hai* (literally, "Nature has

created the potential of deriving pleasure from pain") by the Urdu poet, Nasir Kazmi (1972).

7. Our clinical work is a peculiar amalgam of a warm relationship which we approach with "evenly suspended attention" (Freud, 1912e, p. 111) and "without memory or desire" (Bion, 1967b, p. 272), and a theory-driven deliberateness, hierarchy of interpretation (Loewenstein, 1951), and "strategy" (Levy, 1987) of technique. We respond to the analysand's material with an admixture of "free-floating responsiveness" (Sandler & Sandler, 1998) and selectively paying "attention now to defence, now to what is defended against, depending upon which is apparent in a patient's communications" (Brenner, 2000, p. 548). My proposal of certain guidelines for treating betrayed and betraying patients reflects the spirit of focused attention and strategic interpretation in psychoanalytic technique.
8. This, of course, is the essence of what Freud (1923b) termed "negative therapeutic reaction". He held that unconscious guilt over the wished-for childhood Oedipal transgressions of incest and murder were responsible for such a reaction. Subsequent analysts have, however, added additional dynamics including anxiety over separation from mother (Asch, 1976; Grunert, 1979), envy of the therapist's ability to soothe and help (Kernberg, 1984), and identification with a masochistic parent (Akhtar, 2009).
9. This discussion of betraying and being betrayed has remained patient-focused. It has not addressed betrayals of the patient by the analyst. While their gross forms (e.g., sexual boundary violations) are well-known and written about (Casement, 2006; Celenza, 2006; Gabbard & Lester, 1995), more subtle betrayals by the analyst often go unrecognised or are subsumed—by the analyst—under the rubric of "technical errors" (see Charles, 1997, for a meaningful discussion of this matter).
10. Although the two cases described here involve men betraying women or feeling betrayed by women, this does not mean that women cannot do and feel the same. Moreover, betrayal can also occur in the "non-erotic" realms of money, academic collaboration, national security, etc.

CHAPTER SIX

Revenge

The history of human civilisation is replete with examples of man's destructiveness towards man. Some of these outbursts are impulsive, passionate, and transient. Others are calculated, deliberate, and long-standing. Some involve individuals. Others involve masses. Some occur only in fantasy and, under fortunate circumstances, are turned into defiant poetry, biting fiction, and provocative theatre. Others slit throats, ruin families, and cause bloodshed. Regardless of their extent, all destructive actions somehow or other become justified in the mind of the perpetrator. One's violence is given a patina of reasonableness through all sorts of rationales and rationalisations regardless of whether it involves the plebian tit-for-tat of children or the awesome "messianic sadism" (Akhtar, 2007c) of paranoid fundamentalists. Matters of the former variety fall under the purview of parents, elementary school teachers, and benevolent clergy. Matters of the latter variety belong to interdisciplinary think tanks that can inform sociopolitical praxis.

These two extremes are not encountered in the clinical situation. What one does witness there are "mid-level" destructive aims and fantasies directed at old and new objects as well as their recreations in the transference. Any therapist who has worked with narcissistic, paranoid, and sociopathic individuals would vouch for the veracity of this observation. Given this, it is surprising that the theme of revenge has attracted very little attention from psychoanalysts. The PEP web, which contains over 88,000 entries, comes up with only thirty papers with "revenge" in their titles over the 113-year history of psychoanalysis. Clearly, something is remiss here.

This overview is intended to summarise the scattered writings—psychoanalytic or otherwise—on the topic of revenge and to create some phenomenological and psychodynamic order out of this chaos. In addition, the contribution will make a brief foray into the literary realm and close with elucidating the clinical implications of the observations made during the effort to unfold the nuances of the issues involved here.

Phenomenological aspects

The English word "revenge" is derived from the Old French *vengier*, meaning "to avenge". Its dictionary definition includes phrases such as (i) to avenge by retaliating in kind or degree; (ii) to inflict injury in return for an insult, and (iii) an opportunity for getting satisfaction (*Webster's*, 1987, p. 1009). An unmistakable implication is that revenge has ideational, emotional, and behavioural aspects. In the ideational sphere, revenge is accompanied by a fantasy (conscious or unconscious) of having been grievously harmed by someone and of finding relief from inflicting damage upon the perpetrator. In the emotional sphere, revenge is accompanied by feelings of "mental pain" (Akhtar, 2000; Freud, 1926d; Ramzy & Wallerstein, 1958; Weiss, 1934), bitterness, rage, and defensive exaltation; the vengeful person is often euphoric. In the behavioural sphere, common manifestations of revenge include verbal and physical assaults of varying degrees, ranging from sarcasm, denigration, and hurling obscenities to slapping, hitting, punching, throwing things at someone, knifing, maiming, shooting, and killing. However, gross actions of such a sort do not exhaust the behavioural manifestations of revenge. The phenomena associated with it are complex in many ways.

First: Acts of revenge are not always directed at the individual or organisation that is viewed as having caused harm. Often the rage emanating from feeling hurt is aimed at objects that symbolically stand for the injuring party or are weak and vulnerable, hence suitable for being attacked. Nearly 100 years ago, Rank (1913) pointed out that neurotic acts of revenge are often directed against the "wrong" people. Revenge fantasies in terrorist acts especially depict how victims of the destructive impulse are not truly the targets of it (Akhtar, 2003); innocent civilians are killed and maimed not for rage directed at them but because they are dispensable pawns in a violent game of chess with their governments.

Second: Redirection of vengeful affects and behaviours can involve the self. Thus the chronic self-effacement, self-deprivation, self-denigration, self-mutilation, and self-destructiveness of severely masochistic patients contain a powerful, though unconscious, element of revenge. Freud (1917e, 1921c) had long ago discerned this element in the symptomatology of depression. He stated that

> A leading characteristic of these cases is a cruel self-depreciation of the ego combined with relentless self-criticism and bitter self-reproaches. Analyses have shown that this disparagement and these reproaches apply at bottom to the object and represent the ego's revenge upon it. (1921c, p. 109)

It is as if the patient, in his misery, has become a walking billboard of the parental misconduct during his childhood. His ongoing pain and suffering shouts at the parents with the whole world as their mutual audience, "Look how much you have damaged me! I am a total failure compared to everyone else. I am retarded. I cannot grow and it is all your fault!" (Kramer, 1987, p. 217). Procci's (1987) concept of "mockery through compliance", whereby the individual acts out his or her parents' destructive intent towards himself in an exaggerated way, also applies here. And, so does Ferenczi's (1929) sombre delineation of how the unwanted child turns pessimistic and devoid of life energy. Even more dark is the description of "spite suicides" (Zilboorg, 1936) referring to taking one's life due more to sadism and sarcasm than depressive hopelessness. Maltsberger and Buie (1980) offer a more recent and lucid description of this phenomenon.

> Would-be suicides often daydream of the guilt and sorrow of others gathered about the coffin, an imaginary spectacle which provides much satisfaction. While the contemplation of such a scene is a pleasure in itself, the patient may also consciously entertain the illusion that after the act of suicide he will be present as an unseen observer to enjoy the anguish of those who view his dead body. Such an illusion may be held with such intensity that it supersedes reality in emotional value and forms the basis for action. (p. 61)

Third: Even direct acts of revenge take many forms. Some of them are active (e.g., sarcasm, physical violence), while others are passive (e.g., gaze aversion, refusal to eat). Some involve aggression while others deploy sexuality as a medium. Behaviours that have been linked with an underlying theme of revenge are as varied as frigidity, euphemistically referred as "revenge on the man" (Fenichel, 1945, p. 174), incestuous acting-out (Gordon, 1955), pathological stealing (Castelnuevo-Tedesco, 1974), primal scene reversals (Arlow, 1980), shop-lifting (Ornstein, Gropper & Bogner, 1983), serial killing (Stone, 1989), and sexual betrayal (Akhtar, 2013a). At times, an individual's sexual object choice can also express his or her rebellion and revenge against the cultural strictures of the family (Freud, 1920g). Neurotic fears of being bitten by animals too can contain elements of revenge being taken against oneself for one's original hostility towards parents (Freud, 1926d).

Finally, there exists a relationship between the level of character organisation and the nature of revenge fantasy. At the "higher level of character organization" (Kernberg, 1970), where identity is well-consolidated and defences centre upon repression, revenge fantasies—if they even exist—involve Oedipal issues. Childhood exposure to parental sexuality fuels such fantasies and their subtle and disguised seepage into actual behaviour. At the "intermediate" and "lower" levels of character organisation (ibid.), characterised by identity diffusion and the preponderance of splitting mechanisms, matters appear more stark. Revenge, in this context, is usually overt, cold-blooded, and accompanied by conscious sadistic pleasure. Rosenfeld's (1971) description of narcissistic personalities who idealise their destructive capacity and Kernberg's (1984) delineation of the syndrome of malignant narcissism which combines grandiosity, paranoid traits, and antisocial tendencies are highly pertinent here. Fantasies and actions of violent revenge are common among such individuals and are founded upon severe childhood frustrations and actual trauma; their vindictiveness constitutes the reversal of betrayal and abuse by their parents.

Psychodynamics

Freud's first comment upon revenge was in the context of trauma which, he believed, became more pathogenic when suffered in silence. Taking revenge holds the possibility of getting over the injury, though speaking about what has happened also helps. Here are Freud's own words on this matter.

> An injury that has been repaid, even if only in words, is recollected quite differently from one that has to be accepted. Language recognizes this distinction, too, in its mental and physical consequences; it very characteristically describes an injury that has been suffered in silence as "a mortification" (*Krankung*, literally "making ill"). The injured person's reaction to the trauma only exercises a completely "cathartic" effect if it is an *adequate* reaction—as, for instance, revenge. But language serves as a substitute for action; by its help, an affect can be "abreacted" almost as effectively. (1950a, p. 8, italics in the original)

Freud later evoked the idea of revenge in his elucidation of the dynamics of Little Hans (1909b) and the Wolf Man (1918b). He regarded their fears of being bitten and devoured by animals (in reality and in dreams, respectively) as a boomerang effect of their own hostile fantasies towards their parents, especially in the context of the latter's sexual lives. In *Inhibitions, Symptoms and Anxiety*, written nearly two decades later, Freud reiterated this idea.

> The case of the "Wolf Man" and the somewhat less complicated one of "Little Hans" raise a number of further considerations ... There can be no doubt that the instinctual impulse which was repressed in both phobias was a hostile one against the father. One might say that that impulse had been repressed by the process of being transformed into its opposite. Instead of aggressiveness on the part of the subject towards his father, there appeared aggressiveness (in the shape of revenge) on the part of his father towards the subject. Since this aggressiveness is in any case rooted in the sadistic phase of the libido, only a certain amount of degradation is needed to reduce it to the oral stage. This stage, while only hinted at in "Little Hans's" fear of being bitten, was blatantly exhibited in the "Wolf Man's" terror of being devoured. (1926d, p. 106)

The linkage between a child's sense of betrayal at the discovery of parental sexuality and the resulting desire to take revenge is nowhere more clear in Freud's writings than in his 1910 paper titled "A Special

Type of Choice of Object Made by Men". Explicating the Oedipal situation of the boy, Freud stated:

> He does not forgive his mother for having granted the favour of sexual intercourse not to himself but to his father, and he regards it as an act of unfaithfulness. If these impulses do not quickly pass, there is no outlet for them other than to run their course in phantasies which have as their subject his mother's sexual activities under the most diverse circumstances; and the consequent tension leads particularly readily to his finding relief in masturbation. As a result of the constant combined operation of the two driving forces, [sexual] drive and thirst for revenge, phantasies of his mother's unfaithfulness are by far the most preferred. (1910h, p. 171)

Freud's papers on family romances (1909c) and on a case of female homosexuality (1920a) repeated that revenge originated in the child's feeling humiliation and injury vis-à-vis parental sexuality. A new perspective on revenge was, however, evident in "Mourning and Melancholia" (1917e), where the self-reproaches of both the obsessional and the melancholic were seen as acts of revenge upon the subject's own ego.

> The self-tormenting in melancholia, which is without doubt enjoyable, signifies, just like the corresponding phenomenon in obsessional neurosis, a satisfaction of trends of sadism and hate which relate to an object, and which have been turned around upon the subject's own self. In both disorders, the patients usually still succeed, by the circuitous path of self-punishment, in taking revenge on the original object and in tormenting their loved ones by their illness, having resorted to it in order to express their hostility to him openly. (p. 251)

Freud repeated these ideas in *Group Psychology and the Analysis of the Ego* (1921c, p. 109), though conceding, in *Civilization and Its Discontents* (1930a, p. 130), that the severity of self-reproaches and the underlying revenge motif is only partly due to experiential factors (either via narcissistic injury in the Oedipal phase or via loss of an ambivalently-held but needed object); inborn constitutional factors also contribute to the ferocity of the superego and to the overall propensity for rage and revenge in one's character.

Following Freud, many psychoanalysts enriched the understanding of revenge-related phenomena. Abraham (1920) described a "revenge-type of female castration complex" which, reflecting the phallocentric theorisation of the era, was alleged to cause attacks on the "luckier" male by castrating him. To deprive him of the satisfaction that he has given her sexual pleasure, the woman might become incapable of orgasm. Or, a certain kind of aggressive hypersexuality might develop in her; this is often accompanied by the exploitative fantasies of being a prostitute. Fenichel (1945) later added that since the infantile oral pregnancy themes often include the idea that the woman eats the man's penis, the revenge-type of female castration complex might also result in eating inhibitions. Similarly loyal to the drive theory of psychoanalysis, Klein (1933, 1940) spoke of externalisation of the death instinct and the subsequent creation of "bad objects"; these can then be feared and therefore justifiably attacked. Though the word "revenge" does not constitute an element of her vocabulary (see Hinshelwood, 1991), Klein's description of the "paranoid position" centres upon infantile persecutory anxieties and phantasies of retaliation against "bad objects".

Moving away from this drive-based model, Winnicott (1956a) traced stealing and outrageousness towards others to actual deprivation in childhood. He did not use the word "revenge" (Abram, 2007), but his ideas on what he called "antisocial tendency" are certainly applicable to revenge as well. In his inimitable fashion, Winnicott suggested that insofar as it compels the environment to respond, "antisocial tendency" is an expression of hope. The delinquent's outrageousness is a cry for help. Winnicott (1956a) noted that there are always two trends in antisocial tendency.

> One trend is represented typically in stealing and the other in destructiveness. By one trend, the child is looking for something, somewhere, and failing to find it seeks elsewhere, when hopeful. By the other the child is seeking the amount of environmental stability which will stand the strain resulting from impulsive behavior. This is a search for environmental provision that has been lost, a human attitude, which, because it can be relied on, gives freedom to the individual to move, to act, and to get excited. (p. 310)

The tension between a drive-based and a deprivation-based aetiological model of revenge tilted over time (just as psychoanalytic theory at large did) towards the latter view. Even those contributors (e.g., Arlow, 1980; Socarides, 1966) who employed the vocabulary of drives did so in the context of childhood trauma. Most others (e.g., Boris, 1986; Castelnuovo-Tedesco, 1974; Daniels, 1969; Horney, 1948; Kohut, 1972; Steiner, 1996) emphatically favoured the deprivation and/or humiliation hypothesis of the origin of vindictiveness.

In a remarkable paper titled "The Value of Vindictiveness", Horney (1948) noted that while rational outrage at a frustrating event settles soon after it is vented, vindictiveness, in neurotic characters, can become a way of life. Its aims then are to humiliate, to exploit, and to frustrate others. Its means can be varied and include the induction of guilt and inferiority in others, ingratitude, indifference, and active assaults upon others' valued traits and capacities. Horney described three forms of vindictiveness, namely, (i) openly aggressive vindictiveness that is associated with a certain kind of pride in what is construed as one's honesty and straightforwardness; (ii) self-effacing vindictiveness which operates covertly and exploits others' inclinations towards fairness and justice; vindictiveness of this sort evokes the puzzling impression of being done at the person's expense; and (iii) detached vindictiveness that expresses hostility towards others "by not listening, by disregarding their needs, by forgetting their wishes, by making them feel as disturbing intruders, by withholding praise or affection, and by withdrawing psychically or socially" (p. 4). Horney emphasised that vindictiveness, while destructive in intent, serves some positive functions as well. These include its protective power against real and/or imagined hostility from others, its defensive aim against self-destructiveness, and its promise to restore injured pride. The need for vindictive triumph, in Horney's formulation, arose from many sources, the prime variable being a pressure to reverse the thoughtlessness or openly cruel humiliations experienced at the hands of others. The feeling of vitality and even thrill provided by acts of revenge also counters the inner sense of inferiority and shame.

Searles (1956) also underscored the defensive functions of revenge. He noted that vindictiveness can serve as a defence against repressed emotions, especially those of loss, separation, and mourning. According to him, the vindictive person is unable to let go of his attachment to the object that is indifferent to his desire; seeking revenge against that object maintains the hope of affecting a change in its attitude.

Socarides (1966) noted that the conscious aim of vengeance is retribution and punishment while the unconscious aim is to cover up disastrous damage to the ego that occurred in early childhood and revived in adulthood. Vengeance can also serve as a defence against guilt whereby the self-directed aggression is turned towards the external world. Socarides observed that the vindictive person is "grudging, unforgiving, remorseless, ruthless, heartless, implacable, inflexible [and] lives for revenge with a single-mindedness of purpose" (p. 405). There is a certain kind of "pseudo-courageous" attitude here too since the vengeful individual will go to any extreme to hurt his enemies. Such unrelenting aggression is a product of early, mainly oral, frustration. "Damaged fundamentally in the capacity to love, the vengeful person is unable to withstand future states of deprivation and attacks individuals in the environment as if they were representatives of the depriving breast, frustrating mother, absent father, lost penis" (ibid., p. 410). Envy plays a big role here and the projection of such envy upon superego figures leads to hatred of powerful and secretly idealised others.

Daniels (1969) emphasised that triumph over hated objects is so important for such an individual that he readily cuts ethical corners and uses any weapon in his "war". He strikes first and his pre-emptions betray his paranoia and intense need for control. And, when his victims complain, he accuses them of being hypersensitive and weak. Daniels noted that the vindictive person's hostility goes beyond his explicit "tormentors" since envy plays a great role in his life as well.

> Aside from those who actually "cross him", the vindictive character also perceives as definitely threatening anyone possessing more than he does—materially, intellectually, or psychologically. Bitter envy assails him. Such people must be diminished, reduced to his level; otherwise, his pride suffers and he begins to slide into the depression upon the brink of which he is already standing. Even worse, he begins to be cognizant of the misery of his lot and of his anguished aloneness. He must enter into relation with the envied person and make him miserable too; then he will be less lonely. (pp. 187–188)

Kohut (1972) described the phenomenon of narcissistic rage with great eloquence. He stated that:

> Narcissistic rage occurs in many forms; they all share, however, a specific psychological flavor which gives them a distinct position within the wide realm of human aggressions. The need for revenge,

> for righting a wrong, for undoing a hurt of whatever means, and a deeply-anchored, unrelenting compulsion in the pursuit of all these aims which gives no rest to those who have suffered a narcissistic injury—these are features which are characteristic of narcissistic rage in all its forms and which set it apart from other kinds of aggression. (p. 379)

Kohut went on to note that such rage is only mobilised if there is an archaic grandiose self seeking its preservation and regulating the perception of reality. The "enemy" who incites narcissistic rage is not perceived as a separate individual and an autonomous source of initiative but as a flaw in a narcissistically perceived reality that must be erased and blotted out.

Castelnuovo-Tedesco (1974) termed the triad of entitlement, stealing, and well-rationalised sadomasochism the Monte Cristo complex. Describing the protagonist from Alexandre Dumas's (1802–1870) eponymous novel and adding two clinical cases with similar psychopathology, Castlenuovo-Tedesco proposed that:

> The act of stealing, on close examination, proves to have a variety of discernible meanings and functions, all of which are, broadly speaking, restitutive. It serves, first of all, to undo a loss which is subjectively perceived as a theft where the patient has been the victim. Second, it is seen as an opportunity for revenge, for settling a score and giving back measure for measure. It is my impression, in sum, that the impulse to steal and the urge for revenge are really very close to one another. It is also a way of "turning the tables", of taking the initiative and, in secret, converting a passive experience into an active one. It is further a way of controlling a frightening and dangerous object and rendering it harmless by reinstating a long lost but cherished sense of omnipotence. Finally, it is a channel for discharge of substantial aggressiveness and greed. (p. 175)

The connection between greed and revenge found further exposition in a paper by Boris (1986). Greed, in his conceptualisation, is appetite turned angry and no longer reliant on the actual object. Greed aspires for an idealised object, hence is inconsolable. The next step in the process is the development of spite or the envious nullification of the other's impact and thus, in turn, is followed by seeking revenge. The aim, at this point, is to stimulate greed and envy in the other.

Steiner (1996) elucidated the reverse of this dynamic. He noted that when taking revenge is felt to be too dangerous, grievance is kept under check and becomes a nidus for sadomasochistic retreat. Steiner also noted that the wish for revenge initially represents the pursuit of a just cause but soon gets caught up in destructive motives of diverse, often unrelated origins. Moreover, revenge-seeking serves to protect the split-off good object which can be kept idealised till the time a bad object is found and destroyed.

In contrast to most of the contributors cited above, Arlow (1980) returned to the Oedipal origins of revenge-seeking. He noted that exposure to the primal scene, especially if vivid and frequent, leads to narcissistic mortification and a conviction that one is unloved and unlovable. This trauma gives birth to the wish to wreak vengeance on one or both of the "betraying" parents. A common manifestation of such a wish is the tendency to criticise and demean parents and parental surrogates. More striking are the scenarios where the taking of revenge occurs in sophisticated enactments or reversals of the primal scene.

> In some instances, the individual brings about a repetition of the primal scene in which he casts himself in the role of witness, often enough interrupting and causing distress to a couple making love. Relatively underemphasized, however, are those vengeful repetitions of the primal scene in which the individual causes others to be witness to his sexual activities. The unconscious import of this behavior is to make the betraying parents experience the sense of humiliation, exclusion, and betrayal that the child experienced at the time of the original trauma, except that in this repetition the role of the parent may be assigned to somebody else—spouse, child, lover, etc. (Arlow, 1980, p. 523)

Having covered the multifaceted descriptive and psychoanalytic literature on revenge, I am now in a position to offer a composite profile of phenomena that exist in this realm.

An attempt at synthesis

What becomes clear from this review is that many diverse phenomena are subsumed under the term "revenge". It appears in the vastly different contexts of repressed, disguised, and symbolically represented unconscious fantasies as well as of overtly destructive and violent acts towards others. Confusion also rises from the term "revenge" being employed for a single act of retaliation triggered by hurtful or violating action by someone in external reality and also for the character trait of vindictiveness. Well-justified, rational, and limited acts of retribution also get lumped together here. The fact is that such "good enough revenge" is very different from vindictiveness. "Good enough revenge" meets the following criteria: (i) it is a one-time occurrence, (ii) more of it is in fantasy and less in action, (iii) it avoids self-destructiveness and masochism, and (iv) it takes socially productive forms (e.g., writing a significant book to prove the "enemy" wrong) or carries the potential of initiating (or resuming) a meaningful dialogue between the victim and the perpetrator.[1] In contrast, vindictiveness is chronic, boundless, consuming, and, often, self-destructive besides being grievously harmful to the real or imagined enemy. People who are given to vindictiveness continue to harbour resentment towards their offenders for months, years, and often for their entire life. They are prone to sustained hatred and can disregard all limits in their pursuit of real or imagined offenders. Western literature contains many such characters. *The Merchant of Venice*'s Shylock (Shakespeare, 1596) with his literal-minded insistence upon extracting "a pound of flesh" in lieu of his unpaid debt and *Wuthering Heights*'s Heathcliff (Brontë, 1847) with his bitter rants against the woman by whom he feels betrayed are two outstanding examples. Towering above these is the character of Captain Ahab in Melville's *Moby Dick* (1851). His hunger for revenge against the whale that bit off his leg drives him to such "demonic" revenge-seeking that he ultimately destroys his own self.

The two forms of retaliation (i.e., "good enough revenge" and vindictiveness) stand on opposite poles of the wide spectrum of socioclinical phenomena involved here (see Table 3).

Psychodynamically too, the spectrum of revenge is wide. The phenomena related to revenge seem—like all other psychic phenomena—multiply determined. Although a background of severe childhood frustration does play a major role in it, the dynamics of revenge and vindictiveness exceed it. It comprises variables emanating from all three sources: defect, discharge, and defence. Moreover, the role of these variables and the degree of their contribution to the overt behaviour differs from case to case. *From the perspective of defect*, the truly vengeful individual gives evidence of lacking empathy with his victim. Desperately wishing to inflict pain upon the "enemy", he nonetheless

Table 3. The spectrum of revenge.

Variables	*Good enough revenge*	*Vindictiveness*
Object	External	Internal
Emotion	Rage	Hate
Frequency	Once	Chronic
Scope	Limited	Unlimited
Cognition	Contextual	Narrowed
Ethics	Intact	Compromised
Narcissism	Regained	Regained
Pleasure	Yes	Yes
Masochism	No	Yes
Sublimation	Maybe	No
Consequence	Constructive	Destructive
Time	Heals	Makes no change

cannot empathise with the latter's suffering. The "narrow-mindedness" (Brenman, 1985) that frequently accompanies vengeful actions is also in part due to defects of "mentalization" (Fonagy & Target, 1997) although defensive curtailment of cognitive functions also contributes to it. *From the perspective of discharge,* revenge gives vent, in a more or less aim-inhibited manner, to primitive sadism. Drive components from oral and anal phases are frequently evident in the form of biting sarcasm and defilement of the enemy's life. Hostility felt as a result of humiliating exposure to the primal scene and due to other, more severe trauma also finds discharge in acts of revenge. While sexual acts (e.g., rape, incest) can be used as methods of revenge, it is the satisfaction of destructive aims that is primarily sought and enjoyed. *From the perspective of defence,* revenge constitutes the ego's attempt to reverse humiliating passivity into triumphant activity, to restore traumatically depleted narcissism, and to extrude a malevolent "interject" (Bollas, 1999), that is, an object that has been violently inserted into the self. Revenge, insofar as it carries the hope—mostly unrealistic—permanently erasing the trauma one has suffered, also acts as a preserver of the good internal object and a defence against sadness and mourning.

Technical implications

The theme of revenge appears frequently in the course of intensive treatments. Individuals who seek psychoanalysis or long-term psychoanalytic psychotherapy often have significant childhood trauma in their background and this makes many of them prone to seek revenge against those who have hurt them (usually, though not invariably, the parents), their substitutes, or the world at large. Needless to add, such scenarios are sooner or later created in the transference-countertransference axis as well. Clinical work can thus become quite bloody. The following guidelines might help negotiate the way through such hard-to-tread ground.

First, the patient must be allowed to bring out his grievances and, for quite some time, repeat them as if each rendition is their first exposure to daylight. Balint (1968) emphasises that in the treatment of deeply traumatised individuals the analytic process "must not be hurried by interpretations, however correct, since they may be felt as undue interference, as an attempt at devaluing the justification of their complaint and thus, instead of speeding up, they will slow down the therapeutic processes" (p. 182). To point out discrepancies and contradictions in the patient's story, to bring up the defensive nature of his idealisations and devaluations, and to analyse the potentially masochistic aspects of his outrage, are tasks that must be left for much later.

Second, during this early phase, the analyst's activity should remain restricted to empathic remarks, gentle exploratory comments, and what Killingmo (1989) has termed "affirmative interventions". The psychological essence of such interventions is constituted by four elements: (i) the element of existence, (ii) the element of relating, (iii) the element of worth, and (iv) the element of validity. As a result, affirmative interventions are empathic comments that render plausibility, context-based validity, and historical meaningfulness to the patient's experience. Such remarks are not aimed at revealing meanings; they are directed at establishing the existence of meaning. On a pragmatic level, they consist of objectifying (e.g., you have felt very hurt by this person and are, therefore, very angry with him), justifying (e.g., no wonder you are upset since what this person has done to you felt so unfair and unjust), and contextualising (e.g., you experienced his behaviour as especially discriminating since you have indeed been treated with prejudice before) elements.

Third, if the revenge fantasies of the patient and their associated hostile affects are close to consciousness, the work can move on, after a while, from affirmative to unmasking and interpretive interventions. The analyst must now explore, in a straightforward manner, the scope of revenge fantasies, the dramatis personae in the theatre of vengefulness, the presence or absence of guilt, and the actual and imagined reasons why the revenge the patient so desperately seeks has not been taken and/or how it has, at least partly, been acted out. Clearly such work has to occur in a piecemeal fashion and with continued attention to the analysis of defences and resistances that crop up in this investigative path. Establishing hermeneutic linkages along the axes outlined above gradually would lead to the patient's entertaining healthy forms of "getting even" and also to responsibility, remorse, and even some forgiveness.

Fourth, if the revenge fantasies have been turned upon the self and the clinical picture is mostly masochistic, the analyst must help the patient see, via a moment-to-moment microanalysis of his associations, how the centrifugal pull of masochism operates. Of course, the analyst's comments themselves might be utilised by the patient for self-castigating purposes ("So it is all my fault?"). This has to be watched for and pointed out. Closely associated is such a patient's tendency to develop "negative therapeutic reaction" (Freud, 1923b; see Akhtar, 2009, for a fuller definition), that is, symptomatic worsening instead of improvement as a consequence of a correct interpretation of his malady. In dealing with such occurrences, the analyst must weigh which variable (e.g., unconscious guilt, envious attack on the analyst's goodness, clinging to masochistic pleasure) is the most active, most palatable, and, hence, most interpretable at a given moment. The need for "tact" (Loewenstein, 1951; Poland, 1975) on the analyst's part cannot be overemphasised in this context.

Fifth, in both types of patients (i.e., overtly sadistic and secretly masochistic and overtly masochistic and secretly sadistic), a modicum of limit-setting might become unavoidable. Apt in this context is Hoffer's (1985) reminder that departures from analytic neutrality are permissible when the analyst, the patient, or someone weak and vulnerable in the latter's life is at risk of being harmed. However, the concept of harm must not be restricted to physical harm; violent projections, tenacious false accusations, screaming, and even consistently deploying metaphors of life and death (e.g., "I am drowning and you are just standing on the shore") aimed at rendering the analyst humiliated and helpless have to be "prohibited" sooner or later. The analyst must remind himself that there is a long-held tradition, ranging from Freud's (cited in Alexander & French, 1946) injunction to phobics that they face their feared object, through Ferenczi's (1921) "active technique" and Kolansky and Eisner's (1974) "spoiling" of pre-Oedipal gratifications, to Amati-Mehler and Argentieri's (1989) rupturing of pathologic hope and Akhtar's (2013b) "refusal to listen to certain kinds of material". The analyst must realise that analytic patience, waiting, and tolerance are not there to be idealised by him or to be abused by the patient. Limit-setting is often a necessary step in forcing the enacted material into thought and thus making it subject to exploration and interpretation.

Sixth, in conjunction with attempting interpretive resolution, the analyst—especially when working with tenaciously sadomasochistic patients—must assist the patient's ego in creating choices. Such choices might involve the degree and form of revenge that can be taken safely, the people with whom it should and should not be taken, but most importantly, whether it is essential to take revenge after all. The last-mentioned can lead to the analysis of depressive anxieties underlying the "optimism of revenge" which, in turn, might require some auxiliary ego support and gentle reminders of the love and support that *is* available to the patient and is underutilised by him. This can make mourning bearable.

Seventh, while the foregoing paves the way to forgiveness and it is "good" if that does occur, yet the analyst must not uphold manic ideals for himself and the patient. He must be able to accept that some injuries might not be forgivable, especially if there is no admission of wrong-doing and apology from the perpetrator. In such cases, analytic work should focus upon why the patient cannot forgive himself for being unforgiving and to help the patient find more productive ways of dealing with the unmetabolised residues of his childhood trauma.

Finally, the management of countertransference forms an extremely important dimension in the treatment of severely sadomasochistic patients. This is especially so because the patients' desire for revenge (regardless of whether these are overtly sadistic or masochistic) sooner or later become activated in the transference relationship. The analyst is then mocked, devalued, ignored, and actively or passively thwarted. The patient might act out in his or her actual life in order to hurt the analyst or directly assault the analyst's mind, personality, or technique (Kernberg, 1984, 1992). All this puts a great burden on the analyst and creates many countertransference risks. The first such risk is that of masochistic surrender on the analyst's part. This evolves from the analyst's desperate attempt to show that he is different from the patient's bad internal objects, that he is unerringly tolerant, and that he never retaliates. Such forced "disidentification with the aggressor" (Gabbard, 1997), rationalised by the analyst as a necessary accommodation to the patient's psychopathology, is actually anti-therapeutic since it delays or bypasses the analysis of negative transference. It also carries the risk of conveying to the patient that he or she can get away with unfettered hostility and destructiveness; this, in turn, fuels the patient's deep desire for omnipotence.

A second countertransference pitfall is constituted by the analyst's inability to contain the aggression mobilised by violent projections of bad objects into him. When this happens, the analyst finds himself losing control, raising his voice, becoming sarcastic, unduly rigid in sticking to "rules", and getting into heated arguments about trivial matters. This is hardly helpful since the patient perceives and utilises such behaviours as proof that the world is bad, that no one understands him, and that therapeutic interventions are not invitations to think about oneself but sadistic assaults upon his views of internal and external reality.

A third risk is for the analyst to turn didactic, even moralising. He might find himself appealing to the patient's sense of rationality and reason. Here Kohut's (1972) reminder must be heeded: "The transformation of narcissistic rage is not achieved directly—e.g. via appeals to the patient's ego, to increase its control over the angry impulses—but is brought about indirectly, secondary to gradual transformation of the matrix of narcissism from which the rage arose" (p. 388).

All these risks emanate from the failed containment of the patient's projected hostility. Under ideal circumstances such pitfalls can be avoided. However, in day-to-day clinical work with vengeful patients, enactments of either type often become unavoidable. The analyst's task then involves a post-hoc analysis (and, self-analysis) of such interactions and repair of the disruption caused by them (Akhtar, 2007d; Wolf, 1988).

Concluding remarks

In this chapter, I have provided a wide-ranging survey of the phenomenological, dynamic, literary, and clinical aspects of revenge. My scope has been broad and our theoretical stance multifaceted. Throughout my discourse, I have paid attention to all "four psychologies of psychoanalysis" (Pine, 1988): drive, ego, object relations, and self.

My understanding of the various phenomena related to revenge and vindictiveness and my technical recommendations to deal with them have been similarly broad-based. Two areas have, however, eluded my attention so far. These pertain to the impact of gender and the culture-at-large upon the revenge motif in the human psychic life.

First, there is the variable of gender. Are there differences in the frequency, form, and extent of revenge fantasies and acts in the two sexes? The answer seems far from clear. To be sure, literary and movie protagonists of revenge are more often male but the meaning of this remains ambiguous. Does it simply reflect the male preponderance among the main characters in fiction and movies regardless of their themes? Does it embody an anxious avoidance of depicting and encountering female rage and vindictiveness? Shakespeare's declaration that "hell hath no fury greater than a woman scorned" comes to mind in this context. So does Euripides' *Medea* who killed her two sons as revenge against her husband who had left her for another woman. And then there is Miss Havisham, from Dickens's (1861) *Great Expectations*, who, rejected by a man, seeks revenge on all men by grooming her protégée, Estella, to become the ultimate heartbreaker. So there does not seem to be a shortage of enraged and vindictive feelings in women. However, since men in general are more outwardly aggressive, the prevalence of revenge-related violent acts might be greater in them. In women, this rage might be more disguised or turned inward, resulting in a silently resentful paranoid-masochistic picture. Early literature of descriptive psychiatry (Bleuler, 1908; Kraepelin, 1905, 1921) lends some support to this idea but how far the societal changes over the last century, especially those resulting from the feminist movement, have altered such conceptualisations remains unclear.

This brings up the issue of culture. It is my impression that it harbours very mixed feelings about taking revenge. That revenge is justifiable, even godly, is clearly spelled out in the much-revered citation from the New Testament: "Vengeance is mine; I will repay, saith the Lord" (Romans 12:19) and, before it, the harsh Old Testament's (Deuteronomy 19:21; Exodus 21:24) *Lex Talionis* (the talion principle) dictating that one should extract a tooth for a tooth and an eye for an eye. Moral sanctions of such a sort fuel the hard-wired reflex to retaliate that is our evolutionary legacy.[2] The desire for revenge is thus normalised, even exalted. We accord respect and awe to the vindictive hero in fiction and popular cinema. Captain Ahab from Melville's *Moby Dick*

(1851), and the *Count of Monte Cristo* (1844) from Dumas's eponymous novel mobilise much sympathy and admiration in readers around the globe. And the same is true of the avenging movie characters, ranging from Clint Eastwood's *Dirty Harry* series of the 1970s to the *Angry Young Man* movies of Bollywood cinema (Akhtar & Choksi, 2005). The audience simply laps it all up. It seems as if these books and celluloid dramas afford an abreactive conduit for ubiquitous fantasies of getting even and settling the score. Revenge seems to be "hot" and well accepted in all cultures.

At the same time, children are discouraged from "tit-for-tat" thinking. Vindictiveness is frowned upon. Revenge-seeking is deemed immature and the ideal of forgiveness is upheld by religious and noble men (see the lives of Gandhi, Martin Luther King, Jr., and Nelson Mandela). Parallel to the mesmerising tales of revenge, there exist moving and poignant narratives of forgiveness especially in the traditions of Christianity.

Putting such diverse perspectives together leads one to conclude that society holds ambivalent attitudes about revenge. Consciously, it strives towards responding to injury by forgiving the enemy. Unconsciously, it seeks to redress the trauma by taking revenge. Vicarious enjoyment of "well-justified" revenge in the safety of fiction and movies then becomes a compromise formation for this conflict of our culture. Some tension between the correctness of forgiving and seeking revenge nonetheless remains. Moss (1986) declares the two as competing attempts at reconciliation with the traumatising figures of the Oedipus complex. While the System Conscious might tilt in favour of one or the other strategy, both persist unaltered in the System Unconscious. There, they are represented as self-object pairs involved in the two respective scenarios of revenge and forgiveness. According to Moss, this fiction of symmetry "lies at the base of the civilization-wide proclivity toward the pursuit of revenge and forgiveness as strategies to obliterate the effects of trauma" (p. 209). The implication is clear: the wish to settle a score never entirely leaves the human heart.[3] And this might not be bad. Elsewhere, I have observed that

> Some revenge is actually good for the victim. It puts the victim's hitherto passive ego in an active position. This imparts a sense of mastery and enhances self-esteem. Revenge (in reality or fantasy), allowing the victim to taste the pleasure of sadism, also changes the

> libido-aggression balance in the self-object relationship. The victim no longer remains innocent and the perpetrator no longer the sole cruel party. Now, both seem to have been hurt and to have caused hurt. This shift lays the groundwork for empathy with the enemy and reduces hatred. (Akhtar, 2002, p. 179)

A good way to conclude this discourse is therefore to remind oneself of Nietzsche's remark that "A small revenge is humaner than no revenge at all" (1905, p. 71) and Heine's (cited in Freud, 1930a, p. 110) witticism that "One must, it is true, forgive one's enemies—but not before they've been hanged."

Notes

1. Laura Blumenfeld's (2002) book, *Revenge*, reports her encounter with the Palestinian militant who had shot and wounded her father, a New York rabbi. One of her goals was to see if she could make her father human in the gunman's eyes, since terrorism is not so much about killing people as about dehumanising them to make a political point. In effect, she sought to "punish" the terrorist by showing his victim's humanity. Her unusual form of revenge led to the Palestinian man's apologising to her father and her father's forgiving him.
2. The deterrence function of revenge is what leads evolutionary theorists (Barash & Lipton, 2011; Pinker, 2011) to regard revenge as a part of our evolved human nature. "The necessity of revenge and punishment, from such vantage point, is necessary for the emergence and sustenance of cooperation. It prevents the cooperator from being exploited" (J. Anderson Thomson, Jr., personal communication, June 8, 2013).
3. The idea that the wish for revenge might be ubiquitous does not sit well with everyone. The rejecting response to the movie, *Inglorious Basterds* (2009, directed by Quintin Tarantino), by many Jewish people, is a case in point. The movie depicted the fictional scenario of Jewish violence against the Nazis and thus challenged the apparent absence of revenge fantasies among Jews. In contrast, the movie, *Django Unchained* (2012), showing a freed black slave taking revenge against his white tormentors, was received with relative equanimity by the African American community. The socio-historical reasons that might contribute to this differential response remain unclear.

REFERENCES

Abraham, K. (1913a). Restrictions and transformations of scoptophilia in psycho-neurotics; with remarks on analogous phenomena in folk-psychology. In: *Selected Papers on Psychoanalysis* (pp. 169–234). New York: Brunner/Mazel.

Abraham, K. (1913b). A constitutional basis of locomotor anxiety. In: *Selected Papers on Psychoanalysis* (pp. 235–249). New York: Brunner/Mazel.

Abraham, K. (1920). Manifestations of the female castration complex. In: *Selected Papers on Psychoanalysis* (pp. 338–369). London: Hogarth.

Abraham, K. (1924). The influence of oral eroticism on character formation. In: *Selected Papers of Karl Abraham, M.D.* (pp. 393–406). New York: Brunner/Mazel.

Abraham, K. (1925). The history of an impostor in the light of psychoanalytical knowledge. In: *Clinical Papers and Essays on Psychoanalysis* (pp. 291–305). New York: Brunner/Mazel, 1955.

Abram, J. (2007). *The Language of Winnicott: A Dictionary of Winnicott's Use of Words (2nd edition)*. London: Karnac.

Abrams, S. (1990). Psychoanalytic process: the developmental and the integrative. *Psychoanalytic Quarterly, 59*: 650–677.

Akhtar, S. (1984). The syndrome of identity diffusion. *American Journal of Psychiatry, 141*: 1381–1385.

Akhtar, S. (1985). The other woman: phenomenological, psychodynamic, and therapeutic considerations. In: D. Goldberg (Ed.), *Contemporary Marriage* (pp. 215–240). Homeswood, IL: Dow Jones-Irwin.

Akhtar, S. (1992a). *Broken Structures: Severe Personality Disorders and Their Treatment*. Northvale, NJ: Jason Aronson.

Akhtar, S. (1992b). Tethers, orbits, and invisible fences: clinical, developmental, sociocultural, and technical aspects of optimal distance. In: S. Kramer & S. Akhtar (Eds.), *When the Body Speaks: Psychological Meanings in Kinetic Clues* (pp. 21–57). Northvale, NJ: Jason Aronson.

Akhtar, S. (1994). Object constancy and adult psychopathology. *International Journal of Psychoanalysis, 75*: 441–455.

Akhtar, S. (1996). "Someday …" and "if only …" fantasies: pathological optimism and inordinate nostalgia as related forms of idealization. *Journal of the American Psychoanalytic Association, 44*: 723–753.

Akhtar, S. (1999a). The distinction between needs and wishes: implications for psychoanalytic theory and technique. *Journal of the American Psychoanalytic Association, 47*: 113–151.

Akhtar, S. (1999b). *Immigration and Identity: Turmoil, Treatment, and Transformation*. Northvale, NJ: Jason Aronson.

Akhtar, S. (2000). The shy narcissist. In: J. Sandler, R. Michels, & P. Fonagy (Eds.), *Changing Ideas in a Changing World: Essays in Honor of Arnold Cooper* (pp. 111–119). London: Karnac.

Akhtar, S. (2002). Forgiveness: origins, dynamics, psychopathology, and technical relevance. *Psychoanalytic Quarterly, 71*: 175–212.

Akhtar, S. (2003). Dehumanization: origins, manifestations, and remedies. In: S. Varvin & V. D. Volkan (Eds.), *Violence or Dialogue? Psychoanalytic Insights on Terror and Terrorism*. London: International Psychoanalytical Association.

Akhtar, S. (2007a). *Regarding Others: Reviews, Responses, and Reflections* (pp. 80–94). Charlottesville, VA: Pitchstone.

Akhtar, S. (2007b). Four roadblocks in approaching Masud Khan. *Psychoanalytic Quarterly, 76*: 991–995.

Akhtar, S. (2007c). From unmentalized xenophobia to messianic sadism: some reflections on the phenomenology of prejudice. In: H. Parens, A. Mahfouz, S. W. Twemlow, & D. E. Scharff (Eds.), *The Future of Prejudice: Psychoanalysis and the Prevention of Prejudice* (pp. 7–19). Lanham, MD: Jason Aronson.

Akhtar, S. (2007d). Disruptions in the course of psychotherapy and psychoanalysis. In: B. Van Luyn, S. Akhtar, & W. J. Livesley (Eds.), *Severe Personality Disorders: Everyday Issues in Clinical Practice* (pp. 93–108). Cambridge: Cambridge University Press.

Akhtar, S. (2009). *Comprehensive Dictionary of Psychoanalysis*. London: Karnac.

Akhtar, S. (2010). Freud's *Todesangst* and Ghalib's *Ishrat-e-Qatra*: two perspectives on death. In: S. Akhtar (Ed.), *The Wound of Mortality: Fear, Denial, and Acceptance of Death* (pp. 1–20). Lanham, MD: Jason Aronson.

Akhtar, S. (2011a). *Immigration and Acculturation: Mourning, Adaptation, and the Next Generation*. Lanham, MD: Jason Aronson.

Akhtar, S. (Ed.) (2011b). *Unusual Interventions: Alterations of the Frame, Method, and Relationship in Psychotherapy and Psychoanalysis*. London: Karnac.

Akhtar, S. (2011c). Refusing to listen to certain kinds of material. In: S. Akhtar (Ed.), *Unusual Interventions: Alterations of the Frame, Method, and Relationship in Psychotherapy and Psychoanalysis* (pp. 83–98). London: Karnac.

Akhtar, S. (2012). *The Book of Emotions*. New Delhi, India: Roli.

Akhtar, S. (2013a). *Good Stuff: Courage, Resilience, Gratitude, Generosity, Forgiveness, and Sacrifice*. Lanham, MD: Jason Aronson.

Akhtar, S. (2013b). *Psychoanalytic Listening: Methods, Limits, and Innovations*. London: Karnac.

Akhtar, S. (2013c). Guilt: an introductory overview. In: S. Akhtar (Ed.), *Guilt: Origins, Manifestations, and Management* (pp. 1–14). Lanham, MD: Jason Aronson.

Akhtar, S., & Brown, J. (2005). Animals in psychiatric symptomatology. In: S. Akhtar & V. D. Volkan (Eds.), *Mental Zoo: Animals in the Human Mind and Its Pathology* (pp. 3–38). Madison, CT: International Universities Press.

Akhtar, S., & Byrne, J. (1983). The concept of splitting and its clinical relevance. *American Journal of Psychiatry, 140*: 1016–1018.

Akhtar, S., & Choksi, K. (2005). Bollywood and the Indian unconscious. In: S. Akhtar (Ed.), *Freud Along the Ganges: Psychoanalytic Reflections on the People and Culture of India* (pp. 139–175). New York: Other Press.

Alexander, F., & French, T. (1946). *Psychoanalytic Therapy*. New York: Ronald Press.

Alterman, E. (2004). When presidents lie. *The Nation*, October 5.

Amati-Mehler, J., & Argentieri, S. (1989). Hope and hopelessness: a technical problem? *International Journal of Psychoanalysis, 70*: 295–304.

Arlow, J. H. (1980). The revenge motive in the primal scene. *Journal of the American Psychoanalytic Association, 28*: 519–541.

Asch, S. (1976). Varieties of negative therapeutic reactions and problems of technique. *Journal of the American Psychoanalytic Association, 24*: 383–407.

Asch, S. (1988). The analytic concepts of masochism: a re-evaluation. In: R. A. Glick & D. I. Meyers (Eds.), *Masochism: Current Psychoanalytic Perspectives* (pp. 93–116). Hillsdale, NJ: Analytic Press.

Asher, R. (1951). Munchausen's syndrome. *Lancet, 1*: 339–341.

Bach, S. (1977). On narcissistic state of consciousness. *International Journal of Psychoanalysis, 58*: 209–233.

Balint, M. (1959). *Thrills and Regressions*. London: Hogarth.
Balint, M. (1968). *The Basic Fault: Therapeutic Aspects of Regression*. London: Tavistock.
Barash, D. P., & Lipton, J. E. (2011). *Payback: Why We Retaliate, Redirect Aggression, and Take Revenge*. New York: Oxford University Press.
Barton, R., & Whitehead, J. (1969). The gaslight phenomenon. *Lancet, 1*: 158–160.
Begley, L. (1992). *The Man Who Was Late*. New York: Random House.
Bennett-Levy, J., & Marteau, T. (1984). Fear of animals: what is prepared? *British Journal of Psychology, 75*: 37–42.
Berglas, S. (1986). *The Success Syndrome*. New York: Plenum.
Bergler, E. (1945). Psychopathology of ingratitude. In: C. Socarides (Ed.), *The World of Emotions* (pp. 135–142). New York: International Universities Press, 1977.
Bergler, E. (1949). *The Basic Neurosis*. New York: Harper & Brothers.
Bergler, E. (1961). *Curable and Incurable Neurosis: Problems of Neurotic versus Malignant Masochism*. New York: Liveright.
Berliner, B. (1958). The role of object relations in moral masochism. *Psychoanalytic Quarterly, 27*: 38–56.
Bernstein, D. (1983). The female superego: a different perspective. *International Journal of Psychoanalysis, 64*: 187–200.
Bick, E. (1968). The experience of the skin in early object relations. *International Journal of Psychoanalysis, 49*: 484–486.
Bion, W. R. (1957). Differentiation of the psychotic from the non-psychotic personalities. *International Journal of Psychoanalysis, 38*: 266–275.
Bion, W. R. (1962). A theory of thinking. *International Journal of Psychoanalysis, 43*: 306–310.
Bion, W. R. (1967a). *Second Thoughts*. London: Heinemann.
Bion, W. R. (1967b). Notes on memory and desire. In: *Cogitations*. London: Karnac, 1992.
Bion, W. R. (1970). Lies and the thinker. In: *Attention and Interpretation*. London: Tavistock.
Birds, The (1963). Directed by A. Hitchcock, Universal Pictures production.
Biswas-Diener, R. (2012). *The Courage Quotient: How Science Can Make You Braver*. San Francisco, CA: Jossey-Bass.
Bleuler, E. (1908). *Textbook of Psychiatry*. A. A. Brill (Trans.). New York: MacMillan.
Blum, H. (1981). Object inconstancy and paranoid conspiracy. *Journal of the American Psychoanalytic Association, 29*: 789–813.
Blum, H. (1983). The psychoanalytic process and psychoanalytic inference: a clinical study of a lie and a loss. *International Journal of Psychoanalysis, 64*: 7–33.

Blum, H. (2009). Where does the truth lie? In: S. Akhtar & S. Parens (Eds.), *Lying, Cheating, and Carrying On: Developmental, Clinical, and Sociocultural Aspects of Dishonesty and Deceit* (pp. 59–67). Lanham, MD: Jason Aronson.

Blumenfeld, L. (2002). *Revenge: A Story of Hope*. New York: Simon & Schuster.

Blumenthal, R. (2006). Hotel log hints at illicit desire that Dr Freud did not repress. *New York Times*, p. A-1, December 24.

Bollas, C. (1999). *The Mystery of Things*. London: Routledge.

Bolognini, S. (2011). *Secret Passages: The Theory and Technique of Interpsychic Relations*. G. Atkinson (Trans.). London: Karnac.

Boris, H. N. (1986). The "other" breast—greed, envy, spite and revenge. *Contemporary Psychoanalysis, 22*: 45–59.

Bos, J., & Groenendijk, L. (2006). *The Self-Marginalization of Wilhelm Stekel: Freudian Circles Inside and Out*. New York: Springer.

Brenman, E. (1985). Cruelty and narrow-mindedness. *International Journal of Psychoanalysis, 66*: 273–281.

Brenner, C. (1959). The masochistic character: genesis and treatment. *Journal of the American Psychoanalytic Association, 7*: 197–226.

Brenner, C. (1976). *Psychoanalytic Technique and Psychic Conflict*. New York: International Universities Press.

Brenner, C. (2000). Brief communication: evenly hovering attention. *Psychoanalytic Quarterly, 69*: 545–549.

Brenner, I. (2004). *Psychic Trauma: Dynamics, Symptoms, and Treatment*. Northvale, NJ: Jason Aronson.

Brontë, E. (1847). *Wuthering Heights*. New York: Random House, 2009.

Byrne, R. W., & Whiten, A. (1992). Cognitive evolution in primates: evidence from tactical deception. *Man, 27*: 609–627.

Campbell, J., & Pile, S. (2011). Space travels of the Wolfman: phobia and its worlds. *Psychoanalysis and History, 13*: 69–88.

Cao, L. (1997). *Monkey Bridge*. New York: Penguin.

Casement, P. (1991). *Learning from the Patient*. New York: Guilford.

Casement, P. (2006). *Sexual Boundary Violations: Therapeutic, Supervisory, and Academic Contexts*. Lanham, MD: Jason Aronson.

Castelnuevo-Tedesco, P. (1974). Stealing, revenge, and the Monte Cristo complex. *International Journal of Psychoanalysis, 55*: 169–181.

Catch Me if You Can (2002). Directed by S. Spielberg, Dreamworks production.

Celenza, A. (2006). *Sexual Boundary Violations: Therapeutic, Supervisory, and Academic Contexts*. Lanham, MD: Jason Aronson.

Chadwick, M. (1929). Notes upon the fear of death. *International Journal of Psychoanalysis, 9*: 321–334.

Charles, M. (1997). Betrayal. *Contemporary Psychoanalysis, 33*: 109–122.

Chase, D. (2000). Restorative justice: use of apologies in criminal law. *Virginia Lawyers Weekly*, February 21.

Chasseguet-Smirgel, J. (1984). *Creativity and Perversion*. New York: W. W. Norton.

Clockwork Orange, A (1974). Directed by S. Kubrick, Warner Brothers production.

Cloninger, C. R. (2005). Antisocial personality disorder: a review. In: M. Maj, H. Akiskal, J. Mezzich, & A. Okasha (Eds.), *Personality Disorders (WPA Series in Evidence and Experience in Psychiatry)* (pp. 125–169). Chichester, UK: John Wiley and Sons.

Cloninger, C. R., Reich, T., & Guze, S. B. (1975). The multifactorial model of disease transmission II: sex differences in the familial transmission of sociopathy (antisocial personality). *British Journal of Psychiatry, 127*: 11–22.

Coen, S. J. (1992). *The Misuse of Persons: Analyzing Pathological Dependency*. Hillsdale, NJ: Analytic Press.

Coles, R. (1965). On courage. *Contemporary Psychoanalysis, 1*: 85–98.

Cook, M., & Mineka, S. (1987). Second order conditioning and overshadowing in the observational conditioning of fear in monkeys. *Behavior Research and Therapy, 25*: 349–364.

Cooper, A. M. (1988). The narcissistic-masochistic character. In: R. A. Glick & D. I. Meyers (Eds.), *Masochism: Current Psychoanalytic Perspectives* (pp. 117–138). Hillsdale, NJ: Analytic Press.

Corradi-Fiumara, G. (2009). *Spontaneity: A Psychoanalytic Inquiry*. London: Routledge.

Damasio, A. (1999). *The Feeling of What Happens*. London: Heinemann.

Daniels, M. (1969). Pathological vindictiveness and the vindictive character. *Psychoanalytic Review, 56*: 169–196.

Davey, G. (1992). Characteristics of individuals with fear of spiders. *Anxiety Research, 4*: 299–314.

Davey, G. C. L., Forster, L., & Mayhew, G. (1993). Familial resemblances in disgust sensitivity and animal phobias. *Behavior Research and Therapy, 31*: 41–50.

Davies, M. (2004). Need, greed, and envy in anorexia nervosa and the challenge they present. *Psychoanalytic Psychotherapy, 18*: 432–444.

Davis, D., & Weiss, J. M. (1974). Malingering and associated syndromes. In: S. Arieti & E. B. Brody (Eds.), *American Handbook of Psychiatry* (2nd *Edition), Vol. III* (pp. 270–287). New York: Basic Books.

Delprato, D. (1980). Hereditary determinants of fears and phobias: a critical review. *Behavior Therapy, 11*: 79–103.

Deutsch, H. (1922). On the pathological lie. *Journal of the American Academy of Psychoanalysis, 10*: 386–396 (reprinted 1982).

Deutsch, H. (1929). The genesis of agoraphobia. *International Journal of Psychoanalysis, 10*: 51–69.

Deutsch, H. (1933). *Psychoanalysis of the Neuroses*. London: Hogarth.

Diagnostic and Statistical Manual of Mental Disorders—4th Edition, Text Revision (2000). (pp. 443–450). Washington, DC: American Psychiatric Association.

Diagnostic and Statistical Manual of Mental Disorders—5th Edition (2013). Washington, DC: American Psychiatric Association.

Dickens, C. (1861). *Great Expectations*. New York: W. W. Norton, 1999.

Dirty Rotten Scoundrels (1988). Directed by F. Oz, Orion Pictures production.

Django Unchained (2012). Directed by Q. Tarantino, Columbia Pictures production.

Dumas, A. (1844). *The Count of Monte Cristo*. New York: Bantam Classics, 1984.

Edelsohn, G. (2009). Developmental aspects of lying. In: S. Akhtar and S. Parens (Eds.), *Lying, Cheating, and Carrying On: Developmental, Clinical, and Sociocultural Aspects of Dishonesty and Deceit* (pp. 59–67). Lanham, MD: Jason Aronson.

Eidelberg, L. (1954). *An Outline of the Comparative Pathology of the Neurosis*. New York: International Universities Press.

Eidelberg, L. (Ed.) (1968). *Encyclopedia of Psychoanalysis*. New York: Free Press.

Elson, M. (2001). Silence, its use and abuse: a view from self-psychology. *Clinical Social Work, 29*: 351–360.

Emanuel, R. (2004). Thalamic fear. *Journal of Child Psychotherapy, 30*: 71–87.

Emde, R. (1984). The affective self. In: J. D. Call, E. Galenson, & R. L. Tyson (Eds.), *Frontiers of Infant Psychiatry* (pp. 38–54). New York: Basic Books.

Epstein, L. (1979). Countertransference with borderline patients. In: L. Epstein & A. H. Feiner (Eds.), *Countertransference* (pp. 375–406). New York: Jason Aronson.

Erikson, E. (1950). *Childhood and Society*. New York: W. W. Norton.

Escoll, P. (1992). Vicissitudes of optimal distance through the life cycle. In: S. Kramer & S. Akhtar (Eds.), *When the Body Speaks: Psychological Meanings in Kinetic Clues* (pp. 59–87). Northvale, NJ: Jason Aronson.

Espiritu, Y. L. (2009). Emotions, sex, and money: the lives of Filipino children of immigrants. In: N. Foner (Ed.), *Across Generations: Immigrant Families in America* (pp. 47–71). New York: New York University Press.

Euripides (431 BCE). *Medea*. Las Vegas, NV: On Demand Publishing, 2013.

Exorcist, The (1973). Directed by W. Friedkin, Warner Brothers production.

Eysenck, H. J. (1965). *The Causes and Cures of Neurosis*. London: Routledge & Kegan Paul.

Eysenck, H. J. (1976). The conditioning model of neurosis. *Behavior Research and Therapy, 14*: 251–267.

Fairbairn, W. R. D. (1940). Schizoid factors in the personality. In: *An Object Relations Theory of Personality* (pp. 3–27). New York: Basic Books, 1952.

Feldman, R. (2009). *The Liar in Your Life*. New York: Hachette.

Fenichel, O. (1938). The drive to amass wealth. *Psychoanalytic Quarterly, 7*: 69–95.

Fenichel, O. (1945). *Psychoanalytic Theory of Neurosis*. New York: W. W. Norton.

Ferenczi, S. (1921). The further development of the active therapy in psychoanalysis. In: *Further Contributions to the Theory and Technique of Psychoanalysis* (pp. 198–217). London: Hogarth, 1955.

Ferenczi, S. (1929). The unwelcome child and his death instinct. *International Journal of Psychoanalysis, 10*: 125–129.

Fischer, R. (2009). What it takes to tell a lie. In: S. Akhtar & S. Parens (Eds.), *Lying, Cheating, and Carrying On: Developmental, Clinical, and Sociocultural Aspects of Dishonesty and Deceit* (pp. 17–31). Lanham, MD: Jason Aronson.

Fliess, R. (1942). The metapsychology of the analyst. *Psychoanalytic Quarterly, 11*: 211–227.

Fonagy, P., & Target, M. (1997). Attachment and reflective function: their role in self-organization. *Development and Psychopathology, 9*: 679–700.

Fouts, R. (1997). *Next of Kin: My Conversations with Chimpanzees*. New York: Avon.

Frattaroli, E. (2013). Reflections on the absence of morality in psychoanalytic theory and practice. In: S. Akhtar (Ed.), *Guilt: Origins, Manifestations, and Management* (pp. 83–110). Lanham, MD: Jason Aronson.

Freeman, D. (2009). Sociocultural perspectives on dishonesty. In: S. Akhtar & S. Parens (Eds.), *Lying, Cheating, and Carrying On: Developmental, Clinical, and Sociocultural Aspects of Dishonesty and Deceit* (pp. 111–127). Lanham, MD: Jason Aronson.

Freud, A. (1946). *The Ego and the Mechanisms of Defense*. New York: International Universities Press.

Freud, S. (1896b). Further remarks on the neuro-psychoses of defence. *S. E., 3*: 162–185. London: Hogarth.

Freud, S. (1899a). Screen memories. *S. E., 3*: 301–323. London: Hogarth.

Freud, S. (1900a). *The Interpretation of Dreams. S. E., 4–5*. London: Hogarth.

Freud, S. (1901b). *The Psychopathology of Everyday Life. S. E., 6*: 1–310. London: Hogarth.

Freud, S. (1905a). On psychotherapy. *S. E., 7*: 257–268. London: Hogarth.
Freud, S. (1905d). *Three Essays on the Theory of Sexuality. S. E., 7*: 135–243. London: Hogarth.
Freud, S. (1905e). Fragment of an analysis of a case of hysteria. *S. E., 7*: 1–122. London: Hogarth.
Freud, S. (1906c). Psycho-analysis and the establishment of the facts in legal proceedings. *S. E., 9*: 103–114. London: Hogarth.
Freud, S. (1909b). Analysis of a phobia in a five-year-old boy. *S. E., 10*: 5–149. London: Hogarth.
Freud, S. (1909c). Family romances. *S. E., 9*. London: Hogarth.
Freud, S. (1909d). Notes upon a case of obsessional neurosis. *S. E., 10*: 155–318. London: Hogarth.
Freud, S. (1910h). A special type of choice of object made by men. *S. E., 11*. London: Hogarth.
Freud, S. (1912e). Recommendations to physicians practising psycho-analysis. *S. E., 12*: 109–120. London: Hogarth.
Freud, S. (1912–13). *Totem and Taboo. S. E., 13*: 1–161. London: Hogarth.
Freud, S. (1913c). On beginning the treatment. *S. E., 12*: 97–108. London: Hogarth.
Freud, S. (1915c). Instincts and their vicissitudes. *S. E., 14*: 117–140. London: Hogarth.
Freud, S. (1915d). Repression. *S. E., 14*: 141–158. London: Hogarth.
Freud, S. (1915e). The unconscious. *S. E., 14*: 159–216. London: Hogarth.
Freud, S. (1916d). Some character-types met with in psycho-analytic work. Criminal from a sense of guilt. *S. E., 14*: 310–333. London: Hogarth.
Freud, S. (1916–17). *Introductory Lectures on Psycho-Analysis. S. E., 15–16*. London: Hogarth.
Freud, S. (1917b). A childhood recollection from *Dichtung und Wahrheit. S. E., 17*: 145–157. London: Hogarth.
Freud, S. (1917c). On transformations of instinct as exemplified in anal erotism. *S. E., 17*: 127–133. London: Hogarth.
Freud, S. (1917e). Mourning and melancholia. *S. E., 14*. London: Hogarth.
Freud, S. (1918b). From the history of an infantile neurosis. *S. E., 17*: 1–122. London: Hogarth.
Freud, S. (1919h). The "uncanny". *S. E., 17*: 217–252. London: Hogarth.
Freud, S. (1920a). The psychogenesis of a case of female homosexuality. *S. E., 18*. London: Hogarth.
Freud, S. (1920g). *Beyond the Pleasure Principle. S. E., 18*: 7–64. London: Hogarth.
Freud, S. (1921c). *Group Psychology and the Analysis of the Ego. S. E., 18*. London: Hogarth.
Freud, S. (1923b). *The Ego and the Id. S. E., 19*: 235–259. London: Hogarth.

Freud, S. (1924b). Neurosis and psychosis. *S. E., 19*: 149–153. London: Hogarth.

Freud, S. (1924c). The economic problem of masochism. *S. E., 19*: 157–170. London: Hogarth.

Freud, S. (1924d). The dissolution of the Oedipus complex. *S. E., 19*: 171–188. London: Hogarth.

Freud, S. (1925h). Negation. *S. E., 19*: 235–239. London: Hogarth.

Freud, S. (1925j). Some psychical consequences of the anatomical distinction between the sexes. *S. E., 19*: 241–258. London: Hogarth.

Freud, S. (1926d). *Inhibitions, Symptoms and Anxiety. S. E., 20*. London: Hogarth.

Freud, S. (1930a). *Civilization and Its Discontents. S. E., 21*. London: Hogarth.

Freud, S. (1933a). *New Introductory Lectures on Psycho-Analysis. S. E., 22*: 7–182. London: Hogarth.

Freud, S. (1950a). A project for a scientific psychology. *S. E., 1*: 295–343. London: Hogarth.

Friedman, L. (1969). The therapeutic alliance. *International Journal of Psychoanalysis, 50*: 139–153.

Gabbard, G. (1997). Challenges in the analysis of adult patients with histories of childhood sexual abuse. *Canadian Journal of Psychoanalysis, 5*: 1–25.

Gabbard, G., & Lester, E. (1995). *Boundaries and Boundary Violations in Psychoanalysis*. Washington, DC: American Psychiatric Press.

Gandhi, M. K. (1940). *An Autobiography: The Story of My Experiments with Truth*. M. Desai (Trans.). Boston, MA: Beacon, 1957.

Gediman, H. (1985). Impostor, inauthenticity, and feeling fraudulent. *Journal of American Psychoanalytic Association, 39*: 911–936.

Gellerman, D., & Suddath, R. (2005). Violent fantasy, dangerousness, and the duty to warn and protect. *Journal of the American Academy of Psychiatry and Law, 33*: 484–495.

Gibson, E. J., & Walk, R. D. (1960). The "visual cliff." *Scientific American, 202*: 67–71.

Gilligan, C. (1982). *In a Different Voice: Psychological Theory and Women's Development*. Cambridge, MA: Harvard University Press.

Giovacchini, P. (2000). *Impact of Narcissism: The Errant Therapist in a Chaotic Quest*. Northvale, NJ: Jason Aronson.

Goldstein, J. (1998). *Why We Watch?: The Attractions of Violent Entertainment*. New York: Oxford University Press.

Gordon, L. (1955). Incest as revenge against the pre-oedipal mother. *Psychoanalytic Review, 42*: 284–292.

Grand, S. (2002). *The Reproduction of Evil: A Clinical and Cultural Perspective*. Mahwah, NJ: Analytic Press.

Grant, J. E., Chamberlain, S. R., Schreiber, L. R., & Odlaug, B. L. (2012). Gender-related clinical and neurocognitive differences in individuals seeking treatment for pathological gambling. *Journal of Psychiatric Research, 46*: 1206–1211.

Gray, P. (1994). *The Ego and the Analysis of Defense*. Northvale, NJ: Jason Aronson.

Green, A. (1980). The dead mother. In: *Life Narcissism, Death Narcissism*. A. Weller (Trans.). London: Free Association.

Green, A. (1986). Réponses à des questions inconcevables. *Topique, 37*: 11–30.

Greenacre, P. (1958). Early physical determinants in the development of the sense of identity. *Journal of the American Psychoanalytic Association, 6*: 612–627.

Greenson, R. (1968). Disidentifying from the mother. *International Journal of Psychoanalysis, 49*: 370–374.

Grifters, The (1990). Directed by S. Frears, Cineplex-Odeon Films production.

Grinker, R. (1955). Growth inertia and shame: their therapeutic implications and dangers. *International Journal of Psychoanalysis, 36*: 242–253.

Gross, A. (1951). The secret. *Bulletin of the Menninger Clinic, 15*: 37–44.

Grunberger, B. (1989). *New Essays on Narcissism*. D. Macey (Trans.). London: Free Association.

Grunert, U. (1979). The negative therapeutic reaction as a reactivation of a disturbed process of separation in the transference. *Bulletin of the European Psychoanalytic Federation, 65*: 5–19.

Guarnaccia, P. J., & Rogler, L. H. (1999). Research on culture-bound syndromes: new directions. *American Journal of Psychiatry, 156*: 1322–1327.

Guntrip, H. (1969). *Schizoid Phenomena, Object Relations and the Self*. New York: International Universities Press.

Guttman, S. A., Jones, R. L., & Parrish, S. M. (Eds.) (1980). *The Concordance to the Standard Edition of the Complete Psychological Works of Sigmund Freud*. Boston, MA: G. K. Hall.

Hanly, C. (1990). The concept of truth in psychoanalysis. *International Journal of Psychoanalysis, 71*: 375–384.

Hanly, C. (1992). *The Problem of Truth in Applied Psychoanalysis*. New York: Guilford Press.

Harding, J. (1999). Remorse and rehabilitation. In: M. Cox (Ed.), *Remorse and Reparation* (pp. 107–115). London: Jessica Kingsley.

Hartmann, H. (1958). Comments on the scientific aspects of psychoanalysis. *Psychoanalytic Study of the Child, 13*: 127–146.

Hinshelwood, R. D. (1991). *A Dictionary of Kleinian Thought* (pp. 412–415). Northvale, NJ: Jason Aronson.

Hoffer, A. (1985). Toward a definition of psychoanalytic neutrality. *Journal of the American Psychoanalytic Association, 33*: 771–795.

Hoffman, L., Johnson, E., Foster, M., & Wright, J. (2010). What happens when you die? Three- to- four year olds chatting about death. In: S. Akhtar (Ed.), *The Wound of Mortality: Fear, Denial, and Acceptance of Death* (pp. 21–36). Lanham, MD: Jason Aronson.

Holmes, D. E. (2006). The wrecking effects of race and social class on self and success. *Psychoanalytic Quarterly, 75*: 215–235.

Hopkins, L. (2006). *False Self: The Life of Masud Khan*. New York: Other Press.

Horner, M. (1968). Sex differences in the achievement, motivation, and performance in competitive and non-competitive situations. (Unpublished doctoral dissertation.) Ann Arbor, MI: University of Michigan.

Horney, K. (1948). The value of vindictiveness. *American Journal of Psychoanalysis, 8*: 3–12.

Horowitz, M. (1975). Sliding meanings: a defense against threat in narcissistic personalities. *International Journal of Psychoanalysis, 4*: 167–180.

House of Cards (1993). Directed by M. Lessac, A and M Films production.

Hurvich, M. (2003). The place of annihilation anxieties in psychoanalytic theory. *Journal of the American Psychoanalytic Association, 51*: 579–616.

Inglourious Basterds (2009). Directed by Q. Tarantino, Columbia Pictures production.

Isaacs, K. S., Alexander, J. M., & Haggard, E. A. (1963). Faith, trust, and gullibility. *International Journal of Psychoanalysis, 44*: 461–469.

Issacharoff, A. (1979). Barriers to knowing. In: L. Epstein & A. H. Feiner (Eds.), *Countertransference* (pp. 27–44). New York: Jason Aronson.

Jaws (1975). Directed by S. Spielberg, Universal Pictures production.

Johnson, A., & Szurek, M. (1952). The genesis of antisocial acting out in children and adults. *Psychoanalytic Quarterly, 21*: 323–343.

Jones, E. (1913). The God complex. In: *Essays in Applied Psychoanalysis, Volume II* (pp. 244–265). New York: International Universities Press, 1973.

Jones, E. (1929). Fear, guilt, and hate. *International Journal of Psychoanalysis, 10*: 383–397.

Jones, E. (1948). Theory of symbolism. In: *Papers on Psycho-Analysis, 5th edition* (pp. 116–141). London: Bailliere, Tindall, & Cox, 1959.

Jordan, L. (2002). The analyst's uncertainty and fear. *Journal of the American Psychoanalytic Association, 50*: 989–993.

Joseph, D. I. (1990). Preoedipal factors in "Little Hans". *Journal of the American Psychoanalytic Association, 18*: 206–222.

Kafka, H. (1998). Fear in the countertransference and the mutuality of safety. *International Forum of Psychoanalysis, 7*: 97–103.

Kaplan, H. (1991). Greed: a psychoanalytic perspective. *Psychoanalytic Review, 78*: 505–523.

Kazmi, N. (1972). *Deewan*. Karachi, Pakistan: Urdu Ghar.

Keiser, S. (1969). Superior intelligence: its contribution to neurosogenesis. *Journal of the American Psychoanalytic Association, 17*: 452–473.

Kernberg, O. F. (1967). Borderline personality organization. *Journal of the American Psychoanalytic Association, 15*: 641–685.

Kernberg, O. F. (1970). A psychoanalytic classification of character pathology. *Journal of the American Psychoanalytic Association, 18*: 800–822.

Kernberg, O. F. (1975). *Borderline Conditions and Pathological Narcissism*. New York: Jason Aronson.

Kernberg, O. F. (1980). *Internal World and External Reality*. Northvale, NJ: Jason Aronson.

Kernberg, O. F. (1984). *Severe Personality Disorders: Psychotherapeutic Strategies*. New Haven, CT: Yale University Press.

Kernberg, O. F. (1992). *Aggression in Personality Disorders and Perversions*. New Haven, CT: Yale University Press.

Kernberg, O. F. (1995). *Love Relations: Normality and Pathology*. New Haven, CT: Yale University Press.

Kernberg, O. F., Selzer, M. A., Koenigsberg, H. W., Carr, A. C., & Appelbaum, A. H. (1989). *Psychodynamic Psychotherapy of Borderline Patients*. New York: Basic Books.

Kestenberg, J. (1980). Psychoanalyses of children of Holocaust survivors. *Journal of the American Psychoanalytic Association, 28*: 775–804.

Khan, M. M. R. (1983). Lying fallow. In: *Hidden Selves* (pp. 183–188). New York: International Universities Press.

Kidder, R. M. (2006). *Moral Courage*. New York: Harper Collins.

Kilbourne, B. (2005). Shame conflicts and tragedy in "The Scarlet Letter". *Journal of the American Psychoanalytic Association, 53*: 465–483.

Killingmo, B. (1989). Conflict and deficit: implications for technique. *International Journal of Psychoanalysis, 70*: 65–79.

Kitayama, O. (1997). Psychoanalysis in shame culture. *The Bulletin of the Menninger Clinic, 85*: 47–50.

Klein, M. (1932). *The Psychoanalysis of Children*. New York: Free Press, 1975.

Klein, M. (1933). The early development of conscience in the child. In: *Love, Guilt and Reparation and Other Works—1921–1945* (pp. 262–289). New York: Free Press, 1984.

Klein, M. (1935). A contribution to the psychogenesis of manic depressive states. In: *Love, Guilt and Reparation and Other Works—1921–1945* (pp. 262–289). New York: Free Press, 1975.

Klein, M. (1937). Love, guilt, and reparation. In: *Love, Guilt and Reparation and Other Works—1921–1945* (pp. 306–343). New York: Free Press, 1975.

Klein, M. (1940). Mourning and its relation to manic depressive states. In: *Love, Guilt and Reparation and Other Works—1921–1945* (pp. 344–369). New York: Free Press, 1975.

Klein, M. (1952). The mutual influences in the development of ego and the id. In: *Envy and Gratitude and Other Works—1946–1963* (pp. 57–60). New York: Free Press, 1975.

Klein, M. (1957). Envy and gratitude. In: *Envy and Gratitude and Other Works—1946–1963* (pp. 176–235). New York: Free Press, 1975.

Klein, M. (1959). Our adult world and its roots in infancy. In: *Envy and Gratitude and Other Works—1946–1963* (pp. 247–263). New York: Free Press, 1975.

Kohut, H. (1972). Thoughts on narcissism and narcissistic rage. *Psychoanalytic Study of the Child, 27*: 360–400.

Kohut, H. (1979). The two analyses of Mr Z. *International Journal of Psychoanalysis, 60*: 3–27.

Kohut, H. (1980). *Self Psychology and the Humanities*. New York: W. W. Norton.

Kolansky, H., & Eisner, H. (1974). The psychoanalytic concept of preoedipal developmental arrest. (Paper presented at the fall meetings of the American Psychoanalytic Association.) Cited in: S. Akhtar (Ed.), *Inner Torment: Living Between Conflict and Fragmentation* (p. 231). Northvale, NJ: Jason Aronson, 1999.

Kraepelin, E. (1905). *Einfuehrung in die Psychiatrische Klinik*. Leipzig, Germany: Barth Press.

Kraepelin, E. (1921). *Manic Depressive Insanity and Paranoia*. Edinburgh, UK: Livingston Press.

Krafft-Ebing, R. (1892). *Psychopathia Sexualis with Special Reference to Contrary Sexual Instinct: a Medico-legal Study*. Philadelphia, PA: F. A. Davis, 1978.

Kramer, E. (1987). The analyst's resolution of revenge resulting from the treatment of his parents. *Modern Psychoanalysis, 12*: 207–219.

Kris, E. (1956). The recovery of childhood memories in psychoanalysis. *Psychoanalytic Study of the Child, 11*: 54–88.

Kulish, N. (1996). A phobia of the couch: a clinical study of psychoanalytic process. *Psychoanalytic Quarterly, 65*: 465–494.

Lafarge, L. (1995). Transferences of deception. *Journal of the American Psychoanalytic Association, 48*: 765–792.

Laplanche, J., & Pontalis, J. -B. (1973). *The Language of Psychoanalysis*. D. Nicholson-Smith (Trans.). New York: W. W. Norton.

Lemma, A. (2005). The many faces of lying. *International Journal of Psychoanalysis, 86*: 737–753.

Levin, S. (1967). Some metapsychological considerations on the differentiation between shame and guilt. *International Journal of Psychoanalysis, 48*: 267–276.

Levy, S. (1987). Therapeutic strategy and psychoanalytic technique. *Journal of the American Psychoanalytic Association, 35*: 447–466.

Lewin, B. D. (1935). Claustrophobia. *Psychoanalytic Quarterly, 4*: 227–233.

Lewin, B. D. (1952). Phobic symptoms and dream interpretation. *Psychoanalytic Quarterly, 21*: 295–322.

Lichtenberg, J. D. (1991). Fear, phobia, and panic. *Psychoanalytic Inquiry, 11*: 395–415.

Limentani, A. (1989). *Between Freud and Klein: The Psychoanalytic Quest for Knowledge and Truth*. London: Free Association.

Loewald, H. (1960). On the therapeutic action of psychoanalysis. *Journal of the American Psychoanalytic Association, 41*: 16–33.

Loewenstein, R. (1951). The problem of interpretation. *Psychoanalytic Quarterly, 20*: 1–23.

Mackinnon, R., & Michels, R. (1971). *The Psychiatric Interview in Clinical Practice*. Philadelphia, PA: Saunders.

Madanes, C. (1990). *Sex, Love, and Violence: Strategies for Transformation*. New York: W. W. Norton.

Mahler, M. S., Pine, F., & Bergman, A. (1975). *The Psychological Birth of the Human Infant: Symbiosis and Individuation*. New York: Basic Books.

Maleson, F. (1984). Multiple meanings of masochism in psychoanalytic discourse. *Journal of the American Psychoanalytic Association, 32*: 325–356.

Maltsberger, J., & Buie, D. (1974). Countertransference hate in the treatment of suicidal patients. *Archives of General Psychiatry, 30*: 625–633.

Maltsberger, J., & Buie, D. (1980). The devices of suicide—revenge, riddance, and rebirth. *International Review of Psycho-Analysis, 7*: 61–72.

Mamdani, M. (2004). *Good Muslim, Bad Muslim: America, the Cold War, and the Roots of Terror*. New York: Random House.

Margolis, G. (1966). Secrecy and identity. *International Review of Psycho-Analysis, 47*: 517–522.

Margolis, G. (1974). The psychology of keeping secrets. *International Journal of Psychoanalysis, 1*: 291–296.

Marks, I. (1970). The origins of phobic states. *American Journal of Psychotherapy, 24*: 652–676.

Marks, I. (1987). *Fears, Phobias, and Rituals*. New York: Oxford University Press.

Masson, J. M. (Ed.) (1985). *The Complete Letters of Sigmund Freud to Wilhelm Fliess, 1897–1904*. Cambridge, MA: Harvard University Press.

Mathias, D. (2008). The analyst's fears. *Newsletter of the Psychoanalytic Society of New England East, 20*: 9–12.

Maynard-Smith, J., & Szathmáry, E. (1999). *The Origins of Life: From the Birth of Life to the Origins of Language*. Oxford: Oxford University Press.

McNally, R. J., & Steketee, G. S. (1985). The etiology and maintenance of severe animal phobias. *Behavior Research and Therapy, 23*: 431–435.

Meltzer, D. (1973). *Sexual States of Mind*. London: Karnac, 2008.

Melville, H. (1851). *Moby Dick*. New York: Putnam, 2002.

Menaker, E. (1979). Masochism and the emergent ego. In: L. Lerner (Ed.), *Selected Papers of Esther Menaker* (pp. 72–101). New York: Human Sciences Press.

Meth, J. M. (1974). Exotic psychiatric syndromes. In: S. Arieti & E. B. Brody (Eds.), *American Handbook of Psychiatry, 2nd edition, Vol. III* (pp. 723–739). New York: Basic Books.

Miller, J. R. (1994). Fear of success: psychodynamic implications. *Journal of American Academy of Psychoanalysis, 22*: 129–136.

Mineka, S., Davidson, M., Cook, M., & Keir, R. (1984). Observational conditioning of snake fear in rhesus monkeys. *Journal of Abnormal Psychology, 93*: 355–372.

Mish, F. C. (Ed.) (1998). *Merriam Webster's Collegiate Dictionary (10th edition)*. Springfield, MA: Merriam Webster Press.

Mittleman, B. (1957). Motility in the therapy of children and adults. *Psychoanalytic Study of the Child, 12*: 284–319.

Modell, A. (1965). On aspects of the superego's development. *International Journal of Psychoanalysis, 46*: 323–331.

Moore, B., & Fine, B. (1990). *Psychoanalytic Terms and Concepts*. New Haven, CT: Yale University Press.

Moore, M. (2009). Cultures of dishonesty: from hidden cancers and concealed selves to politics and poker. In: S. Akhtar & S. Parens (Eds.), *Lying, Cheating, and Carrying On: Developmental, Clinical, and Sociocultural Aspects of Dishonesty and Deceit* (pp. 129–140). Lanham, MD: Jason Aronson.

Morrison, A. (1989). *Shame, the Underside of Narcissism*. Hillsdale, NJ: Analytic Press.

Moss, D. B. (1986). Revenge and forgiveness. *American Imago, 43*: 191–210.

Music Man, The (1962). Directed by M. DaCosta, Warner Brothers production.

Natterson, J., & Knudson, A. (1965). Observations concerning fear of death in fatally ill children and their mothers. In: R. Fulton (Ed.), *Death and Identity* (pp. 235–278). New York: John Wiley.

Niederland, W. (1968). Clinical observations on the "survivor syndrome". *International Journal of Psychoanalysis, 49*: 313–315.

Nietzsche, F. (1905). *Thus Spake Zarathustra*. New York: Modern Library Series, 1955.

Nikelly, A. (1992). The pleonexic personality: a new provisional personality disorder. *Individual Psychology: Journal of Adlerian Theory, Research and Practice, 48*: 253–260.

Nikelly, A. (2006). The pathogenesis of greed: causes and consequences. *International Journal of Applied Psychoanalytic Studies, 3*: 65–78.

Nock, K., Borges, G., & Ono, Y. (Eds.) (2012). *Suicide: Global Perspectives from the WHO World Mental Health Surveys*. New York: Cambridge University Press.

O'Shaughnessy, E. (1990). Can a liar be psychoanalyzed? *International Journal of Psychoanalysis, 71*: 187–196.

Ocean's Eleven (2001). Directed by S. Soderbergh, Warner Brothers production.

Olden, C. (1941). About the fascinating effect of the narcissistic personality. *American Imago, 2*: 347–355.

Omen, The (1976). Directed by R. Donner, 20th Century Fox production.

Ornstein, A., Gropper, C., & Bogner, J. Z. (1983). Shoplifting: an expression of revenge and restitution. *Annual of Psychoanalysis, 11*: 311–331.

Otto, R. (2000). Assessing and managing violence risk in outpatient settings. *Journal of Clinical Psychology, 56*: 1239–1262.

Pally, R. (2000). *The Mind-Brain Relationship*. London: Karnac.

Parens, H. (2009). Distortions of truth: from white lies to mass murder. In: S. Akhtar & S. Parens (Eds.), *Lying, Cheating, and Carrying On: Developmental, Clinical, and Sociocultural Aspects of Dishonesty and Deceit* (pp. 141–159). Lanham, MD: Jason Aronson.

Pine, F. (1988). The four psychologies of psychoanalysis and their place in clinical work. *Journal of the American Psychoanalytic Association, 36*: 571–596.

Pine, F. (1997). *Diversity and Direction in Psychoanalytic Technique*. New Haven, CT: Yale University Press.

Pinker, S. (2011). *Better Angels of Our Nature: Why Violence Has Declined*. New York: Penguin.

Poland, W. S. (1975). Tact as a psychoanalytic function. *International Journal of Psychoanalysis, 56*: 155–161.

Potenza, M. N., Steinberg, M. A., McLaughlin, S. D., Wu, R., Rounsaville, B. J., & O'Malley, S. S. (2001). Gender-related differences in the characteristics of problem gamblers using a gambling helpline. *American Journal of Psychiatry, 158*: 1500–1505.

Prathikanti, S. (1997). East-Indian American families. In: E. Lee (Ed.), *Working with Asian Americans: A Guide to Clinicians* (pp. 79–100). New York: Guilford Press.

Procci, W. (1987). Mockery through caricature: a variant of introjection utilized by a masochistic woman. *Journal of American Academy of Psychoanalysis, 15*: 51–66.

Psycho (1960). Directed by A. Hitchcock, Shamley production.

Puppet Masters (1994). Directed by S. Orme, Hollywood Pictures production.

Ramzy, I., & Wallerstein, R. (1958). Pain, fear, and anxiety: a study of interrelationships. *Psychoanalytic Study of the Child, 13*: 147–189.

Rangell, L. (1952). The analysis of a doll phobia. *International Journal of Psychoanalysis, 33*: 43–53.

Rank, O. (1913). "Der Familienroman" in der psychologie des attentäters. *International Zeitschrift Psychoanalyze, 1*: 565–567.

Reich, W. (1933). *Character Analysis*. V. R. Carfagno (Trans.). New York: Farrar, Straus and Giroux, 1972.

Robertson, I. H. (2013). *The Winner Effect: Exploring the Neuroscience of Success and Failure*. New York: St. Martin's Press.

Rohrlich, J. B. (1987). Wall Street's money junkies. *New York Times*, May 7, p. A35.

Rosen, I. (2009). Atonement. In: S. Akhtar (Ed.), *Good Feelings: Psychoanalytic Reflections on Positive Emotions and Attitudes* (pp. 371–390). London: Karnac.

Rosenfeld, H. (1964). On the psychopathology of narcissism: A clinical approach. *International Journal of Psychoanalysis, 45*: 332–337.

Rosenfeld, H. (1971). Theory of life and death instincts: aggressive aspects of narcissism. *International Journal of Psychoanalysis, 45*: 332–337.

Roth, P. (2008). Introduction. In: P. Roth & A. Lemma (Eds.), *Envy and Gratitude Revisited* (pp. 1–18). London: Karnac.

Rudnytsky, P. (2012). *Rescuing Psychoanalysis from Freud*. London: Karnac.

Rycroft, C. (1968). *A Critical Dictionary of Psychoanalysis*. London: Penguin.

Sadock, B. J., & Sadock, V. A. (2007). Factitious disorders. In: *Kaplan and Sadock's Synopsis of Psychiatry* (pp. 658–664). Philadelphia, PA: Lippincott Williams & Wilkens.

Sandler, A. -M. (1989). Comments on phobic mechanisms in childhood. *Psychoanalytic Study of the Child, 44*: 101–114.

Sandler, J., & Sandler, A. -M. (1998). *Internal Objects Revisited*. London: Karnac.

Sass, L. A., & Woolfolk, R. L. (1988). Psychoanalysis and the hermeneutic turn: a critique of "narrative truth and historical truth." *Journal of the American Psychoanalytic Association, 36*: 429–454.

Schafer, R. (1988). Those wrecked by success. In: R. A. Glick and D. Myers (Eds.), *Masochism: Current Psychoanalytic Perspectives* (pp. 81–91). Hillsdale, NJ: Analytic Press.

Searles, H. F. (1956). The psychodynamics of vindictiveness. In: H. F. Searles (Ed.), *Collected Papers on Schizophrenia and Related Subjects*. New York: International Universities Press.

Seedat, S., Scott, K. M., Angermeyer, M. C., Berglund, P., Bromet, E. J., Brugha, T. S., Demyttenaere, K., Girolamo, G., Haro, J. M., Jin, R., Karam, E. G., Kovess-Masfety, V., Levinson, D., Mora, M. E. M., Ono, Y., Ormel, J., Pennell, B. E., Posada-Villa, J., Sampson, N. A., Williams, D. R., & Kessler, R. C. (2009). Cross-national associations between gender and mental disorders in the World Health Organization World Mental Surveys. *Archives of General Psychiatry, 66*: 785–795.

Seelig, B., & Rosof, L. (2001). Normal and pathological altruism. *Journal of the American Psychoanalytic Association, 41*: 179–190.

Shakespeare, W. (1596). *The Merchant of Venice*. New York: Simon & Schuster, 2010.

Shakespeare, W. (1606). *King Lear*. San Francisco, CA: Ignatius Press, 2008.

Shames, L. (1989). *The Hunger for More*. New York: Times Books.

Sharpe, E. F. (1940). Psycho-physical problems revealed in language: an examination of metaphor. *International Journal of Psychoanalysis, 21*: 201–215.

Shengold, L. (1989). *Soul Murder: The Effects of Childhood Abuse and Deprivation*. New Haven, CT: Yale University Press.

Shining, The (1980). Directed by S. Kubrick, Warner Brothers production.

Shneidman, E. S. (2008). *A Commonsense Book of Death*. Lanham, MD: Rowman & Littlefield.

Sievers, B. (2012). Socio-analytic reflections on capitalist greed. *Organizational and Social Dynamics, 12*: 44–69.

Silberer, H. (1909). Report on method of eliciting and observing certain symbolic hallucination-phenomena. In: D. Rapaport (Ed.), *Organization and Pathology of Thought* (pp. 208–233). New York: Columbia University Press, 1951.

Silverman, M. A. (1980). A fresh look of the case of Little Hans. In: M. Kanzer & J. Glenn (Eds.), *Freud and His Patients* (pp. 96–120). New York: Jason Aronson.

Socarides, C. W. (1966). On vengeance: the desire to "get even". *Journal of the American Psychoanalytic Association, 35*: 98–107.

Solyom, L., Beck, P., Solyom, C., & Hugel, R. (1974). Some etiological factors in phobic neurosis. *Canadian Psychiatric Association Journal, 19*: 69–78.

Spence, D. P. (1982). Narrative truth and historical truth. *Psychoanalytic Quarterly, 51*: 43–61.

Spero, M. H. (1984). Shame: an object relational formulation. *Psychoanalytic Study of the Child, 39*: 259–282.

Stanton, A. H. (1978). Personality disorders. In: A. M. Nicoli (Ed.), *The Harvard Guide to Modern Psychiatry* (pp. 283–295). Cambridge, MA: Belknap Press.

Steiner, J. (1996). Revenge and resentment in the "Oedipus situation". *International Journal of Psychoanalysis, 77*: 433–443.

Sting, The (1973). Directed by G. R. Hill, Zanuck/Hill production.

Stone, M. (1980). *The Borderline Syndrome*. New York: McGraw Hill.

Stone, M. (1989). Murder. *Psychiatric Clinics of North America, 12*: 643–651.

Stone, M. (2007). Treatability in severe personality disorders: how far do the science and art of psychotherapy carry us? In: B. van Luyn, S. Akhtar, & W. J. Livesley (Eds.), *Severe Personality Disorders: Everyday Issues in Clinical Practice* (pp. 1–29). Cambridge: Cambridge University Press.

Stone, M. (2009). Lying and deceitfulness in personality disorders. In: S. Akhtar & S. Parens (Eds.), *Lying, Cheating, and Carrying On: Developmental, Clinical, and Sociocultural Aspects of Dishonesty and Deceit* (pp. 69–92). Lanham, MD: Jason Aronson.

Strozier, C. (2004). *Heinz Kohut: The Making of a Psychoanalyst*. New York: Other Press.

Sulzberger, C. (1953). Why it is hard to keep secrets. *Psychoanalysis, 2*: 37–43.

Sundeen, M. (2012). *The Man Who Quit Money*. New York: Riverhead Trade.

Symonds, A. (1985). Separation and loss: significance for women. *American Journal of Psychoanalysis, 45*: 53–58.

Talwar, V., & Lee, K. (2002). Development of lying to conceal a transgression: children's control of expressive behavior during verbal deception. *International Journal of Behavioral Development, 26*: 436–444.

Texas Chain Saw Massacre, The (1974). Directed by T. Hooper, Vortex Pictures production.

Tobak, M. (1989). Lying and the paranoid personality (letter to editor). *American Journal of Psychiatry, 146*: 125.

Tyson, R. L. (1978). Notes on the analysis of a prelatency boy with a dog phobia. *Psychoanalytic Study of the Child, 33*: 427–458.

Volkan, V. D. (1976). *Primitive Internalized Object Relations*. New York: International Universities Press.

Volkan, V. D. (1987). Psychological concepts useful in the building of political foundations between nations (Track II diplomacy). *Journal of the American Psychoanalytic Association, 35*: 903–935.

Volkan, V. D. (1988). *The Need for Enemies and Allies*. Northvale, NJ: Jason Aronson.

Volkan, V. D. (1997). *Bloodlines: From Ethnic Pride to Ethnic Terrorism.* New York: Farrar, Straus and Giroux.

Wachtel, P. L. (2003). Full pockets, empty lives: a psychoanalytic exploration of the contemporary culture of greed. *American Journal of Psychoanalysis, 63*: 103–122.

Waelder, R. (1936). The principle of multiple function; observations on multiple determination. *Psychoanalytic Quarterly, 5*: 45–62.

Wall Street (1987). Directed by O. Stone, a 20th Century Fox production.

Wangh, M. (1959). Structural determinants of phobia. *Journal of the American Psychoanalytic Association, 7*: 675–695.

War of the Worlds, The (1953). Directed by J. Carpenter, Paramount Pictures production.

Waska, R. (2002). Craving, longing, denial, and the dangers of change: clinical manifestations of greed. *Psychoanalytic Review, 89*: 505–531.

Waska, R. (2003a). Greed, idealization, and the paranoid-schizoid experience of instability. *The Scandinavian Psychoanalytic Review, 26*: 41–50.

Waska, R. (2003b). The impossible dream and the endless nightmare. *Canadian Journal of Psychoanalysis, 11*: 379–397.

Watson, C. (2009). Lies and their detection. In: S. Akhtar & S. Parens (Eds.), *Lying, Cheating, and Carrying On: Developmental, Clinical, and Sociocultural Aspects of Dishonesty and Deceit* (pp. 93–110). Lanham, MD: Jason Aronson.

Webster's Ninth New Collegiate Dictionary (1987). Springfield, MA: Merriam Webster Press.

Weiss, E. (1934). Bodily pain and mental pain. *International Journal of Psychoanalysis, 15*: 1–13.

Weiss, E. (1964). *Agoraphobia in the Light of Ego Psychology.* New York: Grune & Stratton.

Weiss, J. M. A. (1974). Suicide. In: S. Arieti & E. B. Brody (Eds.), *American Handbook of Psychiatry, Second Edition, Volume III* (pp. 743–765). New York: Basic Books.

Winnicott, D. W. (1954). The depressive position in normal emotional development. In: *Collected Papers: Through Paediatrics to Psychoanalysis* (pp. 262–277). London: Tavistock.

Winnicott, D. W. (1956a). The antisocial tendency. In: *Collected Papers: Through Paediatrics to Psychoanalysis* (pp. 306–316). New York: Basic Books, 1958.

Winnicott, D. W. (1956b). Psychoanalysis and the sense of guilt. In: *The Maturational Processes and the Facilitating Environment* (pp. 15–28). New York: International Universities Press.

Winnicott, D. W. (1958). The capacity to be alone. *International Journal of Psychoanalysis, 39*: 416–420.

Winnicott, D. W. (1960). The theory of parent–infant relationship. In: *The Maturational Processes and the Facilitating Environment* (pp. 37–55). New York: International Universities Press, 1965.

Winnicott, D. W. (1962). Ego integration in child development. In: *The Maturational Processes and the Facilitating Environment* (pp. 45–53). New York: International Universities Press.

Winnicott, D. W. (1968). Use of an object and relating through identifications. In: *Playing and Reality* (pp. 86–94). London: Tavistock, 1971.

Winnicott, D. W. (1974). Fear of breakdown. *International Review of Psycho-Analysis, 1*: 103–107.

Wolpe, J., & Rachman, R. (1960). Psychoanalytic evidence: a critique based on Freud's case of Little Hans. *Journal of Nervous and Mental Disorders, 131*: 135–148.

Wurmser, L. (1994). *The Mask of Shame*. Northvale, NJ: Jason Aronson.

Yap, P. M. (1969). Classification of the culture-bound reactive syndromes. *Australian and New Zealand Journal of Psychiatry, 3*: 172–179.

Yeomans, F., Selzer, M., & Clarkin, J. (1992). *Treating the Borderline Patient: A Contract Based Approach*. New York: Basic Books.

Zibel, A. (2008). Truth time: lenders are about to pay the price for handing out "liar loans." *The Philadelphia Inquirer*, p. c-1, August 19.

Zilboorg, G. (1936). Differential diagnostic types of suicide. *Archives of Neurological Psychiatry, 35*: 270–291.

Zilboorg, G. (1943). Fear of death. *Psychoanalytic Quarterly, 12*: 465–475.

INDEX